**Favorite Recipes
of South Texas**

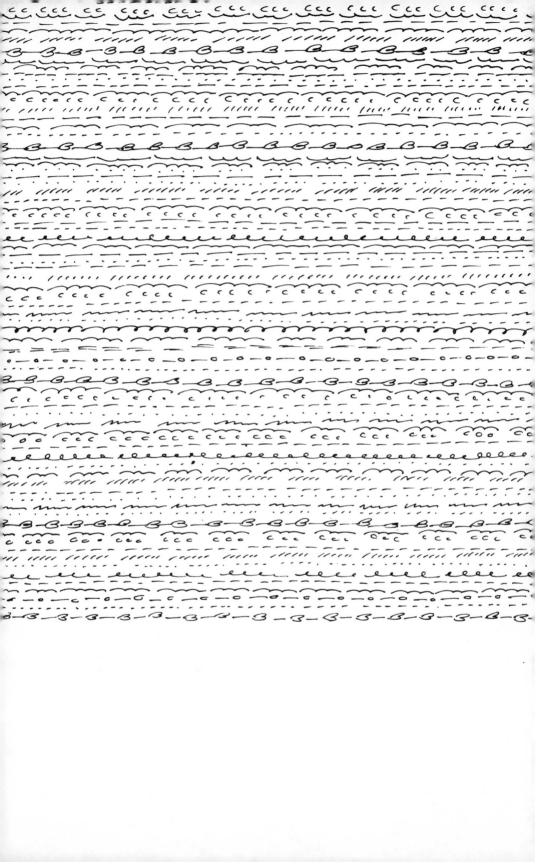

Fiesta

Favorite Recipes of South Texas

Published by
The Junior League of Corpus Christi
Corpus Christi, Texas

Copies of **FIESTA** may be obtained for $12.95 plus $2.25 for postage and handling. (Texas residents add $.97 for state tax.) Make checks payable to **FIESTA**.

Copies of **¡DELICIOSO!** also may be obtained for $12.95 plus $2.25 for postage and handling. (Texas residents add $.97 for state tax.) Make checks payable to **¡DELICIOSO!**

Junior League of Corpus Christi, Inc.
P.O. Box 837
Corpus Christi, Texas 78403

1st printing	September 1973	8,000 copies
2nd printing	December 1973	10,00 copies
3rd printing	August 1975	10,000 copies
4th printing	August 1976	10,000 copies
5th printing	August 1978	12,000 copies
6th printing	August 1985	5,000 copies
7th printing	July 1988	5,000 copies

"The purpose of the Junior League is exclusively educational and charitable and is: to promote voluntarism; to develop the potential of its members for voluntary participation in community affairs; and to demonstrate the effectiveness of trained volunteers."

Printed in the United States
Hart Graphics, Inc.
8000 Shoal Creek Blvd.
Austin, Texas 78758

FOREWORD

South Texas is more than just a place. It is a way of life dictated by its geography and culture.

It is an area whose history includes tales of cannabalistic Indians, plunderous buccaneers, and Spanish *conquistadores* — a history as colorful as its surroundings.

Its boundary extends East from Del Rio almost to San Antonio and then Southward past Corpus Christi to Brownsville and back up the Rio Grande Valley to Del Rio. It is bounded on the Southeast by the Gulf of Mexico and the Southwest by Mexico.

Travelers would have a difficult time finding a more picturesque, semi-tropical haven within the United States. It is an area lush with palm fronds, banana trees, and citrus groves, and beautiful with its ubiquitous bougainvillea in shades ranging from hot pink to majestic red.

It is a place in the sun, where winters are short and mild and summers are long. Constant cool Gulf breezes temper the heat and provide energy for weekend sailing ventures.

South Texas is an area where the cultures of the South, the West, and Mexico blend harmoniously. The influence of Mexico is visibly evident in the architecture, landscaping, customs, and even the culinary arts. In South Texas, *picante* sauce is an everyday staple, and *tortillas* and *tacos* are as commonplace as hot dogs and hamburgers. One is as likely to be serenaded at dinner by a colorful *mariachi* group as by a contemporary combo or a Western band.

Because of the tropical climate, or perhaps the area's proximity to Mexico, South Texas encourages a way of life that is casual, relaxed, and unhurried. It is a life characterized by warm hospitality, informality, and frequent gatherings of *amigos* for back yard barbecues, beach parties, patio suppers, *tamale* and beer socials, or even dinner on board a boat. These are activities that can be enjoyed almost year 'round.

In FIESTA, members of the Junior League of Corpus Christi have brought together the feel, gusto, and uniqueness of the area. These recipes have been collected by natives of South Texas or developed by newcomers who have succumbed to the easygoing way of life. The recipes capitalize on favorite native products, utilizing fresh seafood from the Gulf of Mexico, beef and game from area ranches, citrus fruit and produce from the fertile Rio Grande Valley, and foods and spices from Mexico.

The recipes have all been carefully tested. When necessary, minor changes have been made in ingredients so the dishes can be made as easily in Bronxville, New York, and Boise, Idaho, as in Corpus Christi, Texas. Those recipes marked with an * can be prepared quickly and easily at the end of a busy day.

FIESTA is a taste of Texas — South Texas!

This book encourages hospitality, gaiety, informal fun, excitement, color, and great food. As you prepare and enjoy these foods, you will experience some of the South Texas way of life and understand some of our reasons for naming this book

Fiesta

TABLE OF CONTENTS

		Page
1.	Mexican Food	3
2.	Beverages	37
3.	Appetizers	45
4.	Sandwiches	65
5.	Soups	73
6.	Salads and Salad Dressings	85
7.	Eggs, Cheese, Grains, and Pasta	113
8.	Seafood	125
9.	Poultry	145
10.	Meat	163
11.	Game	193
12.	Vegetables	203
13.	Sauces and Condiments	223
14.	Breads	233
15.	Desserts	249
16.	Dining Under Sail	291
	Index	299
	Order Form	311

EDITORS

Mrs. Lev H. Prichard, III   Mrs. William N. Woolsey

ASSISTANT TO THE EDITORS
Mrs. Gerald Heinzelmann

SUSTAINING ADVISOR
Mrs. Gerald A. Reeves

ILLUSTRATOR
Mrs. Leroy Taylor

COMMITTEE

Mrs. Sam L. Allen
Mrs. A. Jackson Ashmore
Mrs. William H. Barth
Mrs. Jack Best
Mrs. Richard Scott Bonner
Mrs. Charles Bonniwell
Mrs. John C. Brooke
Mrs. Charles Canfield
Mrs. John W. Creveling, Jr.
Mrs. Austin Davies
Mrs. Charles DeCou
Mrs. Ben Donnell
Mrs. R. Michael Dulaney
Mrs. Edwin A. Durham, II

Mrs. A. C. Gilmore
Mrs. Irvin C. Hatridge, Jr.
Mrs. Henry R. Hausman
Mrs. Donald Everett Jackson
Mrs. Lowell Kepp
Mrs. William Hall Keys
Mrs. Earl Sams Lightner
Miss Coleene McCracken
Mrs. W. Richard McCracken
Mrs. Joseph P. Mueller
Mrs. Gary Norton
Mrs. Jack M. Painter
Mrs. Jack Rice Turner
Mrs. Lawrence Riley Williams

**Favorite Recipes
of South Texas**

Mexican Food

1. MEXICAN FOOD

Mrs. Gerald Heinzelmann, Mrs. Lawrence Riley Williams,
Editors

Mexican food is such an integral part of South Texas cuisine that one living in this area will seldom spend many days without lunching or dining on at least an enchilada or a taco. The good Mexican cooks of South Texas have given us a legacy that is clearly woven into our lifestyle — ranging from the simplest to the most elegant of living and entertaining.

There are, of course, authentic Mexican dishes that can be utilized for lunch or dinner, but many recipes are of "Anglo" derivation, with the addition of generous amounts of ingredients and spices common to Mexican food. With a wealth of Mexican food ingredients becoming increasingly available throughout the United States, assembling a complete Mexican menu becomes a simple task.

Corn tortillas are a basic necessity when planning, and if one trembles at the thought of contructing her own, tortillas are almost nationally available in a canned version and are often found packaged in plastic on the grocers' shelves or in the freezer. Corn chips are a successful substitute for dipping and scooping.

Chilies are available in all phases of Mexican cooking. They vary in size, color, shape, and flavor. Generally, the smaller the chili, the hotter it is. In Mexico, fresh chilies are most often roasted in a hot oven, wrapped in moist towels, then skinned to achieve a milder flavor. They are also chopped raw to be used in the fiery sauces so often associated with cooking South of the Border.

A Mexican fiesta is conveniently adaptable to house or patio. On pleasant evenings in the spring and fall, patios are lit with luminarios, and mariachis serenade the guests. Hot colors — pinks, lime, orange — decorate the buffet table and complement the spicy food.

Whatever the occasion, South Texans of Mexican descent are at their happiest entertaining. They are warm and hospitable, eager to have you share with them. From their influence, we have collected favorite recipes to comprise this chapter. To aid those unfamiliar with Mexican cookery, suggested menus using recipes found later in this chapter are listed.

As the Mexicans would say, "Salud, amor, pesetas, y tiempo para gozarlas!" ("Health, love, wealth, and the time to enjoy them!")

Brunch

Sangrita

Huevos rancheros   Assorted fresh fruits

Pan dulce
SWEET ROLLS

Ladies' Luncheon

Border buttermilk

Sopa de flor de calabaza

Jalapeño pie   *or*   Mexican chef salad

Flan with caramel topping

Cocktails

Sangria   Margaritas

Picadillo   Nachos   Chili con queso

Dinner

Guacamole Salad

Marca's enchiladas Suissas   *or*   Chicken enchiladas

Josefinas

Cajeta   *or*   Kahlua over ice cream

Beverages

Mexico brews some of the world's best beers and ales, and these probably are the most appropriate beverages with a Mexican meal. Kahlua, an excellent coffee liqueur from Mexico, is a delicious conclusion for a South-of-the-Border evening.

Allie's Yacht Club Margaritas

1½ ounces tequila
Juice of 1 lime
½ ounce Triple Sec

1 cup ice
Salt

Blend all ingredients in an electric blender. Wet the rim of a glass; invert on a heavily salted towel. Strain the mixture into the glass and serve. Serves 1.

Mrs. Lawrence Riley Williams (Ann Reading Parsley)

Tequila Sunrise

1 ounce tequila
3 ounces lemon- or limeade

3 ounces orange juice

Fill a tall glass with crushed ice. Add tequila and fruit juices. Serves 1.

Mrs. Lawrence Riley Williams (Ann Reading Parsley)

Border Buttermilk

1 6-ounce can frozen pink lemonade (or limeade) concentrate
1 can tequila

Place ingredients in an electric blender and fill with ice. Blend until slushy. Serve in stemmed glasses. Garnish with a sprig of mint if desired. Serves 6 to 8.

Mrs. Charles DeCou (Martha McKamey)
Mrs. Lowell Kepp (Betty Ellis)

Juan's Tequila Sour

2 ounces tequila
2 ounces simple syrup

2 ounces fresh lime juice

Mix the above ingredients. The proportions may be varied to suit individual tastes. Serve over cracked ice. Serves 1.

Mrs. John W. Creveling, Jr. (Judy Hoepfner)

Sangrita

1 46-ounce can tomato juice
2 cups orange juice
6 tablespoons lime juice
6 tablespoons Worcestershire
  sauce

Tabasco brand pepper sauce
2 teaspoons onion juice
Salt
Pepper
1 cup tequila

Mix all ingredients and pour over a block of ice in a punch bowl. Serve as a before-lunch drink or with light brunch. Makes 10 cups.

Mrs. Leroy Taylor (Marcie Michels)

Sangria

6 oranges, sliced
3 lemons, sliced
1 lime, sliced

1 cup sugar
½ pint brandy
1 gallon dry red wine

Arrange the lemons, limes, and oranges in the bottom of a very large pitcher or crock. Sprinkle sugar over fruit. More sugar may be added if oranges are sour. Add the brandy and allow to sit at least 1 hour. Add wine, stir well, and allow to sit 30 minutes. Serve over ice in stemmed glasses. Makes 18 cups.

Mrs. Jack Modesett, Jr. (Marcia Heyne)

Sangria crossed the Atlantic with the Spanish to Mexico. Fruity and refreshing, it is widely served, the perfect beginning for a Mexican "fiesta"!

Tequila Brandy

1 fifth tequila   Rind of 1 orange
1 cup sugar

Remove 1 cup tequila from the bottle. Add sugar and orange rind cut in long strips to remaining tequila in bottle. Shake until sugar is dissolved. After 10 days remove orange peel, and you have a delicious after-dinner liqueur.

Mrs. Charles Canfield (Patricia Kitchen)

Coffee Liqueur

1 quart water   1 teaspoon vanilla
2½ cups sugar   2½ cups vodka
3 tablespoons instant coffee

Bring water, sugar, and coffee to a boil; barely simmer for 3 hours. Cool. Add vanilla and vodka; mix. Serve chilled or at room temperature. Keeps indefinitely. Makes about 1 fifth.

Mrs. Lawrence Riley Williams (Ann Reading Parsley)

Tortillas

Few South Texans, even those of Mexican descent, make corn tortillas "from scratch" today. Masa Harina, an instant masa made by Quaker Oats, makes a superior tortilla with a minimum of effort. As a bread, tortillas are wrapped in foil and steamed in the oven to soften and heat them, then served at once. Diners butter and salt the tortillas and roll them up to eat with their fingers. Cut in quarters and then fried crisp and drained, the tortilla becomes a tostado, the base for nachos and a dipper for numerous Mexican cocktail foods.

Flour tortillas are not difficult to make and are far better than those available in the grocery store. They are served hot from the griddle to be buttered, salted, and rolled up.

Tortillas de Harina No. 1

4 cups flour
2 teaspoons salt

6 tablespoons shortening
1 to 1¼ cups lukewarm water

Sift flour and salt; work in the shortening; stir in a cup of water; then form a ball. If necessary, use more water until the bowl is clear of all dough. Knead dough on a lightly floured board. Shape into biscuit-sized balls and let stand about 15 minutes. Roll out thin. Bake on a hot ungreased griddle or skillet for 2 minutes on 1 side; turn and cook about 1 minute on the other side. Makes 24.

Mrs. Thomas W. Marshall (Florence Deutz)

Tortillas de Harina No. 2

1½ cups flour
1 teaspoon baking powder
1 scant teaspoon salt

1 tablespoon shortening
½ to 1 cup very hot water

Combine dry ingredients. Cut in shortening. Add enough hot water to make dough stick together. Shape into biscuit-sized patties, roll out thin, and cook on a hot griddle until brown. Makes 8.

Though *tortillas de harina* are traditionally made without baking powder, its addition makes a lighter *tortilla*.

Mrs. Charles DeCou (Martha McKamey)

Appetizers

Chili con Queso
CHEESE WITH CHILIES

1 large onion, chopped
¼ cup bacon drippings
1 4-ounce can pickled whole
jalapeño peppers, drained and
chopped

1 13-ounce can evaporated milk
1 16-ounce box Old English
brand process cheese
½ teaspoon Tabasco brand
pepper sauce

Sauté chopped onion in hot bacon drippings. Add chopped jalapeños. Put remaining ingredients in the top of a double boiler. Stir until cheese is melted and mixture has thickened. Serve in a chafing dish with *tostados* or *tortilla* chips. For a milder *chili con queso*, use 2 or 3 chopped peppers and omit the Tabasco sauce. Makes 1 quart.

Mrs. Lawrence Riley Williams (Ann Reading Parsley)

Chili con queso *is not only a classic Mexican appetizer, but also an excellent first course. Put* tostados *on a small plate, pour the* chili con queso *over, and eat with a fork.*

Jalapeño Dip

2 pounds Velveeta brand process
cheese
1 large onion
2 to 3 tomatoes

1 pint pickled seeded jalapeño
peppers
1 tablespoon pepper
2 teaspoons salt

Grate cheese and melt in the top of a double boiler. Combine onion, tomatoes, jalapeños, salt, and pepper in a blender. Add mixture to melted cheese; stir and heat. Serve in a chafing dish with *tostados* for dipping. Makes 2 quarts.

Mrs. Gordon Heaney (Elizabeth Van Westrum)

Chili Dip

2 pounds ground beef	2 teaspoons cumin
1 tablespoon cooking oil	2 tablespoons chili powder
2 cans condensed tomato soup	⅛ teaspoon garlic salt
1 envelope dry onion soup mix	1 pound Velveeta brand
⅛ teaspoon pepper	process cheese
2 teaspoons oregano	

Sauté beef in hot oil. Add remaining ingredients except cheese; simmer 5 minutes. Add cheese and stir until melted. If too thick, add water. Serve in a chafing dish with *tostados*. Makes 2 quarts.

Mrs. Mercer T. Ivey (Jean Nunn)

Cut canned tamales in bite-sized pieces and wrap half a slice of bacon around each piece of tamale. Secure with a toothpick. Bake at 350 degrees 30 to 45 minutes or until bacon is crisp. They may be frozen before baking.

Picadillo

1 pound ground beef	2/3 cup water
(or venison)	¼ teaspoon oregano
½ bell pepper, chopped	½ cup dark raisins,
4 medium tomatoes, peeled	rinsed and drained
and chopped	½ cup white raisins,
6 tablespoons tomato paste	rinsed and drained
½ cup tomato sauce	Salt
1 tablespoon instant minced	Pepper
onion	Slivered almonds

Sauté meat and drain fat. Add remaining ingredients except almonds. Simmer slowly until well mixed, about 30 minutes. If meat mixture is too thick to use as a dip, add water. Serve in a chafing dish with almonds sprinkled on top. Use *tostados* for dipping. Serves 20.

Mrs. Earl Sams Lightner (Robin Holmes)
Mrs. Richard W. Sallee (Alice Heldenfels)

Bean Dip

1 can condensed black bean
  soup
1 can condensed bean with
  bacon soup
¼ cup water
1 teaspoon dry mustard
½ teaspoon cayenne pepper

½ teaspoon chili powder
2 cloves garlic, pressed
4 to 5 drops Tabasco brand
  pepper sauce
1 tablespoon vinegar
½ cup sour cream

Heat all ingredients except sour cream, stirring constantly. Add sour cream and simmer 10 minutes. Can be served warm or chilled. Serve with *tostados* for dipping. Makes 3 cups.

Mrs. Robert G. Kipp (Peggy Alcorn)

Queso y Carne
CHEESE AND BEEF

2 pounds Velveeta brand
  process cheese
1 large tomato, chopped
1 19-ounce can chili without
  beans

2 cloves garlic, pressed
1 medium onion, grated
1 tablespoon Worcestershire
  sauce

Melt cheese in the top of a double boiler. Add remaining ingredients. Cook until well blended and heated through. Serve in a chafing dish with *tostados*. Makes 2 quarts.

Mrs. Gerald Heinzelmann (Carolyn Jones)

Chalupas Compuestas

1 16-ounce can tomatoes	*Tabasco brand pepper sauce*
1 teaspoon thyme	*Tortillas*
1 teaspoon vinegar or lemon	*Shortening*
juice	*Refried beans*
1 teaspoon salt	*Shredded lettuce*
1 tablespoon minced onion	*Sliced avocado*

Simmer tomatoes and seasoning together to make a sauce. Fry *tortillas* in hot shortening until crisp; salt lightly. Spread refried beans on each *tortilla*. Sprinkle with shredded lettuce. Add a few slices of avocado. Top with tomato sauce and serve. Allow 2 per person for dinner.

Mrs. Robert G. Kipp (Peggy Alcorn)

Chalupas compuestas *make a great buffet-style, build-it-yourself dinner. Have platters of* tortillas *spread with refried beans, the lettuce and sliced avocados, and a bowl of the tomato sauce. Additions to the buffet table might include Quick Tortilla Stuffer, grated cheese, shredded chicken, and* guacamole.

Nachos

Tortillas	*Grated Cheddar cheese*
Refried beans	*Sliced pickled jalapeño peppers*

For appetizers, cut *tortillas* into quarters before frying. Otherwise, leave whole. Fry *tortillas* until crisp, spread with refried beans, sprinkle with grated cheese, and top with sliced jalapeño peppers. Broil until cheese melts. Serve hot. An excellent accompaniment to beer.

Mrs. Robert G. Kipp (Peggy Alcorn)

Cut jalapeño peppers in half, remove seeds, and stuff with pineapple cream cheese, pimiento cheese, chicken salad, or tuna fish salad. Refrigerate about 30 minutes before serving.

Soups

Peggy's Chili

1 pound lean ground beef
¼ cup bacon drippings
½ teaspoon salt
½ teaspoon pepper
2 tablespoons chili powder
1 tablespoon flour
1 teaspoon cocoa

1 teaspoon sugar
1 medium bell pepper, chopped
1 medium onion, chopped
2 cloves garlic, chopped
1 6-ounce can tomato paste
Water

Brown meat in bacon drippings. Add dry ingredients and mix thoroughly over low heat. Add bell pepper, onion, and garlic. Cook until onion is clear, add tomato paste, and mix thoroughly. Add enough water to cover the mixture in the pan. Simmer 45 minutes. Serves 4.

Mrs. Robert G. Kipp (Peggy Alcorn)

Chili con Carne

2 pounds chili meat (or venison
    and pork)
2 tablespoons chili powder
2 cloves garlic, minced
3 tablespoons flour
¼ cup shortening

2 tablespoons chopped suet
1 large onion, chopped
2 teaspoons salt
1/3 teaspoon crushed cumin seed
4 dried chili pods

Mix meat thoroughly with chili powder, garlic, and flour. Melt shortening and suet (if meat is lean) in a large, deep pot and sauté onion slowly until tender; add meat mixture. Cook slowly for 15 minutes or until meat falls apart and doesn't stick together. Add salt and gradually pour on hot water as needed, covering the meat. Simmer until meat is tender, 1 hour or more. While the chili is cooking, wash the dried chili pods and remove the seeds and stems. Boil the chili pods in a pot of water until the pulp becomes soft. Then remove from water and press the chili pods through a sieve with a wooden spoon. Add pulp to the chili. When chili is almost done, add the cumin. Serves 8.

Mrs. Robert Biel (Corinne Vauter)

Mother's Chili

2 pounds chili meat*
2 tablespoons corn oil
2 cloves garlic, minced
1 large onion, chopped
2 tablespoons chili powder
    (or more)
3 tablespoons flour

2 teaspoons salt
¼ teaspoon pepper
1 teaspoon oregano
1 teaspoon cumin seed
2 cups hot water
Juice of 1 lime

Brown meat in oil; add garlic and onion. Mix together chili powder, flour, salt, pepper, oregano, and cumin seed and add to meat mixture. Add water and lime juice. Simmer covered for 1 to 2 hours. Serves 8.

*South Texas butchers prepare a coarse-ground, almost a chopped, beef labeled as chili meat. Many cooks prefer this chunkier meat to ground beef.

Mrs. A. Jackson Ashmore (Gay Griffith)

Sopa de Flor de Calabaza
SQUASH-FLOWER SOUP

3 tablespoons butter
1 onion, chopped
1 quart squash flowers*
1 quart cream or milk

2 tablespoons flour
Salt
Pepper

Heat butter in a skillet; add onion and squash flowers. Sauté until the flowers collapse and the onions are transparent. Put into an electric blender with the milk and flour; blend until smooth. Return to heat, stirring until thickened. Add salt and pepper to taste. This cream soup has a very delicate flavor and a pale gold color. Makes 4 servings.

*Each morning gather the male flowers from the squash plants. Male flowers have no tiny fruits behind them, only stems. Rinse and shake them; then store them in a plastic bag in the refrigerator until 1 quart of flowers is accumulated.

Mrs. Dudley A. Chatham (Melba Welsh)

Salads

Mexican Chef Salad

4 tomatoes, chopped
1 large head lettuce, chopped
1 bunch green onions, chopped
6 ounces grated Cheddar cheese
2 avocados, chopped
Italian salad dressing

1 6¼-ounce bag tortilla chips
1 pound ground beef
1 15-ounce can Ranch Style
  brand beans
Salt
Pepper

Mix the first 5 ingredients and moisten with Italian salad dressing. Crush *tortilla* chips and mix into salad. Brown ground beef and add 1 can Ranch Style beans with juice to ground beef. Simmer 10 minutes. Salt and pepper to taste. When ready to serve, mix meat mixture with salad mixture and garnish with tomato and avocado wedges. Serves 6 to 8.

Mrs. Joe Browning (Anne Ahern)

Taco Salad

1 pound ground beef
1 package Lawry's brand taco
  sauce mix
¾ pound Velveeta brand
  process cheese

1/3 cup Ro-Tel brand tomatoes
  and green chilies
¾ head lettuce, shredded
2 tomatoes, chopped
1 6-ounce package corn chips

Make *taco* filling with ground beef and *taco* sauce mix. Melt cheese with Ro-Tel tomatoes. Mix shredded lettuce, tomatoes, meat, and ¼ the corn chips in a salad bowl. Pour cheese mixture over and top with remaining corn chips. Serve immediately. Serves 4. This is a complete meal and needs nothing else. Makes a good family supper or lunch.

Mrs. Jack M. Painter (Darlene Downer)

Guacamole Salad

6 *very ripe avocados*   Salt
3 *medium tomatoes, chopped*   1 *to 2 cloves garlic, minced*
1 *large onion, chopped*   *Lemon juice (optional)*
Tabasco brand pepper sauce

Peel and dice avocados; add tomatoes, onion, and seasonings. Mash with a potato masher to blend, leaving a few lumps. Variations to the basic *guacamole* may be achieved by adding grated Cheddar cheese, chopped jalapeño peppers, or Worcestershire sauce. Serves 12.

Serve as a salad, atop a slice of tomato, with a few *tostados* for decoration, or as a dip for raw vegetables or *tostados*. *Guacamole* is also used as a topping for *chalupas* and in *tacos*.

If made ahead, *guacamole* will turn dark unless preventative measures are taken. Return the avocado pits to the top of the salad and either sprinkle with lemon or lime juice or cover with plastic wrap to prevent air from reaching the *guacamole*. Remove the pits before serving.

Mrs. A. C. Gilmore (Clydell Hollon)

Eggs and Cheese

Border-Style Eggs

3 *sausage patties*, ½-*inch thick*   1 *teaspoon chili powder*
¼ *bell pepper, chopped*   1 *cup tomato juice*
1 *small onion, chopped*   *Eggs*
1 *teaspoon flour*

Crumble sausage into skillet over low heat. Add bell pepper and onion and sauté slowly until onion is clear. Add chili powder mixed with flour, stirring. Pour in tomato juice. Salt to taste, cover, and simmer over very low heat while you prepare eggs: scrambled, fried, or poached. Serve sauce over eggs. Serves 2.

Mrs. Lawrence Riley Williams (Ann Reading Parsley)

Huevos Rancheros
RANCH-STYLE EGGS

1½ cups chopped onion
1 clove garlic, minced
¼ cup bacon drippings
4 tomatoes, chopped

Jalapeño peppers, minced
½ teaspoon salt
6 eggs
6 fried tortillas

Sauté onion and garlic in bacon drippings for 5 minutes. Add tomatoes, jalapeños, and salt; cover and simmer for 10 minutes. Uncover and simmer an additional 10 minutes. Fry eggs and put 1 on top of each fried *tortilla*. Spoon sauce over each. Serves 6.

Mrs. Robert C. Wolter (Frances Overton)

Huevos rancheros are a popular breakfast across South Texas, cooked in the kitchen or over an open fire. Traditionally a fried egg on a tortilla topped with ranchero sauce, the sauce is also served with poached and scrambled eggs and is used as a filling for omelets.

Ann Lively's Ranchero Sauce

½ cup chopped onion
½ cup chopped celery
Butter
6 fresh tomatoes, peeled and
  chopped (or 2 cups canned
  tomatoes)

2 to 3 green chilies
1 8-ounce can tomato sauce
1 clove garlic, pressed
Cumin seed
Salt
Pepper

Sauté onions and celery in butter until soft. Add tomatoes, chilies, tomato sauce, and garlic. Add cumin seed, salt, and pepper. Cook until sauce and tomatoes look like gumbo; then cover and simmer for 45 minutes to 1 hour. Serve over eggs or any vegetable.

Mrs. Richard W. Sallee (Alice Heldenfels)

Ranchero Sauce

2 tablespoons butter
2 onions, chopped
1 clove garlic, minced
1 jalapeño pepper, chopped
2 tablespoons pimiento, chopped

1 tablespoon Worcestershire
   sauce
1 28-ounce can tomatoes
Salt
Pepper

Combine all ingredients and simmer 45 minutes to 1 hour or until thick.

Robert W. Woolsey

Chili Soufflé

4 4-ounce cans green chilies
   (sliced and seeded)
1½ cups shredded Cheddar and
   Jack cheeses

6 eggs, beaten
Salt
Pepper

Butter baking dish and line with green chilies. Top with remaining ingredients. Bake at 325 degrees for 30 minutes. Serves 8.

Mrs. Wayne Lundquist (Nina Gillespie)

Jalapeño Pie

1 11-ounce can pickled seeded
   jalapeño peppers

10 ounces sharp Cheddar cheese,
   grated
4 eggs, beaten

Line a glass pie pan with jalapeños that have been cut in slices lengthwise. Pat cheese over jalapeños, rounding slightly in the middle. Slowly pour in the beaten eggs. Bake at 275 degrees for 45 minutes. Slice and serve hot or at room temperature as a first course. Serves 8. Freeze after baking.

Green chilies may be substituted for a milder flavor.

Mrs. Nixon McNeil (Margaret Beecroft)

Cindy Ryder's White Smash

12 ounces Jack cheese
12 flour tortillas
Corn oil
1 pickled seeded jalapeño
   pepper, minced
¼ cup picante sauce

3 tablespoons butter
3 tablespoons flour
1 cup milk
1 cup sour cream
Garlic powder

Grease an 8-by-12-inch baking dish. Cut cheese into 24 finger-sized pieces. Dip *tortillas* in hot corn oil to soften. Place 2 pieces of cheese, a few pieces of minced pepper, and 1 teaspoon *picante* sauce on each *tortilla* and roll up. Place rolled *tortillas* in a row in the baking dish. Make a white sauce with butter, flour, and milk. Remove from heat and blend in sour cream and garlic powder. Pour over *tortillas*. Garnish with strips of pepper and additional *picante* sauce. Bake at 350 degrees about 20 minutes or until brown and bubbly. Serves 6.

Bell pepper can be substituted for the jalapeño pepper for a milder flavor. The casserole can be prepared several days in advance and refrigerated until ready to bake. If prepared ahead of time, make a thinner white sauce.

Mrs. John H. Yochem (Phyllis Nigh)

Green Chili Enchiladas

10 corn tortillas
Shortening
1 onion, chopped
1 to 2 cloves garlic, minced
2 tablespoons butter
1 16-ounce can tomatoes

1 pound American cheese,
   grated
8 ounces sour cream
1 4-ounce can green chilies,
   chopped

Dip *tortillas* in hot shortening to soften. In another skillet, sauté onion and garlic in butter until translucent; remove from heat and blend in remaining ingredients. Spread sauce in the middle of each *tortilla* and roll up. Place rolled *tortillas* in a greased 8-by-12-inch baking dish. Bake 30 minutes at 350 degrees. Serves 4 to 5.

Mrs. James C. Sharp, Jr. (Amber DeForest)

Poultry and Meat

Chicken Casserole Mexico

1 large onion, chopped
1 4-ounce can green chilies
¼ cup butter
1 can condensed cream of
chicken soup
1 5-1/3-ounce can evaporated
milk

2 cups chicken broth
10 corn tortillas
1 10-ounce can enchilada sauce
1 3-pound chicken, cooked,
boned, and diced
2 cups grated Cheddar cheese

Sauté onion and chilies in melted butter. Add soup, milk, and broth. Heat *enchilada* sauce; dip *tortillas* into sauce to soften. In a 3-quart casserole, layer the *tortillas*, chicken, half the cheese, and soup mixture. Top with remaining cheese. Refrigerate overnight. Bake at 350 degrees for 1 hour. Serves 6 to 8.

Mrs. William N. Woolsey (Sandra Callaway)

Creamed Chicken Tacos

24 tortillas
Cooking oil
2 small onions, diced
2 tablespoons butter
4 cups tomato juice
1 teaspoon salt

Pepper
2 4-ounce cans green chilies
4 cups grated Cheddar cheese
1 pint heavy cream
2 hens, boiled, boned, and cut up

Quarter *tortillas* and fry until crisp, as if making *tostados*. Drain on paper towels. Sauté onions in butter; add tomato juice, salt, and pepper. Add chilies; cover and simmer 30 minutes. Add grated cheese, cream, and chicken and heat until cheese is melted. Dip *tortillas* into chicken mixture. Alternate layers of chicken and *tortillas* in a 3-quart casserole. Allow to set 2 hours. Bake at 350 degrees for 30 minutes. Serves 10 to 12. Freezes well.

Mrs. George Wilson (Kathleen Coleman)

Chicken Enchiladas

1 3- to 4-pound hen
½ cup butter
1½ cups chopped onion
2 10-ounce cans Ro-Tel brand
  tomatoes and green chilies
1 28-ounce can tomatoes

1 2-pound box Velveeta brand
  process cheese
30 corn tortillas
Cooking oil
2 cups sour cream

Boil and bone chicken. Cool and tear into bite-sized pieces. Sauté onions slowly in butter until very tender. Drain tomatoes, reserving liquid. Add drained tomatoes to onions and simmer until mixture cooks down. Cut up cheese and add, stirring until melted. Add chicken. Mixture should be thick. If too thin, add more cheese. If too thick, add tomato juice. Mixture also will thicken as it cools. Fry *tortillas* in oil over medium heat to soften, about 1 minute. Drain on paper towels. Place a heaping tablespoon of chicken mixture in each *tortilla* and roll up. Place in 2 9-by-13-inch baking dishes. Pour remaining chicken mixture on top of *enchiladas*. Spread with sour cream and bake at 350 degrees about 30 minutes or until hot and bubbly. Serves 12 to 15. This can be made ahead of time and refrigerated or frozen, but do not add sour cream until ready to bake.

Mrs. Earl Sams Lightner (Robin Holmes)

Marca's Enchiladas Suissas*

10 to 12 corn tortillas
Cooking oil
4 cups boned chicken
1 cup sour cream

2 cans condensed cream of
  chicken soup
Instant minced onion
8 slices Swiss cheese

Fry *tortillas* quickly in oil to soften; drain. Heat remaining ingredients except for Swiss cheese. Fill each *tortilla* with a spoonful of chicken mixture, roll, and put in a 9-by-13-inch baking dish seamside down. Pour remaining mixture over *tortillas* and top with Swiss cheese. Bake at 350 degrees until bubbly, about 30 minutes. Serves 4 to 6.

Mrs. Ronald B. Brin (Lora Lou McCardell)

Chicken Tortilla Casserole

1 can condensed cream of
  mushroom soup
1 can condensed cream of
  chicken soup
1 soup can milk
1 small onion, chopped

1 4-ounce can green chilies,
  chopped
2 5-ounce cans boned chicken
10 corn tortillas, broken in pieces
12 ounces Cheddar cheese, grated

Mix together and heat the soups, milk, chilies, onion, and chicken. In a 3-quart buttered casserole, place a layer of *tortillas*, a layer of soup mixture, and a layer of grated cheese; repeat. Bake 30 minutes at 350 degrees. Serves 6.

Mrs. Kenneth McKamey (Hattie Bell Colston)

Calabaza con Pollo
SQUASH WITH CHICKEN

1 2½-pound chicken, cut up
1 onion, chopped
½ bell pepper, chopped
1 1-inch-long chili serrano,
  minced
2 cloves garlic, pressed
¼ to ½ teaspoon cumin

1 16-ounce can tomatoes
  (or tomato sauce)
Salt
Pepper
1 medium calabaza*
½ cup canned corn

Sauté chicken until well browned; add a little water, cover, and simmer for 15 minutes. Remove chicken to a plate and bone; add onion, bell pepper, chili, and garlic to the chicken fat and sauté for 2 minutes. Add tomatoes, salt, pepper, and cumin and cook for about 5 minutes. Pour sauce into another container, return chicken to the skillet, add calabaza that has been seeded and diced, and cover all with sauce. Cover the pan and simmer for 15 minutes. Add the corn, heat through, and serve at once. Serves 4. Pork chops may be substituted for the chicken.

*Calabaza is a Mexican melon-shaped squash. Any summer squash may be substituted.

Mrs. Dudley A. Chatham (Melba Welsh)

Mamie's Tamales

6½ pounds lean boned
  pork roast
6½ pounds venison or beef roast
5 pounds lard
4 teaspoons ground cumin seed
2 teaspoons ground black pepper
2 whole bulbs garlic, minced
2 teaspoons black pepper corns

1 3-ounce bottle chili powder
1¼ cups salt (or less)
¼ cup picante sauce
2 tablespoons ground fresh green
  chilies (optional)
3 pounds dried corn shucks
15 pounds prepared masa*

Place roasts in separate kettles, cover with water, and boil until roasts are tender. Reserve pork broth. Grind meat with the fine blade of a meat grinder, or mince. Melt 1 pound lard in a large kettle and combine with ground meat; mix together well. Add cumin, peppers, garlic, half the jar of chili powder, 2 to 4 tablespoons salt, *picante* sauce, and green chilies if desired. Stir until ingredients are well mixed. If the mixture seems dry, add pork broth until moist. Simmer uncovered until flavors are absorbed. Skim off any excess grease and reserve to use with the *masa*.

Soak corn shucks in warm water in a large dishpan to soften, overnight if desired. Rinse 2 or 3 times to remove any corn silk. Blot dry on paper towels. If corn shucks are large, cut them in half. Divide *masa* in half. To half of the *masa*, work in lard, ½ pound at a time, until 2 pounds have been added. Add ¼ bottle of chili powder and ½ cup salt. Mix by hand until ingredients are well blended. Put aside and repeat, using the remaining half of ingredients. Add pork broth to *masa* mixtures and mix with your hands until *masa* is a spreadable paste. Spread a thin layer of *masa* on the smooth side of the corn shucks. Place about 1 to 1¼ teaspoons of the meat mixture on each shuck. Roll the corn shuck like a cigar; then fold up the bottom of the shuck to keep the filling from falling out while cooking. Leave the top of the *tamale* open.

Place foil in the bottom of a tall kettle. Invert a stainless steel mixing bowl in the bottom of the kettle and place empty corn shucks around the mixing bowl in pyramid fashion. Add pork broth to a depth of several inches. Fill the kettle with *tamales*, out of the water and standing at a slant so the fillings will not fall out. Cover the top with empty corn shucks and foil. Cover and steam for 1 hour to 1 hour 30 minutes. Check *tamales* periodically; the *masa* will be firm but not dry when *tamales* are done. Makes 38 to 40 dozen.

Tamales can be and usually are frozen by the dozen in plastic bags. They are reheated by steaming, just as when they are first cooked.

*Prepared *masa* may be bought at *tortilla* factories, or you can make your own by using Masa Harina.

Mrs. Richard W. Sallee (Alice Heldenfels)

Tamales *are probably one of the most commonly known and loved varieties of Mexican food. They are delicious on any cocktail table, with any Mexican dinner, or standing alone. Mexican women make* tamales *in large quantities during the Christmas holidays, and hogs' heads, used traditionally instead of pork roast, are featured in all the meat markets in South Texas. Christmas Eve, especially, would not be complete without a steaming container of* tamales. *In fact,* tamales *are in such demand at Christmas time that you must place your order with your favorite* tamale *maker weeks in advance if you don't make your own.*

Mexican Beef Casserole

1½ pounds ground beef	1 can condensed cream of
1 medium onion, chopped	mushroom soup
Cooking oil	1 10-ounce can enchilada sauce
1 4-ounce can green chilies,	Salt
chopped	Pepper
1 can condensed cream of	12 corn tortillas
chicken soup	8 ounces Cheddar cheese, grated

Brown meat and onion in small amount of hot oil. Add chopped chilies, soups, sauce, salt, and pepper. Cook until well mixed. Place a layer of *tortillas* in a 9-by-13-inch baking dish. Cover with a layer of meat sauce. Alternate *tortillas* and meat, ending with meat sauce. Cover with grated cheese. Bake at 350 degrees for 20 minutes or until cheese melts. Serves 8.

Mrs. F. Elsea Peckenpaugh (Billie Stewart)

Ester's Enchiladas

2 pounds lean ground beef
2 tablespoons cooking oil
3 tablespoons chili powder
½ teaspoon salt
½ teaspoon pepper
½ teaspoon cumin

½ teaspoon minced garlic
1½ cups water
2 tablespoons flour
20 corn tortillas
1 onion, minced
1 pound Cheddar cheese, grated

Brown meat in oil. Add chili powder and spices. Mix flour with water and add to meat. Soften *tortillas* in hot oil. Dip warm *tortillas* in meat sauce. Fill *tortillas* with cheese and onion, roll up, and place in a 9-by-13-inch baking dish. Pour remaining meat sauce on top of *enchiladas*. Bake at 300 degrees for 30 minutes. Serves 10.

Mrs. Charles K. McCauley (Claire Jo Cummings)

Peggy's Enchiladas

1 tablespoon chili powder
1 10-ounce can enchilada sauce
1 recipe Peggy's Chili
20 corn tortillas

1 cup bacon drippings
2 cups grated Cheddar cheese
1 large onion, minced

Add chili powder and *enchilada* sauce to hot chili. Heat *tortillas* in hot drippings until soft; drain on paper towels. One at a time, place *tortillas* in a 9-by-13-inch baking dish. Put 1 teaspoon chili, 1 tablespoon cheese, and a little minced onion in each *tortilla*. Using your hands or kitchen tongs, roll up the *tortilla*, turn it so the seam is down, and move it to the end of the dish. Repeat until dish is full. Cover *enchiladas* with remaining chili, onion, and cheese, in that order. Bake at 350 degrees for 20 minutes. Serves 10.

To prepare ahead of time, heat *enchiladas* until cheese is bubbly, cool for 30 minutes, cover, and refrigerate. Reheat before serving.

Mrs. Robert G. Kipp (Peggy Alcorn)

Quick Tortilla Stuffer

1 pound lean ground beef
2 cloves garlic, pressed
2 tablespoons instant minced
   onion
1 8-ounce can tomato sauce
1 tablespoon chili powder

½ teaspoon cumin
Salt
Water
20 tortillas
Grated Cheddar cheese

Brown the meat with the garlic. Drain off any excess drippings. Add onion flakes, tomato sauce, chili powder, cumin, salt to taste, and a little water; simmer about 5 minutes. Heat *tortillas* on a griddle. If they are dry, dip them in water first. Put the *tortillas* in a warm earthenware pot with a lid. Cook the meat mixture until it has dried out. Serve in a bowl on the table with the pot of *tortillas* and a bowl of grated cheese. Each person places a spoonful of meat into a *tortilla*, tops with cheese, and folds the *tortilla*. A lettuce and tomato salad will complete a simple meal. Serves 8. Also good as a *taco* filling.

Mrs. Dudley A. Chatham (Melba Welsh)

Flautas

2 pounds ground beef
3 tablespoons chili powder
Salt
Pepper
1 tablespoon ground cumin
2 tablespoons flour
Water

Lettuce, chopped
Tomatoes, chopped
Grated Cheddar cheese
Sour cream
Guacamole
20 tortillas

Sauté ground beef until all the pink has disappeared. Add chili powder, salt, pepper, and cumin. Sprinkle flour over the meat. When the flour is absorbed, add enough water to moisten the meat mixture. Place the meat mixture, lettuce, tomatoes, and cheese in hot *tortillas*. Fold *tortillas* and top with *guacamole* and dabs of sour cream. Serve at once. Serves 10.

Mrs. Lawrence Riley Williams (Ann Reading Parsley)

Tacos

2 onions, chopped
1 clove garlic, pressed
Shortening
1 pound lean ground beef
1 teaspoon salt
2 teaspoons chili powder

¼ cup chili sauce (or more)
½ teaspoon cumin
12 corn tortillas
1 cup shredded lettuce
1 to 2 tomatoes, chopped
8 ounces Cheddar cheese, grated

Sauté half the onion and the garlic in shortening until translucent. Stir in beef, salt, and chili powder; sauté until beef is brown. Add cumin and chili sauce. In a skillet, heat *tortillas* in hot shortening until limp; fold in half and continue to fry until crisp. Spoon the beef mixture into the *taco* shells and top the *tacos* with cheese, onion, lettuce, and tomatoes.

Mrs. John Charles Abbott (Jane Belfour)

South of the Border Spaghetti

2 medium onions, chopped
1 clove garlic, minced
1 medium bell pepper, chopped
3 tablespoons bacon drippings
1 pound ground beef
2 tablespoons chili powder
1 teaspoon salt
Tabasco brand pepper sauce
Cayenne pepper

Paprika
1 tablespoon catsup
1 10-ounce can Ro-Tel brand
  tomatoes and green chilies
  (or less)
2 tablespoons Worcestershire
  sauce
1 8-ounce box thin spaghetti
1 8-ounce can tomato sauce

Brown onions, garlic, and bell pepper in bacon drippings. Add meat and remaining ingredients, except spaghetti and tomato sauce. Cook sauce until meat is tender. Cook spaghetti. Place spaghetti in a 2-quart baking dish; pour meat sauce over spaghetti and pour tomato sauce over all. Cover and bake at 350 degrees for 15 to 20 minutes. Serves 6.

Mrs. Gordon Heaney (Elizabeth Van Westrum)

Chili Casserole*

10 corn tortillas
Shortening
2½ cups chili without beans
1 cup chopped tomato
1 cup chopped green onion,
   including tops

¼ teaspoon cumin
¼ teaspoon oregano
¼ teaspoon pressed garlic
1 cup sour cream
1 cup grated Cheddar cheese

Soften the *tortillas* in hot shortening. In a 2-quart casserole, place in order *tortillas*, chili, tomato, and onion. Sprinkle the garlic and spices on top. Spread with sour cream; sprinkle with cheese. Bake at 350 degrees for 30 minutes. Serves 4 to 6.

Mrs. Leslie Giddens (Frances Quinn)

Chili-Bean Casserole*

1 15-ounce can hominy, drained
1 15-ounce can Ranch Style
   brand beans
1 19-ounce can chili

1 small onion, chopped
1 cup grated Cheddar cheese
1 cup crushed corn chips

Layer hominy, beans, chili, and onion in order listed in a 1½-quart casserole. Sprinkle with cheese and top with crushed corn chips. Bake at 350 degrees for 30 minutes. Serves 6.

Mrs. A. C. Gilmore (Clydell Hollon)

Mexican Meat Loaf

2 pounds lean ground beef
2 eggs, beaten
1 teaspoon dried parsley flakes
1 8-ounce can tomato sauce
1 slice bread, torn
1/3 cup crushed corn chips
1 teaspoon chili powder

1 to 2 tablespoons instant
   minced onion
¼ to ½ teaspoon instant
   minced garlic
Salt
Pepper

Mix all ingredients until well blended. Place in a loaf pan. Bake at 350 degrees for 1 hour 15 minutes. Serves 6 to 8. Can be prepared ahead. Can be frozen uncooked; thaw thoroughly and bake as above.

Mrs. Thomas W. Marshall (Florence Deutz)

Mamie's Calabaza

3½-pound ¼-inch-thick
round steak
3 to 4 tablespoons bacon
drippings
2 onions, chopped
3 large cloves garlic, minced
4 to 4½ pounds calabaza
(or zucchini)

8 ears corn (or 3 17-ounce cans
whole kernel corn)
2 16-ounce cans tomatoes
2 teaspoons ground cumin
1 tablespoon salt
¾ teaspoon pepper

Cut steak into bite-sized cubes; brown in bacon drippings. Add onions and garlic and continue to brown for several minutes. Wash, stem, and seed calabaza and cut into 1 to 1½-inch chunks, but do not peel. Cut corn into 1½-inch chunks, cob and all (or use canned corn). Add remaining ingredients, cover, and simmer 1 hour 30 minutes. Serve in large flat soup dishes. Serves 12.

Mrs. Joe P. Nelson (Harriet Hornish)

Mexican Pork Chop Supper

2 large calabaza
2 pounds pork chops
2 tablespoons cooking oil
¼ teaspoon cumin
¼ teaspoon pepper

2 cloves garlic, minced
½ teaspoon salt (or more)
1 7½-ounce can tomatoes,
drained
1 small onion, chopped

Pare squash and cut in small pieces. Cube pork chops. Cook chops in hot cooking oil until brown. Add squash and remaining ingredients; simmer until squash is tender. Bake in a 2-quart casserole at 350 degrees for 30 minutes. Serves 6.

Chicken may be used in place of pork chops, but pork chops add more flavor.

Mrs. Charles K. McCauley (Claire Jo Cummings)

Vegetables

Spanish Rice

5 tablespoons bacon drippings
1 cup rice
½ medium onion, chopped
½ medium bell pepper, chopped
½ teaspoon whole cumin seed

3 cloves garlic
1 6-ounce can tomato paste
Salt
Pepper
5 cups water

Heat drippings in a cast iron skillet. Add rice and sauté until golden, stirring frequently. Stir in chopped onion and bell pepper and cook about 5 minutes. Mash garlic and cumin together in a mortar; add to the rice. Rinse the mortar with 1 cup water and add to the rice. Add tomato paste and rinse the can with more of the measured water. Mix together well, salt and pepper to taste, and add remains of the 5 cups of water. Reduce heat, cover, and simmer slowly for 45 minutes to 1 hour, stirring occasionally. Serves 6.

Mrs. Gerald Heinzelmann (Carolyn Jones)

Kay's Calabaza

3 pounds calabaza
2 onions, sliced
1¼ teaspoons salt
Water
½ cup celery, minced
1 egg, beaten

3 slices bread, torn
½ teaspoon pepper
¼ teaspoon oregano (optional)
1 cup grated American cheese
Paprika

Slice squash and put in a medium sauce pan. Add onions and ¼ teaspoon salt. Add water and cook until tender; drain. Mash with a potato masher. Add celery. Mix the egg with the bread, remaining salt, pepper, and oregano if desired. Mix bread mixture, squash mixture, and cheese. Pour into a greased 2-quart casserole and sprinkle with paprika. Bake at 350 degrees for 25 minutes. Serves 8.

Mrs. James W. Cottingham (Linda Yancy)

Frijoles
PINTO BEANS

1 pound dried pinto beans
1 tablespoon sugar
1 tablespoon salt (or more)

½ cup bacon drippings
2 to 3 cloves garlic, minced
Cold water

Place beans and sugar in a pan with enough water to cover. Simmer, covered, 3 hours or until beans are soft. Add additional water during cooking if needed. Add bacon drippings, salt, and garlic. Cook at least 1 more hour, stirring occasionally. This can be cooked for more than 4 hours or overnight if there is enough water. Serves 8.

Mrs. Robert G. Kipp (Peggy Alcorn)

Refritos
REFRIED BEANS

¼ to ½ cup bacon drippings
1 pound pinto beans, cooked

Salt

Heat bacon drippings in a skillet; add cold beans. Stir frequently until beans are hot. Mash with a fork or potato masher. Brown beans until dry and a little crusty, stirring frequently.

Mrs. Robert G. Kipp (Peggy Alcorn)

Condiments

Chili Pequin Sauce

1 quart fresh chili pequins
2 cups chopped onion
1 clove garlic, chopped

1 tablespoon salt
1 teaspoon pepper
Vinegar

Cover first 5 ingredients with vinegar. Blend in electric blender until finely chopped. Makes 2 quarts. A very hot sauce for cooking and seasoning.

Mrs. Fred L. Crook, Jr. (Gibbs Beasley)

Alice Eleanora Nesby's Picante Sauce

½ cup chopped onion
3 cloves garlic, pressed
2 tablespoons cooking oil
24 chili pequins

1 16-ounce can tomatoes
(or 2 cups peeled)
1½ tablespoons vinegar
1 teaspoon salt

Sauté onion and garlic in oil. Coarsely blend together the tomatoes and *chili pequins*. Combine all ingredients and cook 45 minutes or until thick. Store in the refrigerator. Makes 1 pint.

Mrs. Richard W. Sallee (Alice Heldenfels)

Jalapeño Jelly

1 cup ground bell pepper
½ cup fresh ground jalapeño
  pepper
1½ cups cider vinegar

6½ cups sugar
1 6-ounce bottle Certo brand
  pectin
Green food coloring

Remove seeds and veins and grind bell peppers and jalapeños. Add vinegar and sugar and boil for 20 minutes. Remove from heat; allow mixture to set for 20 minutes. Return to rolling boil, stirring constantly, for 2 minutes. Add Certo; continue to boil for 5 minutes, stirring constantly. Add green food coloring. Pour into 6 sterile half-pint jars and seal. Excellent as an accompaniment to roast.

Mrs. Henry Gillespie (Cornelia Martin)

Breads

Jalapeño Corn Bread

1 cup corn meal
½ teaspoon baking soda
¾ teaspoon salt
1 cup buttermilk
2 eggs, beaten
½ cup melted butter or bacon
   drippings

1 medium onion, chopped
1 17-ounce can yellow, cream-
   style corn (or 3½ cups
   fresh corn)
1 cup grated Cheddar cheese
1 jalapeño pepper, chopped

Mix all ingredients, except cheese and jalapeño, and pour ½ of mixture into a hot, well-greased 9-by-9-inch pan. Place cheese over the batter; sprinkle with jalapeños. Add remaining batter. Bake at 350 degrees for 45 minutes. Cool before serving. Serves 8 to 10. Green chilies may be substituted for jalapeño pepper if a milder flavor is desired.

Mrs. Jerry E. Fischer (Alice Ann Peters)

Josefinas

8 Mexican hard rolls
1 cup canned green chilies
1 cup butter

1 clove garlic, minced
1 cup mayonnaise
8 ounces Jack cheese, grated

Slice rolls into ½-inch slices; toast on 1 side. Rinse seeds off chilies and chop; mix with butter and garlic. Spread the chili mixture on the untoasted sides of bread slices. Mix mayonnaise and cheese; spread on the bread. Broil until cheese is brown and puffy. Serve at once. Makes about 30. One thin loaf of French bread may be substituted for the rolls.

Mrs. Leroy Taylor (Marcie Michels)

Maximilian and Carlotta brought bread-making methods with them from France in the nineteenth century, as well as the clay ovens in which to bake the bread. Though French rule was short-lived, the bread has remained; and Mexican bakeries on both sides of the Border make excellent hard rolls and loaves. Thus, a hot loaf of French or Italian bread can be successfully served with a Mexican meal.

Desserts

Nogada Amador Ayala
MEXICAN PRALINES

1 pound dark brown sugar
1 cup granulated sugar
1 cup water

1 3-inch-long slice bacon
1 cup pecans

Boil sugars, water, and bacon together, until candy reaches the soft ball stage. Remove bacon. Working very fast, remove candy from heat and beat until creamy. When candy begins to cream, add pecans, beat, and quickly drop on waxed paper. Makes about 4 dozen.

Mrs. C. L. Concklin (Doraine Geiger)

Pour 1 ounce of tequila over a half-cup serving of orange, lemon, lime, or pineapple sherbet.

Pan de Polvo

3 pounds shortening
5 pounds + 2 cups flour
5 cups sugar
1 teaspoon salt

1 cup boiling water
1 tablespoon anise seed
6 sticks Mexican cinnamon

Cut shortening into flour, 2 cups sugar, and salt. Pour boiling water over anise seed to make a strong tea. Add about ¾ cup to the flour mixture to make a dough. Roll the dough out between sheets of waxed paper. Cut into desired shapes and bake at 300 degrees about 20 minutes. Pulverize cinnamon in an electric blender and mix with remaining sugar. Roll the hot cookies in the mixture. Makes several hundred small cookies.

Mrs. Frank B. Adams (Jeanne Stewart)

Flan with Caramel Topping

2½ cups sugar
1 tablespoon water
8 eggs

1 teaspoon vanilla
½ teaspoon salt
1 quart milk, scalded

Caramelize 1 cup sugar. Add water and cook 1 minute, stirring constantly. Pour caramel into 12 custard cups, 1 at a time, tilting each cup to coat the sides. Lightly beat eggs. Add remaining sugar, vanilla, and salt. Stir in milk. Pour into custard cups. Set cups in a pan with 1 inch hot water. Bake in a preheated 350-degree oven for 30 minutes or until a silver knife near the edge comes out clean. Unmold before serving. Serves 12.

Mrs. F. William Foran (Sylvia Sarphie)

Pour 1 ounce of Kahlua over chocolate chip ice cream. Top with toasted coconut.

Cajeta
CARAMELIZED MILK DESSERT

1 14-ounce can condensed milk
2 egg whites

1 to 2 jiggers brandy or rum

Remove paper from milk can. Place can in a sauce pan with enough water to cover can completely. Boil at least 3 hours. Be sure to keep can covered at all times. If it boils dry, it will explode. Open can and pour milk over stiffly beaten egg whites. Fold in the egg whites. If egg whites start to get lumpy, use an electric beater and beat until smooth. As you are mixing the hot caramelized milk with the egg whites, add brandy or rum, a little at a time. Serve in individual ramekins, 4 to 5 tablespoons to a serving. Top with cream or whipped cream. This is very sweet and small servings are advisable. Serves 5.

Mrs. Robert G. Kipp (Peggy Alcorn)

Beverages

2. BEVERAGES

Favorite South Texas beverages include those made with the delicious light rum and tequila from Mexico and juices from the citrus of the Rio Grande Valley. There are tall drinks for thirst-quenchers on hot summer days; and punches for morning coffees, children's birthday parties, and major celebrations like debutante parties and wedding receptions. There are even hot drinks for the few days of winter when there is a log burning in the fireplace and a Norther blowing outside.

Cocktails

Frozen Daiquiri

2 6-ounce cans frozen limeade   6 cans water
1 6-ounce can frozen lemonade   1 fifth light rum

Mix all ingredients together and put in a container in the freezer. Spoon from container into glasses. The mixture will stay slushy indefinitely in freezer. Serves 12.

Mrs. Gerald Heinzelmann (Carolyn Jones)

Vickie's Strawberry Daquiri

1 cup light rum   1 package frozen sliced
¼ cup fresh lemon juice   strawberries

Put all ingredients in the blender container and blend at high speed until smooth. Add a tray of crushed ice cubes and blend again. Serves 6 or 7.

Mrs. Gilbert Wright, III (Rosemary Hume)

Tawhiri Buster

Carbonated grapefruit drink or   1 jigger light rum
   Fresca brand diet drink

Fill a tall glass with ice; add rum and grapefruit drink. Stir. Serves 1.

Mrs. Earl Sams Lightner (Robin Holmes)

Pineapple Refresher

1 8¼-ounce can crushed
   pineapple
4 ounces light rum

¼ cup confectioners sugar
2 cups cracked ice
2 sprigs mint

Blend first 3 ingredients together at high speed until smooth. Add cracked ice. Pour into tall glasses and top with fresh mint. Serves 2. This makes a smooth ladies' drink.

Mrs. Maurice Priday (Joan McCroskey)

Whiskey Sour Old South

½ lemon, rind and all
Sugar

Bourbon

Place lemon in bottom of silver mint julep cup and sprinkle with sugar. Muddle with wooden muddler. Put in a straw and pack with crushed ice. Fill with bourbon. Serves 1.

Mrs. J. Michael Mahaffey (Lynn Smith)

Bloody Mary

1 jigger vodka
1 6-ounce can tomato juice
Dash Tabasco brand
   pepper sauce

½ teaspoon picante sauce
Salt
Pepper
½ teaspoon Worcestershire sauce

Put ice in a glass, then vodka. Add tomato juice to top and then seasonings. Serves 1. If you prefer your drinks hotter, use Snap-E-Tom brand tomato drink in place of tomato juice.

Mrs. Earl Sams Lightner (Robin Holmes)

"Bloody Shame"

1 46-ounce can tomato juice
1 6-ounce can Snap-E-Tom
  brand tomato drink
1 tablespoon Worcestershire
  sauce

2 tablespoons lemon juice
½ teaspoon Tabasco brand
  pepper sauce
1 teaspoon salt
Dash pepper

Mix ingredients in a pitcher. Serve in tall iced glasses. This is a good eye-opener for a house party. Each guest may add vodka or not as he chooses. Serves 12. This is not too hot, but spicy!

Mrs. Lev H. Prichard, III (Ella Wall)

Wine Punches

Sherry Flip

1½ cups orange juice
1 egg
½ cup lemon juice

1 cup dry Sherry
1 to 2 teaspoons sugar

Blend all ingredients in blender. Serve over ice or chill in refrigerator. Serves 4. This unusual and refreshing drink is good before brunch.

Mrs. Jack Best (Betty Reno)

French 75's

Large chunk of ice
4¼ ounces brandy
1 fifth Sauterne
1 fifth Champagne

1 10-ounce bottle carbonated
  water
1 ounce Curaçao*

Combine ingredients in the order listed and chill. Serves 15 to 20.
  *If unable to get Curacao, soak grated orange rind in 1 ounce Cointreau or Triple Sec for 24 hours, then substitute.

Mrs. A. Jackson Ashmore (Gay Griffith)

Gluehwein

1 bottle dry red wine
1 to 2 cups strong tea
1 cup light rum
3 sticks cinnamon (or less)

½ to 1 cup sugar
Juice of 3 lemons
Juice of 2 oranges

Heat without boiling. Serve hot. Serves 12.

Mrs. Jack M. Painter (Darlene Downer)

Fish House Punch

1 fifth Sauterne
1 fifth Southern Comfort

1 fifth Champagne
1 quart carbonated water

Combine ingredients and chill. When ready to serve, pour over a block of ice in a punch bowl. Serves 30.

Mrs. Charles DeCou (Martha McKamey)

Non-Alcoholic Drinks

Bride's Bowl

2 fifths sparkling Catawba
  grape juice* (or champagne)
2 quarts carbonated water

Juice of 4 lemons
4 cups canned cubed pineapple
1 cup sugar

Add lemon juice and sugar to canned pineapple and let stand several hours. Combine in punch bowl with chilled grape juice and add a small block of ice. Pour in the carbonated water and serve immediately. Garnish with orange slices, pineapple tidbits, maraschino cherries, or strawberries. Serves 20.

This resembles champagne punch when made with Catawba grape juice and is excellent when you want festive bubbles without alcohol.

*Catawba grape juice can be found in the gourmet section of food stores.

Mrs. Lev H. Prichard, III (Ella Wall)

Golden Wedding Punch

2 cups lemon juice
2 cups orange juice
2 cups sugar
2 cups water
4 quarts chilled ginger ale

Combine all ingredients except ginger ale. Let stand several hours. When ready to serve, add ginger ale. This is pretty served with decorated ice ring in punch bowl. Serves 24. Fresh mint sprigs lend color and make a refreshing flavor addition.

Mrs. Max J. Luther, III (Maxine Jenkins)

Basic Fruit Punch

2 6-ounce cans frozen orange juice
2 6-ounce cans frozen lemonade
1 46-ounce can pineapple juice
2 quarts water
1 28-ounce bottle ginger ale
Maraschino cherries

Combine all juices and water. Add ginger ale and maraschino cherries when ready to serve. Makes about 35 4-ounce cups.

CRANBERRY PUNCH:

8 cups basic fruit punch
2½ cups lemon-lime rickey mix
2 cups cranberry juice
1 quart orange sherbet

Combine basic fruit punch with lemon-lime rickey mix and cranberry juice. Add orange sherbet and serve. Makes about 25 4-ounce punch cups.

LIME PUNCH:

10 cups basic fruit punch
2½ cups lemon-lime rickey mix
1 quart lime sherbet

Combine basic fruit punch with lemon-lime rickey mix. Add sherbet and serve. Makes 25 4-ounce punch cups.

Mrs. Garnett Tabor Brooks, Jr. (Patsy Linkenhoger)

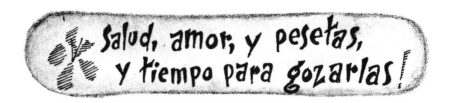

Salud, amor, y pesetas, y tiempo para gozarlas!

Christmas Party Punch

1 3-ounce package
  cherry-flavored gelatin
1 cup boiling water
1 6-ounce can frozen lemonade

3 cups cold water
1 quart cranberry juice
1 28-ounce bottle ginger ale

Dissolve gelatin in boiling water. Add remaining ingredients. Chill or serve over ice. This can be made ahead of time except for the ginger ale, which must be added just before serving. Serves 25.

Mrs. Ben Donnell (Elinor Drake)

Coffee Punch

1 quart heavy cream
1/3 to ½ cup sugar
4 teaspoons vanilla

1 gallon strong coffee, chilled
1 quart vanilla ice cream
Cinnamon sticks

Whip cream and add sugar and vanilla. Fold cream into chilled coffee. Just before serving stir in ice cream. Serve in glasses with a stick of cinnamon. Serves 30.

Mrs. Edwin A. Durham, II (Kaye Tarrant)

Wassail

1 quart hot tea
1 quart cranberry juice
1 quart apple juice
3 sticks cinnamon
12 whole cloves

1 cup sugar
2 cups orange juice
¾ cup lemon juice
1 orange, sliced
1 lemon, sliced

Combine all ingredients except orange and lemon slices. Bring to a boil. Pour into a bowl and float fruit slices. Serves 16 to 20.

Mrs. Ben Donnell (Elinor Drake)

Hot Spiced Percolator Punch*

3 cups pineapple juice
3 cups water
1 tablespoon whole cloves
½ tablespoon whole allspice

3 sticks cinnamon, broken
¼ teaspoon salt
½ cup brown sugar,
    lightly packed

Put pineapple juice and water in bottom of an 8-cup percolator. Put the rest of the ingredients in the top. Perk for 10 minutes. Serve hot in mugs. Serves 6.

Mrs. R. Michael Dulaney (Florence "Sue" Williams)

Hot Apricot Drink

1 cup water
2 tablespoons sugar
4 whole cloves

1 3-inch stick cinnamon
1 12-ounce can apricot nectar
2 tablespoons lemon juice

Boil the first 4 ingredients for 5 minutes and then strain. Add apricot nectar and lemon juice; heat and serve. Serves 4.

Mrs. William N. Woolsey (Sandra Callaway)

Mulled Grape Juice

1 cup sugar
2 cups water
12 whole cloves
2 sticks cinnamon

1 quart grape juice
2 tablespoons lemon juice
½ teaspoon grated lemon rind

Combine first 4 ingredients and boil for a few minutes. Then add remaining ingredients; bring to a boil and serve in mugs. Serves 6. Adding 1 jigger of kirsch to each mug makes a nice change.

Mrs. Richard King, III (Jimmie Rose Harrison)

Beverage recipes found in Chapter 1. MEXICAN FOOD:

Allie's Yacht Club Margaritas
Tequila Sunrise
Border Buttermilk
Juan's Tequila Sour

Sangrita
Sangria
Tequila Brandy
Coffee Liqueur

Appetizers

3. APPETIZERS

The cocktail table is as likely a place as any to reveal the multitude of influences on the South Texas cook and hostess. Fresh seafood from the nearby Gulf served hot or cold, a barbecued tenderloin of beef with tiny biscuits, a platter of raw vegetables, Mexican food.

Regardless of what is served, two things are almost always certain: the food will be spicy, and it can be prepared ahead of time. Southern hospitality combines with Western informality in Corpus Christi, and few specialties call for a cook in the kitchen or a butler with a silver tray.

Meats

Spicy Sausage Balls

2 pounds hot bulk sausage
2 eggs, well beaten
2/3 cup Progresso brand
    seasoned bread crumbs
4 teaspoons curry powder
½ teaspoon chili powder
1/3 cup catsup

2 8-ounce cans tomato sauce
    with mushrooms
2 tablespoons soy sauce
2 tablespoons Worcestershire
    sauce
1 3-ounce can mushroom crowns
    (optional)

Break up sausage; add eggs, bread crumbs, curry powder, and chili powder and mix well. Shape into ¾-inch balls and brown over low heat on all sides, draining off fat as it accumulates. Put sausage balls on paper towels to drain. Combine remaining ingredients in sauce pan. Add sausage balls. Simmer, covered, 15 minutes. Serve in chafing dish. Makes 100.

This freezes beautifully. Thaw completely before removing from freezer container to keep from breaking meat balls. Add 1 8-ounce can tomato sauce to pan when reheating.

Mrs. Lev H. Prichard, III (Ella Wall)

Swedish Meat Balls

3 slices white bread, crusts
   removed
½ cup half and half
¾ cup minced onion
¼ cup butter or olive oil
1 pound lean ground beef,
   ground twice
2 eggs
1 clove garlic, pressed

½ teaspoon mace or nutmeg
1 teaspoon salt
1 teaspoon seasoned salt
½ teaspoon pepper
2 tablespoons chopped chives
2 tablespoons flour
½ teaspoon tomato paste
1 cup beef stock
1 cup sour cream

Soak bread in half and half. Sauté the onion in 1 tablespoon oil until soft. Cool. Place ground beef in large mixing bowl with the 2 lightly beaten eggs, garlic, mace, salts, pepper, chives, sautéed onion, and the bread from which most of the cream has been squeezed. Work with hands until well blended. Form into large meat balls for a main course, or into thumbnail-sized balls for *hor d'oeuvres*. Heat the remaining oil and slowly brown the meat balls. Remove the meat balls from the skillet and blend into the drippings the flour and tomato paste. Stir until well blended, then slowly add stock. Cook over low heat until thick. Before serving, gradually stir in the sour cream, taste for seasoning, then return meat balls to this mixture and slowly reheat. Serve from a chafing dish with toothpicks. Serves 12 to 16.

Mrs. Gerald Heinzelmann (Carolyn Jones)

Rumaki

16 chicken livers
8 water chestnuts

8 slices bacon, halved

Wash the livers and drain on paper towel. Large livers should be cut in half. Cut chestnuts into halves. Wrap bacon around livers with chestnuts. Broil, turning once, until bacon is crisp. Makes 16.

Mrs. Earl Sams Lightner (Robin Holmes)

Paté de Fois Gras in Aspic

1 can condensed beef broth   ½ cup butter
1 tablespoon unflavored gelatin   ¾ cup dry Sherry
1 pound liverwurst

Heat beef broth and add gelatin. When cool, add Sherry. Cover bottom of mold with beef broth and chill until firm. Cream liverwurst and butter and place in center of 1-quart mold. Pour remaining liquid around the liverwurst. Chill until firm. Unmold and serve with crackers.

Mrs. Verne E. Powell (Elizabeth Hunter)

Seafood

Frosted Caviar Cheese Mold

Dash Tabasco brand   1 cup cottage cheese
  pepper sauce   1 clove garlic, pressed
Juice of ½ lemon   1½ tablespoons gelatin
1 tablespoon soy sauce   2 tablespoons dry Sherry
1 tablespoon seasoned salt   1 to 2 2-ounce jars imported
1 cup sour cream   caviar

Mix all seasonings, sour cream, and cottage cheese in blender. Mix gelatin and Sherry and dissolve in top of double boiler. Add to sour cream and cheese mixture; blend again. Put in lightly greased 1-quart mold; refrigerate 24 hours. Unmold on tray and frost with caviar. Garnish with parsley and serve with crackers or melba toast.

Mrs. A. C. Gilmore (Clydell Hollon)

Easy Crab Spread*

1 7½-ounce can crab meat,
    drained and flaked
¼ cup mayonnaise
Dash Worcestershire sauce

Dash Tabasco brand pepper sauce
1 teaspoon lemon juice
2 tablespoons prepared
    horseradish

Mix the above ingredients and chill. Serve with crackers. Makes about 1 cup.

Mrs. A. Jackson Ashmore (Gay Griffith)

Gray's Crab Dip Provençal

1 cup chopped onion
1 cup chopped celery
1 cup minced parsley
1 cup chopped bell pepper
7 tablespoons butter

6 tablespoons flour
1 quart milk
2 cups cooked white crab meat
1 cup grated Parmesan cheese
    (or more)

Sauté vegetables in ¼ cup melted butter over low heat for 5 minutes; do not brown. In a double boiler, prepare a white sauce with remaining butter, flour, and milk. Add well cleaned crab, vegetables, and cheese. Serve in a chafing dish with chips or crackers. Makes about 2 quarts.

Mrs. Robert C. Wood (Helen Heaney)

Hot Cheese and Crab Dip

1 7½-ounce can crab meat
1 8-ounce box Old English brand
    process cheese

10 ounces sharp Cheddar cheese
¼ cup butter
½ cup Sauterne

Reserving few pieces for garnish, shred crab meat. Cut cheese in small pieces; melt with crab, butter, and Sauterne over low heat. Pour into chafing dish; garnish with reserved crab meat pieces. Serve with wheat wafers or chunks of crusty bread and fondue forks. Makes about 3 cups.

Mrs. Gerald A. Reeves (Lois Arnett)
Mrs. Robert C. Wood (Helen Heaney)

Baked Crab Dip

1 8-ounce package cream cheese,   ½ teaspoon creamed
   softened   horseradish
1 tablespoon milk   ¼ teaspoon salt
1 6½-ounce can flaked crab meat   Tabasco brand pepper sauce
2 tablespoons minced onion   (optional)
   (or more)   Toasted almonds

Mix all ingredients except almonds in an electric mixer until smooth. Pour in a small round casserole dish. Sprinkle generously with toasted almonds. Bake at 375 degrees for 15 minutes. Serve with potato chips for dippers.

Mrs. A. C. Gilmore (Clydell Hollon)

Baked Crab and Shrimp*

1 bell pepper, chopped   1 cup mayonnaise
1 onion, chopped   ½ teaspoon salt
1 cup chopped celery   ¼ teaspoon pepper
1 6½-ounce can crab meat   1 teaspoon Worcestershire sauce
1 6½-ounce can shrimp

Combine ingredients and pour into greased baking dish. Bake 30 minutes at 350 degrees. When done, spoon into bite-sized pastry shells for party *hors d'oeuvres*. Serve hot. Makes 20 to 24.

Mrs. A. C. Gilmore (Clydell Hollon)

Oyster Tidbits

1 clove garlic   Bacon
Picante sauce   Catsup
Fresh oysters

Use oyster shells or ramekins. Rub shell or dish with garlic. Put dash of *picante* in shell; then place oyster on top. Top this with a 1-inch piece of bacon and a dash of catsup. Broil 15 minutes at 350 degrees.

Mrs. Earl Sams Lightner (Robin Holmes)

Oysters Box Ranch

½ cup butter   1 quart oysters
1 cup A-1 brand sauce   Dry white wine to cover

Place butter and A-1 Sauce in a large skillet to simmer over low heat. Place oysters, liquid and all, in a smaller pan and cover with white wine. Simmer until edges of oysters are ruffly and plump, 5 to 8 minutes. Gently remove oysters with a slotted spoon and drain very, very well. Slip into A-1 Sauce and simmer gently 15 to 20 minutes. Serve warm, in sauce, as an *hors d'oeuvre*, or in a chafing dish on the cocktail table. Serves 4.

Mrs. J. Franklin Critz (Isabelle Pattee)

Chris' Oyster Loaf

2 8-ounce packages cream   1 tablespoon Worcestershire
  cheese   sauce
2 3¾-ounce cans smoked   Dash Tabasco brand pepper sauce
  oysters   Salt to taste
¼ cup milk or cream   Chopped parsley
2 to 3 tablespoons mayonnaise   Paprika
1 tablespoon lemon juice

Cream the cheese; chop oysters; mix all above ingredients except parsley and paprika together. (Or use blender.) Cover and refrigerate for several hours to season. Then form into 1 large loaf for a big party or make 2 smaller loaves and freeze 1. Cover with chopped parsley and paprika. Serve with buttery sesame seed crackers.

Mrs. A. C. Skinner (Marshall Elmore)

Gray's Salmon Party Mound

1 16-ounce can salmon
1 8-ounce package cream cheese
1 teaspoon lemon juice
2 teaspoons grated onion
1 teaspoon prepared horseradish

¼ teaspoon salt
¼ teaspoon liquid smoke
½ cup chopped pecans
3 tablespoons minced parsley

Drain and flake salmon, removing skin and bones. Combine all ingredients except parsley and pecans. Mix well and shape into mold or ball. Then cover mound with mixture of parsley and nuts and chill well. Serve with crackers.

Mrs. Robert C. Wood (Helen Heaney)

Garnelen Bollen
SHRIMP PUFFS

1 pound bread
Milk
2 pounds cleaned shrimp,
   finely ground

1 pound potatoes, cooked and
   mashed
2 teaspoons salt
Pepper

Soak bread in milk; squeeze dry. Mix all ingredients together, kneading mixture with hands until smooth. Form in 1-inch balls and fry until brown in deep fat heated to 370 degrees. Drain on paper towels. Reheat in a 350-degree oven before serving. Makes 100 puffs.

Mrs. Lowell Kepp (Betty Ellis)

Shrimp Canapés

Bread rounds
Mayonnaise
Prepared mustard (or curry
   powder)

Boiled shrimp
Paprika

Spread bread rounds with stiff mayonnaise seasoned with either prepared mustard or curry powder. Press a boiled shrimp into the mayonnaise; garnish with paprika.

Mrs. Lowell Kepp (Betty Ellis)

Ginger Pickled Shrimp

3 pounds shrimp
¾ cup celery tops
½ cup mixed pickling spices
1 tablespoon salt

2½ cups sliced onion
10 bay leaves
1 recipe pickling marinade

Bring water to boil; add celery tops, spices, salt, and shrimp. Stir gently until water returns to a boil. Drain, peel, and devein shrimp. Rinse with cold water and drain thoroughly. Alternate shrimp, bay leaves, and onion in a non-metallic casserole. Pour marinade over shrimp and cover. Chill at least 24 hours, stirring occasionally. Drain well before serving. Will keep a week but it is best at 2 or 3 days. Makes about 3 quarts.

MARINADE:

2 cups salad oil
1 cup white vinegar
1 tablespoon celery seed
2 teaspoons salt

½ teaspoon Tabasco brand
   pepper sauce
¼ cup peeled and minced ginger
   root (or more)

Mix all ingredients together.

Mrs. Charles Bonniwell (Lynn Eichelkraut)

Deviled Shrimp

2 pounds shrimp, boiled and
   peeled
1 lemon, sliced thin
1 onion, sliced thin
2 tablespoons chopped pimiento
½ cup pitted ripe olives, sliced
½ cup vegetable oil

2 tablespoons wine vinegar
1 cup lemon juice
1 teaspoon salt
1 teaspoon black pepper
¼ teaspoon cayenne pepper
¼ teaspoon dry mustard
1 bay leaf, broken

Mix shrimp, lemon, onion, pimiento, and olives. In second container, mix all other ingredients. Mix all ingredients and toss. Chill 24 hours and serve ice cold. This will keep a week in the refrigerator. Toss occasionally. Makes 2 quarts.

Mrs. Lev H. Prichard, III (Ella Wall)

Shrimp Dip*

1 can condensed tomato soup 1 8-ounce package cream cheese
1 cup salad dressing   1½ cups boiled chopped shrimp
Garlic salt

Mix all ingredients and serve chilled with crackers or chips. Makes about 1 quart.

Mrs. Gerald Heinzelmann (Carolyn Jones)

Gray's Shrimp Dip

2 pounds boiled, cleaned shrimp Mayonnaise
1 8-ounce package cream cheese Worcestershire sauce
Juice of 1 lemon   8 green onions, minced

Chop shrimp coarsely. Soften cheese; mix with all other ingredients. Adjust amount of mayonnaise, using more for a dip, less for a spread. Serve with potato chips or crackers. Serves about 16.

Mrs. Robert C. Wood (Helen Heaney)

Shrimp on Cucumber à la San Miguel

1 pound cooked shrimp   Cayenne pepper
Mayonnaise   Dill weed
Salt   4 cucumbers
Black pepper

Put cooked shrimp through grinder. Add mayonnaise until spreadable; season to taste with salt, peppers, and dill weed. Chill. Peel cucumbers and cut in slices ¼- to ½-inch thick. Place on paper towels separately in rows. Cover with more towels, roll up, and chill until ready to use. Just before serving, heap shrimp on cucumber rounds. Place on paper doily on serving dish to make cucumbers easier to pick up. Makes about 50.

Mrs. Joseph P. Mueller (Patty Puig)

Vegetables

Gray's Hot Broccoli Dip

3 ribs celery, chopped
1 small onion, chopped
1 4-ounce can mushroom stems
  and pieces, drained
3 tablespoons butter
1 6-ounce roll sharp process
  cheese
1 teaspoon garlic salt

1 can condensed cream of
  mushroom soup
1 10-ounce package frozen
  chopped broccoli, cooked
Tabasco brand pepper sauce
Worcestershire sauce
Soy sauce (optional)

Sauté celery, onion, and mushrooms in butter until translucent. In a double boiler, heat cheese and soup seasoned with garlic salt until cheese melts. Stir in broccoli. Combine vegetables and cheese mixture and put through blender or food mill. Season to taste. Serve in a chafing dish with potato chips. Makes about 1 quart.

Mrs. Robert C. Wood (Helen Heaney)

Gray's Cucumber Dip

1 6-inch-long cucumber
1 8-ounce package cream cheese
1 small onion (or less)

½ teaspoon salt
Juice of ½ lemon

Put all ingredients in blender. Serve with crackers. Makes about 1 pint.

Mrs. Robert C. Wood (Helen Heaney)

Gray's Pickled Mushrooms

2 cups canned button
  mushrooms, drained
½ cup dry vermouth
1 cup corn oil
½ cup red wine vinegar
1 clove garlic, pressed

2 tablespoons minced onion
1 tablespoon basil
1 teaspoon salt
½ teaspoon pepper
½ teaspoon sugar
½ teaspoon dry mustard

Put mushrooms in Mason jar with tight lid. Combine remaining ingredients and beat well. Pour into jar over mushrooms and stir. Keep in refrigerator for 2 months, or

Combine button mushrooms with Italian salad dressing. Add chopped onions and jalapeños if desired. Refrigerate 30 minutes before serving.

Mrs. Robert C. Wood (Helen Heaney)

Cocktail Water Chestnuts

1 6-ounce can water chestnuts
½ cup vinegar
½ cup liquid from chestnuts

12 slices bacon, halved
¼ cup brown sugar
¼ cup catsup

Marinate whole chestnuts in vinegar and chestnut liquid for 1 hour. Drain. Spread each ½ slice of bacon with brown sugar mixed with catsup. Roll chestnuts in bacon and fasten with toothpicks. Broil on a rack for 5 minutes or until bacon is crisp. Drain on absorbent paper. Serve with cocktail toothpicks. Makes 24.

Mrs. John Charles Abbott (Jane Belfour)

Cheese

Hot Chutney Cheese Ball

1 8-ounce package cream cheese
¼ cup chutney
1 teaspoon curry powder

¼ teaspoon dry mustard
  (or more)
Toasted almonds

Mix all ingredients, except almonds, and shape into a ball. Chill until firm. Roll in toasted almonds. Chill 4 hours before serving.

Mrs. Robert G. Kipp (Peggy Alcorn)

Curry-Chutney Cheese Ball

1 8-ounce package cream cheese 1 9-ounce jar chutney
1 teaspoon curry powder ½ cup almond bits

Mix cheese, curry powder, half the chutney, and almond bits. Form into ball and chill 2 hours. Pour remainder of chutney sauce over ball before serving.

Mrs. Robert G. Kipp (Peggy Alcorn)

Olive Cheese Ball

1 8-ounce package cream cheese 2/3 cup chopped ripe olives,
1 8-ounce package blue cheese,   drained
 crumbled 1/3 cup chopped walnuts, pecans,
¼ cup butter   or toasted diced almonds
1 tablespoon minced chives

Have all ingredients at room temperature. Blend cheeses and butter; stir in olives and chives. Chill slightly. Form into ball on serving dish. Chill thoroughly. Just before serving, sprinkle chopped nuts over ball. Garnish with parsley. Serve with assorted crackers.

Mrs. Charles DeCou (Martha McKamey)

Cocktail Party Cheese Ball

1 pound sharp Cheddar cheese,   2 teaspoons Worcestershire
 grated   sauce
¼ pound Roquefort cheese, ¼ teaspoon cayenne pepper
 crumbled ½ cup chopped pecans
½ pound cream cheese ½ cup minced parsley
2 teaspoons grated onion

Have cheeses at room temperature. Blend well in electric mixer. Add Worcestershire sauce, onion, and pepper. Chill thoroughly. Form into bite-sized balls or 1 or 2 big balls. Mix pecans and parsley on waxed paper. Roll cheese balls in this mixture until completely covered. Place on attractive tray surrounded by assorted crackers. Will freeze.

Mrs. Charles Canfield (Patricia Kitchen)

Cheese Log

1 16-ounce box Old English
  brand process cheese, grated
2 tablespoons chopped onion
3 stuffed olives, chopped
3 tablespoons minced bell pepper
2 tablespoons chopped sour
  pickle

1 pimiento, chopped
1 hard-cooked egg, chopped
  (optional)
½ cup fine cracker crumbs
¼ cup salad dressing
½ teaspoon salt

Mix ingredients; shape into log. Roll in chopped parsley, cayenne pepper, or paprika. Chill until firm.

Mrs. H. R. Arnold (Lucille Word)

Barnett's Cheese Spread

1 12-ounce can beer
1 pound extra sharp Cheddar
  cheese
1 pound mild Cheddar cheese
Juice from 2 to 3 cloves garlic
1 rounded teaspoon dry mustard

4 to 5 dashes Tabasco brand
  pepper sauce
¼ teaspoon salt
3 tablespoons Worcestershire
  sauce

Pour beer into glass; allow it to sit overnight. Grate cheese. Mix all ingredients except beer together thoroughly with your hands. Add beer, a little at a time. Add only enough to make mixture the consistency you want for a dip or spread. Do not allow it to become runny. Cheese will keep, properly covered, at least a month in the refrigerator. Do not freeze. To serve, allow it to come to room temperature for 15 to 20 minutes. Serve with crackers. Makes about 1 pint.

Mrs. Jack Modesett, Jr. (Marcia Heyne)

Pour Pickapeppa brand steak sauce over a softened mound of cream cheese. Serve with chips or crackers.

Dried Beef Log

1 8-ounce package cream cheese
1 tablespoon prepared
  horseradish
1 teaspoon prepared mustard
1 2½-ounce jar dried beef
3 tablespoons butter

Blend cream cheese, horseradish, and mustard. Mince beef and sauté in butter until frizzled. Shape cheese into log and roll in dried beef. Wrap in waxed paper and chill. Serve with crackers or melba toast. Freezes well.

Mrs. Max J. Luther, III (Maxine Jenkins)

Dried Beef Cornucopias

1 8-ounce package cream cheese
2 teaspoons prepared mustard
¼ cup grated onion
1 2½-ounce jar dried beef

Mix cream cheese, mustard, and onion well. Spread a generous teaspoon of mixture on each slice of beef; roll into a cornucopia and fasten with a toothpick. These freeze very successfully. Allow about 1 hour for thawing. Makes about 20.

Mrs. Lev H. Prichard, III (Ella Wall)

The cheese mixtures and the methods of preparation for the Dried Beef Log and the Dried Beef Cornucopias are completely interchangeable. Simply use the flavor you prefer and alternate between the log and the cornucopias, depending on whether you want to use crackers. The cornucopias are a good choice for outside parties when high humidity might wilt crackers.

Bacon Dip

1 8-ounce package cream cheese
Milk
1 teaspoon grated onion
2 tablespoons minced bell
  pepper

Salt
Pepper
5 slices bacon, cooked until crisp
Paprika

Mash cheese with fork. Add milk, 1 tablespoon at a time, mixing well until the mixture is good dipping consistency. Add onion, bell pepper, salt, and pepper to taste. Crush bacon and add to mixture; mix well. Sprinkle with paprika and serve at room temperature.

Mrs. Lawrence Riley Williams (Ann Reading Parsley)

Dana's Dilly Dip*

2/3 cup mayonnaise
2/3 cup sour cream
1 tablespoon shredded green
  onion

1 teaspoon Beau Monde brand
  seasoning
1 tablespoon minced parsley
1 teaspoon dill weed

Mix thoroughly, chill, and serve with chips. Makes about 1½ cups.

Mrs. George Taggart (Ethleen Reimers)

Pastry

1-2-3's*

1 pound bulk pork sausage
2 cups flour

3 5-ounce jars Old English
  brand process cheese

Mix all ingredients. Shape into small balls, flatten into round cookie shapes, and put on an ungreased cookie sheet. For later use, make into long rolls, refrigerate or freeze, slice off later, and put on cookie sheets. Bake at 325 degrees for 20 minutes. Makes about 60.

Mrs. Lawrence Riley Williams (Ann Reading Parsley)

Cheese Snacks

1 cup butter
1 8-ounce box Old English
   brand process cheese
1 teaspoon salt

¾ teaspoon cayenne pepper
   (or less)
2½ cups flour
1 cup chopped nuts

Cream butter. Add grated cheese and mix well. Add flour, seasonings, and nuts. Roll on floured board to shape like ice box cookies into sticks about 1-inch thick. Wrap in waxed paper and store in refrigerator. Slice and bake at 350 degrees 10 to 15 minutes. Makes about 200.

Mrs. Russell Kirkland (Elizabeth Scull)

Cheese Straws

½ cup butter
1 8-ounce package sharp
   Cheddar cheese, grated
Juice of ½ lemon

½ teaspoon salt
½ teaspoon cayenne pepper
   (or less)
1½ cups flour

Cream butter in mixer; add cheese and cream very well. Add lemon juice, salt, and pepper. Add flour. Put in cookie press using a star or ribbon disc. Put full strips on greased cookie sheets. Cut into 2-inch segments and bake at 300 degrees for about 25 minutes. Freezes well; take out 15 minutes before serving.

Mrs. Charles Canfield (Patricia Kitchen)

Olive-Cheese Puffs

½ cup butter
1 5-ounce jar Old English
   brand process cheese

1 cup flour
1 jar stuffed green olives

Blend butter and cheese; then add flour gradually. Divide into 2 or 3 large balls and place covered in refrigerator for about 2 hours. Drain olives and dry them on paper towels. Flour hands and form balls with an olive in the center of each ball. Bake on cookie sheet at 400 degrees for about 10 minutes.

Mrs. Richard Scott Bonner (Karen Olsen)

Cheese Toasties

1 24-ounce loaf bread
2 cups butter

10 ounces grated Cheddar or
    Parmesan cheese
Cayenne pepper (optional)

Remove crusts from bread; cut bread into strips or cubes. Dip bread in melted butter; roll in cheese, seasoned with cayenne pepper if desired. Place bread on a cookie sheet and bake in a 350-degree oven until crisp and brown. The bread may be prepared ahead, placed on cookie sheet, and refrigerated until time to bake. Makes about 60.

Mrs. Robert L. Browning (Marylee Douglass)
Mrs. George Taggart (Ethleen Reimers)

Blue Cheese Wafers

8 baker's rolls
½ cup butter

4 ounces blue cheese

Slice baker's rolls vertically into thin slices. Melt butter and cheese in a skillet over low heat. Using a fork, dip bread into the mixture, quickly covering both sides. Bake on a cookie sheet at 425 degrees for 5 minutes or until brown. Serves 10.

Mrs. E. Jackson Giles (Mary Kathryn Garrett)

Hot Cheese Squares

1 8-ounce box Old English
    brand process cheese
½ cup margarine

1 egg
1 loaf unsliced sandwich bread

Let cheese and margarine soften; mix together. Add beaten egg. Cut crusts from bread, slice twice lengthwise and then into 1- to 1½-inch cubes. Ice the cubes with cheese mixture and place on ungreased cookie sheet. Refrigerate 12 hours. Bake at 375 degrees for 8 to 10 minutes. Makes about 60.

Mrs. William N. Woolsey (Sandra Callaway)

Cheese Puff Soufflés

2 cups butter
4 5-ounce jars Old English
 brand process cheese
1 teaspoon Tabasco brand
 pepper sauce

Dash cayenne pepper
1 ½ teaspoons dill weed
1 teaspoon Beau Monde brand
 seasoning
2 ½ loaves sandwich bread

Cream butter and cheese in mixer. Add seasonings. Remove crusts from bread. Use 3 slices of bread for each sandwich and spread the cheese mixture between layers. Cut the sandwiches into quarters and ice the top and sides of each quarter with the remaining cheese mixture. Bake on cookie sheets at 350 degrees for about 25 minutes or until brown. To quick-freeze, place the unbaked sandwiches on cookie sheets in the freezer. When frozen, place in plastic bags until ready to use. Makes about 60.

Mrs. Leslie Giddens (Frances Quinn)

Nuts

Deviled Almonds

¼ cup butter
¼ cup corn oil
1 ½ cups almonds
1 tablespoon celery salt

½ teaspoon salt
⅛ teaspoon cayenne pepper
½ teaspoon chili powder

Cook butter, oil, and almonds in skillet, stirring until nuts are golden; drain. Mix seasonings together and stir into nuts.

Mrs. A. Jackson Ashmore (Gay Griffith)

Sherry's Indian Nuts

PECANS:

2 cups pecan halves
1½ tablespoons melted butter
1 teaspoon salt

2 teaspoons soy sauce
⅛ teaspoon Tabasco brand
   pepper sauce

Preheat oven to 300 degrees. Put pecans in cake pan and pour butter over. Bake 15 or 20 minutes, stirring often. Mix remaining ingredients and toss with toasted pecans.

ALMONDS:

2 cups whole, blanched almonds
1½ tablespoons melted butter

1 tablespoon curry powder
2 tablespoons salt

Prepare as for pecans.

CASHEWS:

2 cups cashews
1½ tablespoons melted butter

1 tablespoon chili powder
Salt (optional)

Prepare as for pecans.

Mrs. Richard Scott Bonner (Karen Olsen)

Roquefort Pecans

3 ounces crumbled Roquefort
   cheese

1 3-ounce package cream cheese
120 pecan halves

Mix the cheeses together when both are at room temperature. Then spread on flat side of pecan halves and press together, sandwich fashion. Makes about 60.

Mrs. A. Jackson Ashmore (Gay Griffith)

Appetizer recipes found in Chapter 1. MEXICAN FOOD:

Chili con Queso
Jalapeño Dip
Chili Dip
Picadillo

Bean Dip
Queso y Carne
Nachos
Guacamole Salad

Sandwiches

4. SANDWICHES

Whether it's a bridge foursome, a crowd to watch a football game on television, a picnic on Padre Island, or a teenager's party, sandwiches often seem to be the main attraction on South Texas tables. These are sandwiches with a difference, good enough and unusual enough to earn a place in a cookbook.

Gulf Coast Poor Boys

Skinny French bread or individual French loaves

FILLINGS:

1. Spread toasted bread with lots of tartar sauce. Top with fried oysters. One pint of oysters serves 4.
2. Spread toasted bread with lots of tartar sauce. Top with fried shrimp. One pound raw shrimp serves 4.
3. Van Cleve Special: Spread toasted bread with deviled crab meat and top with cheese. Heat until cheese melts. One pound crab meat serves 6.
4. Spread toasted bread with mayonnaise. Top with fried soft shell crabs. Add lettuce and tomato slices.

Mrs. Earl Sams Lightner (Robin Holmes)

Crab Burgers

1 cup crab meat	*½ cup mayonnaise*
¼ cup minced celery	*½ cup shredded Cheddar cheese*
2 teaspoons dried minced onion	*4 hamburger buns*

Combine all ingredients, spread on ·buttered buns, and broil. Makes about 8 halves, using small hamburger buns. May be served on Melba rounds for cocktails.

Mrs. Edwin Prichard, Jr. (Marjorie Reynolds)

Tuna Fish Spread

1 7-ounce can Albacore tuna
2 hard-cooked eggs
1 green onion, minced
2 tablespoons sweet pickle relish
1 heaping teaspoon prepared
mustard
Mayonnaise

Drain tuna and turn into mixing bowl. Add chopped egg, minced onion, relish, and mustard. Mix well and add enough mayonnaise to mixture to moisten it heavily. Add salt and pepper to taste. Serves 4. May be served on lettuce leaf garnished with tomato wedges, olives, and pickles; as a cold sandwich spread; or on split English muffins topped with American cheese and toasted until bubbly.

Mrs. Earl Sams Lightner (Robin Holmes)

Football Feed

1 onion, chopped
½ cup chopped celery
  (or celery seed)
2 tablespoons butter
2 tablespoons vinegar
1 14-ounce bottle catsup
1 teaspoon prepared mustard
4 teaspoons lemon juice
2 tablespoons brown sugar
1 tablespoon Worcestershire
  sauce
½ cup stock from meat
3 pounds chuck roast
Hot rolls

Sauté onion and celery in butter. Add other ingredients; cook 10 minutes. Stew chuck roast in water until meat falls apart. When meat is done, shred, removing gristle, etc.; then mix with sauce. This is better if done the day before using. Refrigerate. Before serving, heat slowly and serve with hot rolls to make sloppy Joe sandwiches. Serves 8 to 10. These sandwiches served with a green salad and a pot of beans make for good fare after a Saturday of football watching.

Mrs. Leslie Giddens (Frances Quinn)

Sloppy Joes

1 pound ground beef
2/3 cup chopped onion
2 tablespoons shortening
1/4 cup water
1 heaping tablespoon prepared
   mustard

1/2 cup catsup
1/2 teaspoon salt
1/4 teaspoon pepper
1 can condensed chicken
   gumbo soup
4 seeded buns

Cook meat and onion together in hot shortening until meat is
lightly browned. Stir frequently with a wooden spoon. Add other
ingredients. Cover and simmer gently over low heat for 30 minutes.
Stir occasionally. Spoon onto seeded sandwich buns and serve with
dill pickles. Serves 4. A sure child pleaser.

Mrs. John Charles Abbott (Jane Belfour)
Mrs. Charles Canfield (Patricia Kitchen)

Pizzaz Hamburgers

2 pounds ground beef
1 3-ounce package cream
   cheese, softened
1 tablespoon crumbled blue
   cheese
1 tablespoon minced onion

1 teaspoon prepared horseradish
1 teaspoon prepared mustard
12 slices bacon, slightly precooked
Salt
Pepper

Divide beef into 12 mounds. Flatten each between squares of
waxed paper to 1/2-inch thickness. For the filling, cream the cheeses
together; stir in onion, horseradish, and mustard. Top 6 of the patties
with filling, leaving 1/2-inch margins for sealing. Cover filled patties
with remaining patties, sealing edges well. Wrap edges with bacon,
using 2 slices. Broil 5 inches from heat for 6 minutes. Turn; broil
5 minutes more. Add salt and pepper to taste. Serves 6.

Mrs. Curtis B. Dyer, Jr. (Jerry Bramlet)

Croque Monsieur
FRIED HAM AND CHEESE SANDWICH

2 tablespoons grated Swiss
   cheese
1 tablespoon cream

2 slices French bread
1 thin slice ham
2 tablespoons butter

Mix cheese and cream until spreadable and cover 1 side of each slice of bread with mixture; place ham between the 2 slices. Melt 1 tablespoon butter in a small skillet over moderate heat; add sandwich and cook slowly until golden brown. Remove sandwich, add remaining butter, and cook other side. Serves 1.

Mrs. Lev H. Prichard, III (Ella Wall)

Tasty Frank Sandwich

1 slice bread
Mayonnaise
Mustard
2 frankfurters, halved
   lengthwise

Onion
Lettuce
Tomato
1 slice Swiss cheese

Toast bread on 1 side and spread with mayonnaise and mustard. Slice frankfurters that have been heated and lay them across bread. Add thin sliced onion, lettuce, sliced tomato, and top with 1 slice of cheese. Broil until cheese melts. Serves 1.

Mrs. James Cliff Avant (Sally Dixon)

Broiler Bacon and Tomato Sandwiches

Sliced white or French bread
Mayonnaise
Tomato, sliced

Cheddar cheese
Bacon slices
Worcestershire sauce

Toast bread under broiler on 1 side. Turn over and spread mayonnaise on untoasted side. Place slices of tomato on this, then slices of Cheddar cheese, then half-cooked slices of bacon. Sprinkle with Worcestershire sauce. Broil until cheese bubbles.

Mrs. Jack Best (Betty Reno)
Mrs. Robert L. Browning (Marylee Douglass)
Mrs. Jack M. Painter (Darlene Downer)

Bean-Bacon-Onion Broil

8 slices bread   1 onion, sliced very thin
1 16-ounce can pork and beans   8 slices bacon

Toast bread under broiler on 1 side. Turn untoasted sides up and generously cover with pork and beans. Top beans with sliced onions. Top onions with bacon (1 slice cut in half). Put under broiler until bacon is done. (Be sure to have broiler shelf at lowest position in oven.) Serves 8.

Mrs. James D. Cable (Mary Pearle Garrett)

Open-Faced Turkey Sandwich

Toast   Slices white turkey meat
Mayonnaise   Thousand Island dressing
Shredded lettuce

Spread toast with mayonnaise. Top each slice of toast with a generous amount of shredded lettuce, then turkey slices. Top with Thousand Island dressing.

Mrs. Austin Davies (Kathy Jones)

Hot Avocado Sandwiches

3 12-inch-long loaves French   18 thin slices tomato
   bread   18 slices crisply fried bacon
Butter   18 slices American cheese
2 or 3 avocados, sliced thin and   Salt
   sprinkled with lemon juice   Pepper
2 medium onions, sliced and
   separated into rings

Cut loaves lengthwise and butter cut side. Place buttered side up on cookie sheets. Layer ingredients in order given above. Salt and pepper each layer lightly. Bake at 400 degrees for 5 to 10 minutes or until cheese begins to bubble. Makes 6 meal-sized servings or 12 sandwiches, if cut in half. Excellent with soup.

Mrs. Charles Bonniwell (Lynn Eichelkraut)

Pizza Snacks

1 2¼-ounce can chopped ripe olives
½ cup stewed tomatoes, well drained and chopped
1 cup grated sharp Cheddar cheese
1 teaspoon grated Parmesan cheese
1 teaspoon grated onion
⅛ teaspoon oregano
⅛ teaspoon garlic salt
7 slices toast, buttered

Mix all ingredients together except the toast. Spread mixture on toast. Cut each slice of toast into 4 squares or smaller if serving as an appetizer and bake at 400 degrees for 10 minutes. Serve immediately. Can be made in advance and put in the oven just before serving. Can be kept frozen for as long as 3 weeks. Completely thaw before baking. Makes 28 *hors d'oeuvres* or 7 sandwiches.

Mrs. Charles DeCou (Martha McKamey)

Cucumber Sandwiches

1 3-ounce package cream cheese
1 medium cucumber, peeled, seeded, and minced
1 tablespoon minced onion
½ teaspoon salt
⅛ teaspoon pepper
Very thinly sliced white bread
Butter

Mix first 5 ingredients thoroughly. Spread 2 slices of the bread with butter; then spread cucumber mixture on 1 slice and top with the other. Makes 4 to 5 sandwiches. Do not use the electric blender for the cucumber mixture.

Mrs. Mercer T. Ivey (Jean Nunn)

Olive Broiler Sandwiches

1 cup chopped ripe olives
½ cup thinly sliced green
   onions
1½ cups shredded American
   cheese

½ cup mayonnaise
½ teaspoon salt
½ teaspoon curry powder
   (or chili powder)
6 English muffins, split in half

Mix olives, onion, cheese, mayonnaise, salt, and curry or chili powder. Toast muffins. Spread with cheese filling. Broil until filling is heated and cheese melts. Use 2 muffin halves per serving. Serves 6.

Mrs Max J. Luther, III (Maxine Jenkins)

Egg Salad Sandwich Filling

8 to 10 hard-cooked eggs,
   chopped
1 tablespoon dill seed
Big pinch tarragon
Sweet pickle relish (optional)

3 tablespoons chopped pimiento
Salt
Pepper
½ cup homemade mayonnaise

Mix well ahead, if possible, so flavors may blend. Serves 8.

Mrs. William H. Hawn (Ester Jane Roark)

Sandwich Loaf

1 unsliced pullman loaf bread
Pimiento cheese spread
Chicken or tuna salad
2 8-ounce packages cream cheese

Cream
Mayonnaise
Pecans
Stuffed green olives, chopped

Trim crusts of bread and slice lengthwise 3 times. Spread pimiento cheese on bottom layer, chicken or tuna salad on middle layer. Mix cream cheese with enough cream and mayonnaise to make a spreading consistency. Add chopped pecans and chopped green stuffed olives to about 1/3 mixture and spread on top layer; reserve other part to ice the whole loaf. Decorate with sliced olives, both green and ripe, and pimiento. Chill; slice with an electric knife. Serves 12.

Mrs. William N. Woolsey (Sandra Callaway)

Soups

5. SOUPS

The South Texas soup pot may contain the bounty of the sea or the market basket of the Rio Grande Valley. There are probably as many gumbo recipes in the area as there are cooks, and everyone thinks hers is the best. Each of those included here is distinctive; there is one for everybody's taste. There are spicy gumbos for hearty winter suppers and chilled soups for luncheons during the long summertime.

Captain Max Luther's Fish Chowder

3- to 4-pound redfish, red
    snapper, or sheepshead
4 slices bacon
2 large potatoes, sliced thin
1 large onion, sliced
1 16-ounce can tomatoes
1 to 2 bay leaves, crumbled

1 clove garlic, minced
Minced parsley (optional)
1 to 2 lemons, sliced
Salt
Pepper
¾ cup red Bordeaux wine

Bone the fish and cut into slices about 3 inches square. Fry bacon until crisp; crumble. In the bottom of a pot with a lid, place a layer of potatoes, onions, and tomatoes; then a layer of fish, the spices, lemon, and bacon. Sprinkle with salt and pepper. Add a small amount of water, barely covering the other ingredients. Cover and simmer until potatoes are done. Just before removing from heat, add wine. Makes about 4 quarts.

Mrs. Max J. Luther, III (Maxine Jenkins)

At the turn of the century, beach parties were the center of Corpus Christians' social life. These were carefully planned cookouts: shrimp boils and gumbo and chowder parties. The young men of the community took great pride in overseeing the cooking at these affairs. Captain Luther was one of them. His descendants have reduced his original recipe, which served up to 200 persons.

Ceviche
MODIFIED

1 pound fresh scallops or red snapper, cut in 1½-inch pieces	1 2-ounce bottle stuffed olives, chopped
2 cans frozen lemon juice, thawed	½ 7-ounce can pickled seeded mild jalapeño peppers, minced
1 28-ounce can tomatoes, chopped	½ cup olive oil
	½ 14-ounce bottle catsup
1 small onion, minced	Pinch oregano

Marinate fish in lemon juice 4 hours. Drain tomatoes and reserve juice. Combine all ingredients, using juice from jalapeños as desired, according to how hot you want soup. Add juice from tomatoes, if needed, to obtain desired consistency. Refrigerate overnight and serve cold as soup. The *ceviche* may be drained and served as an *hors d'oeuvre*. Makes about 1½ quarts.

Mrs. Gerald Heinzelmann (Carolyn Jones)

Coquina Broth

4 quarts fresh coquinas	Juice of ½ lemon
2 cups water	1/3 cup dry Sherry
1 lemon, sliced	Salt
1 teaspoon butter	

Wash coquinas in several waters as you would beans. Pick through and discard any foreign matter. Place coquinas, sliced lemon, and water in a large pot and steam or simmer 30 minutes. Stir once. Pour broth through cheesecloth into a sauce pan. Add butter, lemon juice, and Sherry. Season to taste. Serve hot in *demitasse* cups as a first course. Serves 8. The broth freezes well.

Mrs. Franklin Critz (Isabelle Pattee)

Coquinas are miniscule mussels found buried in the sands of the Gulf beaches of Padre Island. A simple way to gather coquinas is to dig them up and fill mesh citrus sacks. Rinse the sacks in the waves to remove the sand. Then transfer the coquinas to a heavy duty plastic bag or to a bucket for transporting to the kitchen. Sort them at once.

Spicy Seafood Gumbo

3 cups bacon drippings
1 cup flour
4 pounds sliced okra
1 tablespoon paprika
3 cups chopped onion
2 cups chopped bell pepper
2 cups chopped celery
2 cups chopped parsley
4 8-ounce cans tomato sauce
4 10-ounce cans Ro-Tel brand
   tomatoes and green chilies
2 gallons chicken stock
4 bay leaves
4 teaspoons thyme
Pepper to taste
¼ cup Worcestershire sauce
¼ cup salt
2 tablespoons oregano
Tabasco brand pepper sauce
Dry white wine (optional)
4 to 5 pounds peeled shrimp
2 to 3 pounds crab meat
6 to 8 pints oysters
Cooked rice (optional)
Gumbo filé (optional)

Make a roux in a 12- to 14-quart kettle by heating 2 cups bacon drippings and adding flour. Cook over low heat, stirring constantly, until roux is brown. Add okra and paprika and cook over low heat, stirring constantly, until okra is brown and ropy.

In a large skillet, heat remaining cup of drippings and sauté onion, bell pepper, celery, and parsley until onion is clear. Add the mixture to the roux. Add tomato sauce, tomatoes, stock, and seasoning and simmer for 5 hours. Maintain the liquid level by adding wine or water as needed. About 30 minutes before serving, add seafood. Serve in deep soup bowls, over rice if desired. Gumbo filé may be sprinkled lightly in the gumbo. Makes 3 gallons.

For a chicken gumbo, omit seafood and add the cooked meat from a 3- to 4-pound hen and 2 to 3 pounds cooked ham.

Mrs. Gerald A. Reeves (Lois Arnett)

Dick Picton's Gumbo

1 pound bacon or salt pork
1 pound large onions, sliced
1 clove garlic
½ cup flour
1 small rib celery
½ cup minced parsley
½ pound okra (optional)
1 28-ounce can tomatoes
1 10-ounce can Ro-Tel brand
  tomatoes and green chilies

3 tablespoons Worcestershire
  sauce
1 tablespoon salt
1 tablespoon Tabasco brand
  pepper sauce
Pepper
Water
3 pounds shrimp
2 pounds crab, including claws

Fry bacon, onions, and garlic in large skillet. Remove pieces of bacon and onion and discard all but about 1½ cups drippings. Add flour and slowly brown until dark. Add other ingredients except seafood and browned bacon and onion. Simmer at least 1 hour. Add water if needed. Add seafood and simmer 30 to 40 minutes longer. Serves 10.

Mrs. Mitchell Wommack (Barbara Ballard)

Betsy's Shrimp Gumbo with Curry

1 large bell pepper, sliced
1 rib celery, including leaves,
  sliced
5 cups sliced onion
1 cup cooking oil
1 cup chili sauce
1 teaspoon thyme
1 teaspoon curry powder
Salt

Black pepper
Cayenne pepper
3 bay leaves
½ cup minced parsley
2 10-ounce packages frozen
  sliced okra
2 16-ounce cans tomatoes
1 16-ounce can tomato juice
5 pounds cleaned shrimp

Sauté bell pepper, celery, and onion in hot oil until onion is clear. Add all other ingredients except shrimp and simmer 1 hour. Remove from heat. Refrigerate 24 hours. Simmer the gumbo 1 hour. Add shrimp about 10 to 20 minutes before serving. Shrimp are cooked when they are no longer translucent. Serve over rice in soup bowls. Serves at least 12 as main course.

Mrs. William N. Woolsey (Sandra Callaway)

Seafood Gumbo with Chicken and Veal

3 slices bacon
4 onions, chopped
2 bay leaves
½ bell pepper, chopped
4 cloves garlic
1 teaspoon thyme
2 pounds okra, sliced
1 pound veal, cubed
Ham bone
1 28-ounce can tomatoes

1/3 cup minced parsley
1 teaspoon sugar
Tabasco brand pepper sauce
Worcestershire sauce
Juice of 1 lemon
1 pint oysters
1 cup crab meat
2 pounds cleaned shrimp
Gumbo filé

Fry bacon; brown onion in drippings; add bay leaves, bell pepper. garlic, thyme, and okra. In another large pot, brown veal; add ham bone, tomatoes, parsley, sugar, Tabasco, Worcestershire sauce, and lemon; cover with water and simmer 2½ hours. Add chicken and seafood and simmer until shrimp is no longer clear. Remove from heat and stir in gumbo filé to taste. Serves 20.

Mrs. Frank B. Adams (Jeanne Stewart)

Shrimp Bisque

12 ounces cooked, cleaned
   shrimp
½ cup fish stock (or more) or
   canned clam juice
1½ cups heavy cream
¼ teaspoon paprika

Salt
Freshly ground pepper
¼ to 1/3 cup dry Sherry
1 tablespoon minced parsley
   and chives

Place 8 ounces shrimp and fish stock or clam juice in an electric blender; blend for 1 minute. Remove to the top of a double boiler, add cream and paprika, and season to taste with salt and freshly ground pepper. Cook over hot water, stirring from time to time, until soup comes to a boil. Thin to taste with additional fish stock or clam juice. Add Sherry and serve immediately in individual cups, garnished with remaining chopped shrimp, parsley, and chives. Serves 4 to 6.

Mrs. Richard King, III (Jimmie Rose Harrison)

Neely's Oyster Bisque

1 quart oysters, minced
1 bunch shallots, minced
1 clove garlic, minced
½ cup butter
2 tablespoons flour

1 pint heavy cream
1 pint half and half
Salt
Pepper
Dry Sherry

Heat oysters, shallots, and garlic in hot butter until oysters curl. Stir in flour. In a double boiler, heat creams and add oyster mixture. Add salt, pepper, and Sherry to taste. Serves 8 to 12.

Mrs. Mitchell Wommack (Barbara Ballard)

Purée of Vegetable Soup

3 carrots
2 ribs celery
1 small onion
1 tablespoon butter
1 quart chicken stock
¼ cup dry vermouth

1 tablespoon sugar
½ teaspoon salt
¼ teaspoon celery salt
Freshly ground pepper
Parsley

Scrape and dice carrots, celery, and onion. In a large sauce pan, cook about ¾ of the vegetables in butter over low heat, covered, until they are tender. Reserve and chop finer the remaining vegetables. Purée the cooked vegetables with 1 cup chicken stock in a blender. In a sauce pan combine the vegetable purée with the reserved vegetables, 3 cups chicken stock, vermouth, sugar, salt, celery salt, and pepper to taste. Bring the soup to a boil, reduce the heat, and simmer 5 minutes. Put a pinch of minced parsley in the bottom of each soup cup and pour soup over it. Serves 4 to 6.

Mrs. Vernon Medlin (Mamie Smith)

Fresh Vegetable Soup

5 onions	3 or 4 soup bones
5 potatoes	4 16-ounce cans tomato sauce
1 pound carrots	4 46-ounce cans V-8 brand
1 whole stalk celery	vegetable juice
Fresh green beans	Salt
5 ears corn	Pepper
2 pounds stew meat	

Scrub all vegetables well. Do not peel them. Cut onions, potatoes, carrots, celery, and green beans into fairly large bite-sized pieces. Cut corn off the cob and scrape the cobs' juice into a 12-quart soup kettle. Use some of the celery leaves. Combine all ingredients in soup kettle and add water to 1 inch from top of kettle. Cook until all vegetables are tender. Soup freezes well.

Mrs. Lawrence Riley Williams (Ann Reading Parsley)

Lettuce and Green Pea Soup

3 tablespoons butter	1 20-ounce package frozen
1½ cups sliced onion	green peas
3 cups shredded green lettuce	1½ teaspoons salt
¼ cup minced parsley	1/8 teaspoon pepper
4 13¾-ounce cans chicken broth	1 cup heavy cream

Melt butter and sauté onions, lettuce, and parsley for about 15 minutes. In another pan, let chicken broth come to a boil, add vegetables, and cook about 5 minutes or until tender. Cool and put all ingredients in blender. Blend until smooth. Soup may be frozen at this point. When ready to use, heat in double boiler and add 1 cup heavy cream. Serves 12.

Mrs. Kenneth McKamey (Hattie Bell Colston)

Cream of Corn Soup*

1 16-ounce can cream-style corn   Garlic salt
1 cup half and half   Curry powder
1 onion, minced

Simmer corn, half and half, and onion in an uncovered sauce pan. Do not boil, or soup will curdle. Put soup through a colander. Season to taste with garlic salt and curry powder. Serve hot or chilled. Serves 4.

Mrs. Edwin A. Durham, II (Kaye Tarrant)

Cold Cucumber Soup*

1 cucumber, peeled and chopped   1 teaspoon curry powder
2 tablespoons diced shallots   1 to 2 teaspoons Worcestershire
1 can condensed green pea soup   sauce
   (without ham)   Herb-seasoned croutons
1 8-ounce carton sour cream

In blender, mince the cucumber; add shallots and mince. Blend in soup, then sour cream. Add curry and Worcestershire sauce. Serve chilled in cups with croutons. This tastes best when it is prepared 1 day ahead and refrigerated. Serves 4 to 6.

Mrs. Joe P. Nelson (Harriet Hornish)

Cream of Potato Soup

2 onions, chopped   1 cup heavy cream
4 white potatoes, sliced   Salt
2 tablespoons butter   White pepper
4 cups chicken broth   1 tablespoon chives, chopped

Simmer onions, potatoes, butter, and broth in a covered sauce pan for about 15 minutes or until potatoes are tender. Put through blender and return to very low heat. Stir in cream and season to taste. Serve with chopped chives sprinkled on top. Serves 4 to 6.

Mrs. Lev H. Prichard, III (Ella Wall)

Luella's Gazpacho

1 can condensed tomato soup
1 can water
1 tablespoon olive oil
1 tablespoon garlic wine vinegar
1 teaspoon garlic salt (or less)
⅛ teaspoon cayenne pepper

1 green onion, stem included
½ small cucumber, peeled
2 small tomatoes, peeled and
   seeded
1 tablespoon lime juice
Tomato juice

A day before serving, blend first 8 ingredients and refrigerate overnight. Shortly before serving, return to blender and add tomatoes and lime juice. Stir in tomato juice as necessary to adjust consistency. Adjust seasonings to taste. Serve cold with garnishes of sliced ripe olives, chopped avocado, cucumber, tomato, onion, and croutons as desired.

Mrs. Thomas L. Goad (Elizabeth Vickers)

Glorious Gazpacho

¼ cup olive oil
2 tablespoons lemon juice
3 cups tomato juice
1 cup beef broth
¼ cup minced onion
1 tomato, cubed
1 cup minced celery
Dash Tabasco brand pepper
   sauce

1 teaspoon salt
⅛ teaspoon freshly ground
   pepper
1 bell pepper, minced
   (red or green)
1 cucumber, diced
Croutons

Beat together the oil and lemon juice. Stir in the tomato juice, broth, onion, tomato, celery, Tabasco, salt, and pepper. Chill 3 hours. Serve bell peppers, cucumbers, and croutons as garnishes. Keeps several weeks in refrigerator. Serves 4.

Mrs. H. C. Heldenfels (Hazel Norvell)

Blender Gazpacho*

2 cloves garlic
5 ripe tomatoes, quartered
½ bell pepper, seeded and sliced
1 small onion, peeled and
    coarsely chopped

1 teaspoon salt
½ teaspoon pepper
3 tablespoons olive oil
¼ cup wine vinegar
½ cup ice water

Place above ingredients in blender; cover and blend on high speed for 2 to 3 seconds only. Chill well and pour into cups or mugs, as it is good to drink. Garnish with chopped pepper or as desired.

Mrs. George S. Hawn (Gippie Walling)

Iced Tomato Soup with Dill

1 onion, chopped
8 large vine-ripened tomatoes,
    peeled and chopped
1 tablespoon salt
White pepper
¼ cup water

2 tablespoons tomato paste
3 tablespoons flour
2 cups chicken stock
1 cup heavy cream
2 teaspoons freshly chopped dill
    (or ½ teaspoon dried dill weed)

Cook onion, 6 tomatoes, salt, pepper, and water briskly for 6 minutes. Add tomato paste and flour. Add stock and stir until it boils. Strain. Put residue through blender. Strain into soup and chill. When soup is cool, add cream, dill, and the 2 remaining tomatoes. Chill several hours before serving. Serves 8.

Mrs. Edwin A. Durham, II (Kaye Tarrant)

French Onion Soup

4 large onions, chopped
2 large onions, sliced
2 2/3 tablespoons butter
6 cups chicken broth

Dash Worcestershire sauce
1 cup dry red wine
¼ to ½ teaspoon pepper
1 teaspoon salt

Sauté onion in butter over moderate heat until very soft, about 3 minutes. Add broth. Bring to a boil, then reduce heat. Add Worcestershire sauce and wine and simmer about 30 minutes. It is better served the next day. Serve with toasted cubed French bread and lots of grated Parmesan cheese. Serves 10.

A. C. Gilmore

Spicy Bean Soup

1 cup dried Great Northern
  beans
2½ quarts water
Ham bone, ham hock, or 2
  ounces salt pork + 1 cup
  cubed ham

½ cup chopped onion
2 teaspoons salt
2 chorizo sausages
1 bunch turnip greens
2 small potatoes, diced

Boil beans and water for 2 minutes. Remove from heat. Soak for 1 hour. Add ham bone or ham and salt pork. Bring to a boil, lower heat, and simmer 1 hour 30 minutes. Remove bone or salt pork. Prick sausages with a fork and add to soup with potatoes. Simmer at least 30 minutes. About 15 minutes before serving, remove sausages and discard. Add turnip greens that have been shredded finely with a knife. Serves 6.

Mrs. Charles Bonniwell (Lynn Eichelkraut)

Soup recipes found in Chapter 1. MEXICAN FOOD:

Peggy's Chili
Mother's Chili

Chili con Carne
Sopa de Flor de Calabaza

Salads

6. SALADS AND SALAD DRESSINGS

Many a Corpus Christian has a vegetable garden in his back yard, where tomatoes grow the year 'round in the mild, sub-tropical climate. Similarly, citrus trees are decorative accents on many lawns. For non-gardeners, vegetables and fruits from the Texas-Mexico border are trucked in daily all year, providing a choice and a quality of produce few other areas can match. How better to enjoy the freshness of produce than in a salad, especially on a warm summer day? Add equally fresh seafood, and you have a summer supper.

Seafood

Crab New Orleans

1 cup mayonnaise	Salt
2 tablespoons catsup	Black pepper
Tabasco brand pepper sauce	Cayenne pepper
3 tablespoons olive oil	1 to 2 tablespoons chopped
1 tablespoon wine vinegar	ripe olives
2 tablespoons grated onion	1 pound flaked crab meat
2 tablespoons minced parsley	4 to 6 large tomatoes
6 tablespoons heavy cream,	Lettuce
whipped	Sliced hard-cooked eggs

Blend together mayonnaise, catsup, Tabasco, olive oil, vinegar, onion, parsley, and whipped cream. Add salt and pepper to taste. Stir in olives and chill 1 to 2 hours. Add crab meat. Slice tomatoes in half; place on salad plates. Pile crab salad on tomatoes; garnish with lettuce and eggs. Serves 8 to 12. The sauce is delicious for all seafood cocktails and doubles very well. This salad can be used either as a first course or as a luncheon salad.

Mrs. Richard King, III (Jimmie Rose Harrison)

Crab Meat and Artichoke Hearts

6 artichoke hearts
1 pound crab meat
½ cup mayonnaise
2 tablespoons capers
1 tablespoon minced onion

1 tablespoon chopped parsley
1 tablespoon lemon juice
½ teaspoon Dijon mustard
Salt
Pepper

Place artichoke hearts on a glass dish. Cover with crab meat. Combine remaining ingredients. Pour over crab meat and serve cold. Serves 6. Also an excellent first course.

Mrs. Ben Donnell (Elinor Drake)

Crab Louis

1 cup blender mayonnaise
½ cup chili sauce
1/3 cup vinegar and oil
  French dressing
1½ teaspoons Worcestershire
  sauce
1/3 teaspoon coarsely ground
  black pepper
1 tablespoon minced green
  onion

2 teaspoons fresh hot
  horseradish
2 tablespoons sweet pickle
  relish, drained
Juice of 1 lime
Lettuce
½ avocado
1 pound lump crab meat
2 hard-cooked eggs
Cherry tomatoes

Mix first 9 ingredients to make Sauce Louis and refrigerate. Place lettuce on a serving plate; cut ½ avocado into 4 slices. Mound well picked crab meat on lettuce and surround with avocado strips, sliced hard-cooked eggs, and cherry tomatoes. Top with Sauce Louis. Serves 4. Serve with hot cheese sticks and fruit cobbler.

Mrs. J. Franklin Critz (Isabelle Pattee)

Green Lobster Salad

½ cup mayonnaise
6 tablespoons puréed spinach
Salt
Freshly ground black pepper
Cayenne pepper
Lemon juice
1 lobster, cooked in court
   bouillon (or 3 to 4 pounds
   shrimp)

½ cucumber
2 hard-cooked eggs
3 ripe avocados
Juice of 2 lemons
Minced tarragon
Minced chives
Minced parsley

Combine mayonnaise with puréed spinach to make a green sauce. Season to taste with salt, peppers, and a little lemon juice. Pass through a fine sieve. Dice lobster meat. Dice cucumber and eggs. Cut avocado in half, removing meat without piercing the skin. Dice avocado and marinate in lemon juice. Brush inside of avocado shells with lemon juice. Combine drained diced avocado, cucumber, lobster, and eggs. Add green sauce; toss carefully. Fill avocado shells with the salad. Chill. Just before serving, sprinkle with minced tarragon, chives, and parsley. Serves 6.

Mrs. Richard King, III (Jimmie Rose Harrison)

Congealed Shrimp Salad

1 tablespoon unflavored gelatin
2 cups water
1 3-ounce box lemon-flavored
   gelatin
1 can condensed tomato soup
2 3-ounce packages cream cheese
1 cup chopped celery

½ cup chopped nuts
½ cup chopped bell pepper
1 cup mayonnaise
1 tablespoon grated onion
½ to 1 pound boiled shrimp,
   chopped

Soften unflavored gelatin in ¼ cup cold water. Dissolve with lemon-flavored gelatin in 1¾ cups boiling water. Let cool. Beat in tomato soup and cream cheese. Fold in other ingredients. Chill. Serve on lettuce leaves. Serves 6 to 8. This is a good choice for a ladies' luncheon.

Mrs. Jack M. Painter (Darlene Downer)

Mary's Shrimp and Macaroni Salad

1 onion, minced
3 ribs celery, chopped
1 bell pepper, chopped
Butter
2 pounds cleaned, cooked shrimp
¼ cup lemon juice

7 ounces macaroni, cooked and
* drained (may be cooked in*
* shrimp water)*
Mayonnaise
Seasoned salt

Sauté together the onion, celery, and bell pepper in melted butter. Mix all ingredients together and add mayonnaise to taste. Chill. Season with seasoned salt. Serves 10.

Mrs. Donald Everett Jackson (Patricia Ann Alexander)

Mary's Shrimp Mold

2½ cups boiled, peeled shrimp
1½ cups salad dressing
1 medium onion, grated

2 hard-cooked eggs, grated
2 tablespoons unflavored gelatin

Cut shrimp into bite-sized pieces. Mix remaining ingredients together with the shrimp and pour into a mold. Chill in refrigerator. Serve with crackers for supper. Serves 4.

Mrs. James W. Cottingham (Linda Yancy)

Shrimp Salad New Orleans

¾ cup cooked wild rice
1 pound boiled shrimp
¾ teaspoon salt
1 tablespoon lemon juice
1 tablespoon chopped scallion
1 tablespoon sliced stuffed olives

¼ cup slivered bell pepper
¾ cup diced raw cauliflower
1/3 cup mayonnaise
1 cup finely shredded lettuce
2 tablespoons Miracle brand
* French dressing*

Mix all ingredients together, including lettuce; chill and serve on lettuce leaves. Serves 4.

Mrs. James C. Freeman (Cornelia Herz)

Party Aspic

2 tablespoons unflavored gelatin
3½ cups tomato juice
½ teaspoon salt
1 teaspoon sugar
¼ teaspoon Tabasco brand
    pepper sauce

1 teaspoon Worcestershire sauce
¼ cup lemon juice
½ onion, grated
½ cup minced celery
1 8¼-ounce can green peas
20 boiled, cleaned shrimp

Sprinkle gelatin on 1 cup of the tomato juice to soften. Combine remainder of tomato juice, salt, sugar, Worcestershire sauce, Tabasco, lemon juice, onion, and celery. Simmer about 10 minutes. Remove from heat and combine with softened gelatin mixture. Add peas and chill until gelatin becomes syrupy. Fold in shrimp cut into bite-sized pieces. Turn into a 2-quart mold and chill until firm. Serve on lettuce cups with your favorite dressing. Serves 4 to 5.

If desired, 1 cup crab meat may be substituted for the shrimp and a chopped avocado or artichoke hearts for the peas. This recipe multiplies indefinitely.

Mrs. Joe P. Nelson (Harriet Hornish)

Seafood Mold

1 can condensed tomato soup
2 tablespoons unflavored gelatin
1 cup water
1 8-ounce package cream cheese
1 cup mayonnaise
3 7-ounce cans seafood (lobster,
    shrimp, crab, or water-packed
    tuna) or the equivalent of fresh
    seafood, minced or shredded

½ cup minced green onion
1 cup minced celery
Juice of 2 lemons
Tabasco brand pepper sauce
Dill weed
Basil
Salt
White pepper

Heat undiluted soup and add gelatin dissolved in water. Soften cream cheese and mix with mayonnaise. Add soup and remaining ingredients, flavoring with lemon juice, Tabasco, dill, basil, salt, and white pepper to taste. Pour into 1 large mold for an *hors d'oeuvre* or individual molds for a salad course. Serves 8 to 10.

Mrs. Gerald Heinzelmann (Carolyn Jones)

Pimiento-Tuna Molded Salad

1 can condensed cream of
  celery soup
2 tablespoons unflavored gelatin
1 cup cold water
1 3-ounce package cream cheese

1 cup mayonnaise
1 cup diced celery
1 tablespoon minced onion
1 2-ounce jar pimiento
1 7-ounce can white flake tuna

Heat soup; soften gelatin in cold water; combine mixture and stir over low heat until gelatin dissolves; cool. Mix cream cheese and mayonnaise until smooth. Mix celery, onion, pimiento, and tuna together. Add mayonnaise mixture; stir in gelatin mixture. Pour into lightly oiled molds; chill until firm; serve on lettuce leaves. Serves 8.

Mrs. Lev H. Prichard, III (Ella Wall)

Chicken

Hot Chicken Salad

3 cups chopped cooked white
  chicken meat
2 tablespoons onion juice
¾ cup slivered almonds
2 tablespoons lemon juice

2 cups minced celery
1 cup mayonnaise
1 cup grated Velveeta brand
  process cheese
Crushed potato chips

Mix all ingredients except potato chips. Pour in a 2-quart baking dish. Top with crushed potato chips. Bake at 350 degrees until warm. Serves 6.

Mrs. George Taggart (Ethleen Reimers)

Celestial Chicken Salad

4 cups diced cooked chicken
2 cups diced celery
1 4½-ounce jar whole
  mushrooms, drained
½ cup pecan halves, toasted*
4 slices crisp fried bacon,
  crumbled

1 cup mayonnaise or salad
  dressing
1 cup sour cream
1½ teaspoons salt
2 tablespoons lemon juice

Combine chicken, celery, mushrooms, pecans, and crumbled bacon in a large bowl. Blend mayonnaise or salad dressing with remaining ingredients. Add to chicken mixture, tossing lightly to mix. Chill thoroughly. Serve in crisp lettuce cups, if desired. Serves 6 to 8.

*To toast pecans, place in shallow baking pan in preheated 350-degree oven for about 15 minutes.

Mrs. Joseph P. Mueller (Patty Puig)

Crown Jewel Ham and Chicken Molds

1 tablespoon unflavored gelatin
¾ cup water
1 can condensed cream of
  celery soup
1 tablespoon lemon juice
  (or more)

Dash pepper
2 tablespoons minced onion
1 cup diced cooked chicken
4 slices boiled ham
Stuffed olives, sliced

Sprinkle gelatin over ½ cup cold water. Let stand 5 minutes. Place over low heat and stir until dissolved. Combine soup, ¼ cup water, lemon juice, pepper, and onion. Add to gelatin. Carefully stir in chicken. Lightly grease 4 individual molds or custard cups with salad oil. Line sides of molds with strips of ham. Arrange sliced olives on bottom. Fill with chicken mixture. Chill until firm. Unmold and serve on lettuce. Serves 4.

Mrs. Max J. Luther, III (Maxine Jenkins)

Chicken Mousse

6 cups cooked minced
  chicken breasts
3 cups chopped celery
1/4 cup chopped bell pepper
1/4 cup minced chives

6 tablespoons unflavored gelatin
1 quart homemade unsalted
  mayonnaise
1 quart unsalted chicken broth*
1 teaspoon white pepper

Mix chicken, celery, bell pepper, and chives. Soften gelatin in 1 cup cooled broth. Bring remaining broth to a boil; add to gelatin mixture and stir until dissolved. Cool and add to chicken mixture. Blend in mayonnaise. Add pepper. Pour into a 5-quart mold and chill until firm. Serves 12.

*To make a strong, flavorful broth, add chicken bouillon cubes to the broth the chicken was boiled in.

Mrs. Tom McArdle (Marion Hall)

Meat

Enid's Pressed Veal

1 1/2 pounds veal
1 small onion
2 ribs celery
2 teaspoons salt
1/8 teaspoon pepper
1 tablespoon unflavored gelatin
1/4 cup water

1 1/2 cups broth
1 cup chopped celery
3 hard-cooked eggs, chopped
1 cup mayonnaise
1 hard-cooked egg, sliced
Stuffed olives, sliced

Boil veal with 1 onion, 2 ribs celery, 1 teaspoon salt, and pepper until tender. Reserve broth. Grind meat. Soften gelatin in water; add hot broth and stir until gelatin is dissolved. Fold in ground meat, chopped celery and eggs, mayonnaise. and 1 teaspoon salt. Decorate the bottom of a 1-quart mold with sliced eggs and olives. Pour in gelatin mixture. Chill overnight. Serves 8. Doubles well.

Mrs. William N. Woolsey (Sandra Callaway)

Fruit Salads

Midsummer Salad

½ *watermelon*
1 *large cantaloupe*
1 *large honeydew melon*
1 *cup pineapple chunks*
  (canned)
1 *cup seedless green grapes*
  (cut in halves if they are
  large)

1 *cup strawberries, cut in halves*
  or large pieces
¾ *cup sugar*
½ *cup water*
1 *tablespoon grated lemon rind*
1 *tablespoon grated orange rind*
¼ *cup lemon juice*
3 *tablespoons lime juice*

Cut melons into balls with melon baller. Mix all fruit and put in glass bowl. Mix together remaining ingredients; stir until sugar is dissolved. Boil 5 minutes. Cool; pour over mixed fruit. Chill for a few hours or overnight. Serves 10 to 15.

Mrs. Max J. Luther, III (Maxine Jenkins)

24-Hour Salad

3 *eggs, beaten*
¼ *cup sugar*
¼ *cup vinegar*
2 *tablespoons butter*
1 *cup heavy cream, whipped*

3 *cups pineapple chunks*
  (canned)
3 *cups light, sweet cherries*
  (canned)
3 *cups oranges, chopped*
2 *cups marshmallows, chopped*

Put eggs in double boiler. Add sugar and vinegar and beat continuously until thick and smooth. Remove from heat and add butter. Cool. When cool, fold in whipped cream, fruit, and marshmallows. Chill in refrigerator overnight. Serves 10 to 12.

Mrs. Max J. Luther, III (Maxine Jenkins)

Fruit Salad*

1 20-ounce can cubed pineapple
2 11-ounce cans mandarin
   oranges
1 3½-ounce can angel
   flake coconut
1 pint sour cream

Refrigerate all ingredients. Drain fruit. Mix together all ingredients. Serve on lettuce leaf. Serves 10 to 12.

Mrs. George Taggart (Ethleen Reimers)

Individual Frozen Salad*

2 cups sour cream
2 tablespoons lemon juice
½ cup sugar
⅛ teaspoon salt
1 10-ounce can crushed
   pineapple
1 banana, diced
4 drops red food coloring
¼ cup chopped pecans
1 16-ounce can pitted dark, sweet
   cherries, drained

Combine sour cream, lemon juice, sugar, salt, pineapple, and banana. Then fold in food coloring, pecans, and cherries. Freeze in paper baking cups placed in muffin tins. Remove and place in plastic bag in freezer. Serves 16.

Mrs. A. Jackson Ashmore (Gay Griffith)

Mandarin Orange Salad

1 3-ounce package orange-
   flavored gelatin
1 cup boiling water
1 11-ounce can mandarin
   oranges
1 6-ounce can frozen orange
   juice concentrate
Sliced white grapes (optional)

Mix gelatin with boiling water until gelatin is dissolved. Drain oranges. Add syrup and frozen orange juice to the gelatin. Stir until orange juice melts. Fold in oranges and grapes if desired. Chill until set. Serves 6. Can also be used as a summer dessert.

Mrs. William N. Woolsey (Sandra Callaway)

Pineapple-Cucumber Salad

1 3-ounce package lemon- or
   lime-flavored gelatin
1½ cups hot water
¼ cup vinegar

½ teaspoon salt
1 cup diced cucumber
1 cup crushed pineapple

Dissolve gelatin in hot water. Add vinegar. Cool. Add remaining ingredients. Pour into a 1-quart mold and chill until firm. Serves 4.

Mrs. Walter P. Noe (Jayn Friedlander)

Cam's Lime-Pine Salad

2 3-ounce packages lime-
   flavored gelatin
1½ cups boiling water
½ cup sour cream
½ cup mayonnaise

2 3-ounce packages cream cheese
2 8-ounce cans crushed pineapple
¾ cup chopped pecans
2 tablespoons white vinegar

Pour boiling water over lime-flavored gelatin. Add sour cream and mayonnaise to softened cream cheese. Add to gelatin and stir. This mixture should be as smooth as possible. If necessary, beat with electric mixer until smooth. Add remaining ingredients and chill to set. Serves 16. To vary flavor, substitute salad dressing for mayonnaise and use walnuts in place of pecans.

CHRISTMAS TREE SALAD:

1 recipe Cam's Lime-Pine Salad
1 8-ounce package cream cheese
Sour cream

Mayonnaise
Green food coloring
Maraschino cherries

Get paper cone fountain cups from the drug store. Pour Cam's Lime-Pine Salad in the cone cups, set in glasses to hold the cones, and chill in refrigerator. An hour before dinner, using a knife and tearing cone, invert on lettuce. Soften cream cheese and add a little sour cream, mayonnaise, and green food coloring until the mixture is spreadable. Frost the trees and decorate with a few pieces of maraschino cherries.

Mrs. Earl Sams Lightner (Robin Holmes)

Yum Yum Salad

1 3-ounce package lime-
  flavored gelatin
1 cup hot water
1 cup pineapple juice
3 tablespoons sugar

1 20-ounce can pineapple
1 cup pecans
1 cup grated Cheddar cheese
1 cup heavy cream, whipped

Dissolve lime-flavored gelatin in hot water. Add sugar to pineapple juice and heat to boiling. Remove from heat. Pour in gelatin and pineapple. Refrigerate. When mixture begins to congeal, pour in pecans and cheese and fold in whipped cream. Serves 4 to 6.

Mrs. Walter P. Noe (Jayn Friedlander)

Congealed Cranberry Mold

3 cups cranberries
3 cups water
1¾ cups sugar
2 3-ounce packages lemon-
  flavored gelatin

1 tablespoon unflavored gelatin
1 cup chopped celery
1½ cups chopped apples
1 whole orange, ground
½ cup chopped pecans

Grind cranberries and cook in ½ cup water until tender. Add sugar and cool. Mix gelatin in 2½ cups boiling water and add to cranberry mixture. Stir in apple, celery, orange, and nuts. Chill. Serves 16.

Mrs. E. A. Durham, II (Kaye Tarrant)

Dr Pepper Salad

1 3-ounce package cherry-
  flavored gelatin
1 16-ounce can pitted dark,
  sweet cherries, juice reserved

1 cup drained crushed
  pineapple, juice reserved
1 cup finely diced celery
½ cup chopped pecans
1 10-ounce bottle Dr Pepper

Mix heated reserved cherry and pineapple juice with cherry-flavored gelatin and dissolve. Let cool and add other ingredients. Refrigerate until congealed. Serve on lettuce leaves with mayonnaise. Serves 6 to 8.

Mrs. William Hall Keys (Rose Mary Blackshear)

Wine Salad

1 3-ounce package cherry-
    flavored gelatin
1 17-ounce can dark, sweet
    cherries, liquid reserved

1 cup Port wine
English walnuts, pecans, or
    cream cheese

Heat 1 cup of the reserved cherry liquid and pour over the
cherry-flavored gelatin. Stir until dissolved. Add wine. Stuff the
cherries with walnuts, pecans, or cream cheese, and arrange them
in a mold, pouring a little of the gelatin mixture over them. Put
in the refrigerator until set. Fill with the rest of the gelatin mixture
and return to the refrigerator. Serves 6 to 8. This is especially good
with a Thanksgiving or Christmas turkey.

Mrs. Gerald Heinzelmann (Carolyn Jones)

Congealed Ambrosia Mold

1 3-ounce package orange-
    pineapple or orange-flavored
    gelatin
1 tablespoon sugar
1 cup boiling water
1 cup cold water

1 cup heavy cream, whipped
2 oranges, sectioned and sliced
1 1/4 cups seeded and halved red
    grapes or 1 banana, sliced and
    quartered
2/3 cup angel flake coconut

Dissolve flavored gelatin and sugar in boiling water. Add cold
water. Chill until slightly thickened. Fold in whipped cream. Then
fold in remaining ingredients. Spoon into a 1½-quart mold. Chill.
Serves 8.

Mrs. Lowell Kepp (Betty Ellis)

Mango Mousse

1 14¾-ounce can mangoes
1 8-ounce package cream cheese
2 3-ounce boxes orange-
   flavored gelatin

1 3-ounce box lemon-flavored
   gelatin
2 cups boiling water

Put can of mangoes and cream cheese in a blender; blend until smooth. Dissolve gelatins in boiling water. Add blended mangoes and cream cheese. Pour into a 1½-quart mold. Chill until set. Serves 8. Serve in a ring mold with strawberries in the center for a luncheon, or in squares, topped with curried mayonnaise, as an accompaniment to Mexican food.

Mrs. J. Gordon Bryson (Martha Bell)

Vegetable Salads

Caesar Salad

1 clove garlic
1 2-ounce can flat anchovy
   filets
¼ cup olive oil
2 tablespoons tarragon vinegar
1 teaspoon Worcestershire sauce

1 teaspoon prepared mustard
1 large head romaine lettuce
Freshly cracked pepper
1 egg
Toasted croutons
Grated Parmesan cheese

Crush garlic clove and combine with anchovy filets that have been mulled well with the back of a wooden spoon against a wooden salad bowl. Add 2 tablespoons of the olive oil and mix well. Add remaining olive oil and mix well again. Stir in tarragon vinegar. Last, add Worcestershire sauce and mustard. Set dressing aside and tear up romaine lettuce that has been washed, drained, and wrapped in an absorbent towel in the refrigerator to crisp (preferably the day before). Sprinkle lettuce with pepper and break the egg, which has been coddled for 1 minute, over it. Toss with enough dressing to moisten well. Finally, toss with grated Parmesan cheese and croutons. Serves 4 to 6.

Mrs. Gerald Heinzelmann (Carolyn Jones)

Tossed Salad

1 head bibb lettuce
1 head red leaf lettuce
1 head romaine lettuce
Water cress (if available)
1 large tomato, cut in wedges
1 cucumber, sliced
1 ripe avocado, diced

1 7-ounce can artichoke hearts, quartered
1 small red onion, sliced in rings
¼ cup toasted sesame seeds
½ cup toasted croutons
Grated Parmesan cheese
Italian dressing

Tear up lettuce and greens and mix in a large salad bowl. Add all other vegetables; toss in sesame seeds, croutons, Parmesan cheese, and .dressing at the very last minute. Serves 18.

Mrs. William N. Woolsey (Sandra Callaway)

In any oil and vinegar salad dressing, including the mixes, use olive oil for the oil and old, soured wine instead of vinegar.

Three-Bean Salad

1 16-ounce can green beans
1 16-ounce can wax beans
1 16-ounce can dark red
  kidney beans
1 medium onion, chopped

Salt
Pepper
2/3 cup sugar
½ cup white vinegar
½ cup salad oil

Drain juice from beans; add chopped onion and seasonings. Add sugar that has been dissolved in vinegar. Mix with salad oil. Make 2 or 3 days before needed. Stir once a day and drain before serving. Serves 6.

Mrs. Donald P. McClure (Sally Garrett)

Winter Salad

1 8-ounce can baby lima beans
1 8-ounce can green peas
1 8-ounce can French style
   green beans
1 small purple onion, chopped
2 ribs celery, chopped

1 small bell pepper, chopped
Pimiento
1/2 cup sugar
1/4 cup salad oil
1/2 cup vinegar
1 1/2 teaspoons salt

Drain vegetables; mix with onion, celery, pepper, and pimiento. Mix sugar, oil, vinegar, and salt until sugar dissolves. Pour dressing over vegetables. Refrigerate overnight before serving. This will keep in a tightly sealed container for several days. Makes 1 quart.

Mrs. Lev H. Prichard, III (Ella Wall)

Mixed Vegetable Salad

1 tablespoon mayonnaise
1 8-ounce package cream cheese
Dash Tabasco brand pepper
   sauce
1 green onion, chopped
1 bell pepper, chopped

1/2 cup chopped celery
3 10-ounce packages frozen
   mixed vegetables, cooked and
   chilled
1 teaspoon lemon juice

Cream mayonnaise, cream cheese, and Tabasco until smooth. Add onion, pepper, and celery to chilled vegetables. Fold in cream cheese mixture. Add lemon juice. Serves 10 to 12.

Mrs. Lowell Kepp (Betty Ellis)

Sweet and Sour Asparagus

1/2 teaspoon salt
2/3 cup vinegar
1/4 cup sugar
1 cinnamon stick

5 whole cloves
1 tablespoon celery seed
1/2 cup water
2 15-ounce cans green asparagus

Mix everything except asparagus and bring to a boil. Place drained asparagus in a flat baking dish and pour boiling liquid over it. Cover and refrigerate for 24 hours. Serves 6 to 8.

Mrs. Charles DeCou (Martha McKamey)

Sweet and Sour Salad

½ cup sugar
½ cup vinegar
6 green onions, sliced
1 clove garlic

1 16-ounce can whole green
    beans, drained
½ cup salad oil

Bring sugar and vinegar to a boil. Pour over beans, sliced onions, and garlic. Add oil. Refrigerate. In sealed jars or plastic containers the salad will keep for several weeks in refrigerator. Serves 4.

Mrs. William Hall Keys (Rose Mary Blackshear)

Marinated Broccoli

½ cup tarragon vinegar
½ cup salad oil
1 small clove garlic, minced
1 tablespoon sugar

1 teaspoon salt
Dash Tabasco brand pepper sauce
1 bunch fresh broccoli, cooked

Combine all ingredients except broccoli in glass container. Add broccoli; toss. Cover and chill at least 8 hours. Stir often. If fresh broccoli is not in season, use frozen. Or, use 2 packages frozen brussels sprouts. Serves 6 to 8.

Mrs. Austin Davies (Kathy Jones)

Cole Slaw

1 large head cabbage, diced
1 large onion, sliced in rings
¾ cup sugar
1 teaspoon prepared mustard

1 teaspoon celery seed
1½ teaspoons salt
1 cup vinegar
1 cup corn oil

Place diced cabbage in bowl and put onion rings on top. Mix sugar, mustard, celery seed, salt, and vinegar in sauce pan and bring to a boil. Then add corn oil and mix well. Pour over salad. Seal well and refrigerate for 24 hours. Serves 8.

Mrs. A. Jackson Ashmore (Gay Griffith)

Confetti Slaw

1 medium head green cabbage	Salt
1 small head red cabbage	Pepper
1 bell pepper, seeded	¾ cup white vinegar
4 carrots, scraped	1½ cups salad oil (not olive
10 radishes	oil)
20 stuffed green olives, sliced	2 tablespoons sugar
1 bunch green onions and tops,	2 teaspoons celery seed
chopped	½ cup mayonnaise

Shred washed raw vegetables; combine with olives. Mix salt, pepper, vinegar, oil, sugar, and celery seed. Shake to mix well. Pour over vegetables. Add mayonnaise and toss well. Cover and refrigerate. Chill several hours before serving. This may be prepared the day before serving. Serves 15 to 20.

Mrs. Joe P. Nelson (Harriet Hornish)

The Kings' Copper Penny Carrots

2 pounds carrots	¾ cup vinegar
1 small bell pepper, thinly sliced	1 teaspoon prepared mustard
1 medium onion, thinly sliced	1 teaspoon Worcestershire
1 can condensed tomato soup	sauce
½ cup salad oil	Salt
1 cup sugar	Pepper

Cook carrots in salted water until medium done. Rinse in ice water. Arrange layers of carrots, bell pepper, and onion in container. Make marinade of other ingredients and heat well, until thoroughly blended. Pour over carrots and keep refrigerated. Will keep for weeks and liquid may also be used again. Serves 12. This recipe doubles well for a large group.

Mrs. Lowell Kepp (Betty Ellis)

Hearts of Palm Salad*

2 8-ounce cans hearts of palm
¼ cup salad oil
⅛ cup cider vinegar
½ teaspoon sugar

¼ teaspoon dried dill weed
¼ teaspoon salt
Dash pepper

Arrange hearts of palm on lettuce leaves on individual salad plates. Combine other ingredients and pour over. Chill. Serves 4.

Mrs. Edwin Singer (Patsy Dunn)

Marinated Peas

1 16-ounce can green peas
¼ cup salad oil
¼ cup vinegar
Salt

Pepper
Paprika
2 cloves garlic, chopped

Drain peas; marinate in oil and vinegar. Add salt, pepper, paprika, and garlic. Marinate overnight. Serves 4.

Mrs. Walter P. Noe (Jayn Friedlander)

Potato Salad

6 large potatoes, cooked, peeled, and cubed
1 egg
1 medium onion, chopped
½ bell pepper, chopped
2 ribs celery, chopped
¼ cup sweet pickle relish
1 large dill pickle, chopped
Salt
Pepper

¼ teaspoon celery seed
¼ teaspoon Worcestershire sauce
1½ tablespoons chopped parsley
3 tablespoons chopped stuffed olives
1½ teaspoons mustard
½ cup mayonnaise
2 tablespoons cider vinegar

Mix cubed potatoes with raw egg. Add all other ingredients, mix, and chill. Serves 12.

Mrs. Dudley A. Chatham (Melba Welsh)

Hot Potato Salad

7 medium new potatoes
¼ cup olive oil
2 tablespoons vinegar
1 teaspoon pepper

1 tablespoon chopped chives
½ teaspoon celery seed
½ teaspoon tarragon
Salt

Boil new potatoes. Mix other ingredients together with a silver fork and pour over hot diced potatoes. Serves 6 to 8. This is good with ham, cold beef, or tongue.

Mrs. J. Cary Barton (Pattee Critz)

Spinach Salad

6 cloves garlic, quartered
¾ cup French dressing
3 hard-cooked eggs, chopped

8 slices bacon, fried crisp and
  crumbled
1 pound crisp young spinach,
  washed and refrigerated

Allow garlic to steep in French dressing at least 2 hours. Remove garlic from dressing when ready to toss salad. Sprinkle eggs, bacon, and dressing over spinach. Toss and serve. Serves 6.

Mrs. Jack M. Painter (Darlene Downer)

Russian Tomato Salad

12 plum tomatoes
Olive oil
1 cup heavy cream, whipped
½ cup mayonnaise
2 tablespoons freshly grated
  horseradish

2 to 4 tablespoons minced
  parsley or chives
Salt
Freshly ground black pepper
Paprika

Peel tomatoes; brush with olive oil and chill until ready to serve. Combine whipped cream with mayonnaise, grated horseradish, and parsley or chives. Season to taste with salt and pepper. Chill. When ready to serve, arrange tomatoes on a dish in a pyramid and top with dressing. Sprinkle with paprika. Serves 4 to 6.

Mrs. Richard King, III (Jimmie Rose Harrison)

Tomatoes with Artichoke Hearts

6 large ripe tomatoes
Salt
Pepper
Powdered dill weed
6 canned artichoke hearts

1 pint mayonnaise
1 cup sour cream
1 teaspoon curry powder
1 teaspoon lemon juice
1 teaspoon grated onion

Scald tomatoes to remove skins. Scoop out centers and season them inside and out with salt, freshly ground pepper, and powdered dill. Put an artichoke heart in each tomato. Chill. One hour before serving, cover each tomato with a sauce made by combining mayonnaise with sour cream, curry powder, grated onion, and lemon juice. Add more curry powder if desired. Serve very cold on bibb lettuce. Serves 6.

Mrs. Edwin A. Durham, II (Kaye Tarrant)

Spring Salad Soufflé

1 3-ounce package lime-flavored
  gelatin
½ cup water
1 can condensed cream of
  asparagus soup
½ cup mayonnaise
1 tablespoon vinegar

1 teaspoon grated onion
Dash pepper
½ cup shredded unpared
  cucumber
¼ cup diced celery
1 tablespoon minced parsley

Mix gelatin and water in a sauce pan. Gradually blend in soup. Heat and stir until gelatin is dissolved. Add mayonnaise, vinegar, onion, and pepper to gelatin. Beat with a rotary beater until mixture is smooth. Chill until partially set. Pour gelatin into a large chilled bowl; beat until thick and fluffy. Fold in remaining ingredients. Pour into a 1½-quart ring mold; chill until firm. Serves 4 to 6. Excellent for a ladies' luncheon.

Mrs. Gary Dukes (Bonnie Jean Cameron)

Asparagus Mold

1 can condensed cream of asparagus soup	½ cup cold water
1 3-ounce package lemon-flavored gelatin	½ cup mayonnaise
	¾ cup celery, minced
1 8-ounce package cream cheese, room temperature	½ cup bell pepper, minced
	½ cup pecans, minced
	1 tablespoon grated onion

Heat soup to boiling. Remove from fire and add lemon-flavored gelatin until dissolved. Add cheese and stir until melted and mixed. Stir in remaining ingredients. Turn into mold or dish and chill. Serves 6 to 8.

Mrs. Edwin Prichard, Jr. (Marjorie Reynolds)

Avocado Aspic

2 cups tomato juice	1 tablespoon Worcestershire sauce
2 tablespoons unflavored gelatin	½ teaspoon salt
2 teaspoons dill pickle juice	½ teaspoon pepper
2 teaspoons grated onion	¼ cup cold water
2 teaspoons minced bell pepper	2 cups small curd cottage cheese
3 tablespoons lemon juice	¼ cup mayonnaise
½ teaspoon Tabasco brand pepper sauce	1 cup evaporated milk
	2 to 3 medium avocados, diced
	½ to 1 cup minced celery

Heat 1 cup tomato juice to boiling and pour over 1 tablespoon of the gelatin, which has been softened in small amount of water. Stir well; add unheated tomato juice. Add dill pickle juice, grated onion, bell pepper, lemon juice, Tabasco Sauce, Worcestershire sauce, salt, and pepper. Chill until slightly thickened. Combine remaining gelatin and cold water; let stand. Combine cottage cheese, mayonnaise, evaporated milk, avocados, and celery. Add to gelatin. Combine this with the tomato juice mixture, pour into a mold or dish, and chill thoroughly. Makes 2 quarts.

Mrs. Emil Tejml (Sue Rosson)

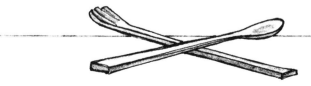

Avocado Salad

2 3-ounce packages lime- or
   lemon-flavored gelatin
2 cups hot water
2 cups minced celery
1 medium bell pepper, diced

12 ounces cream cheese
1 cup mayonnaise
2 large, barely ripe avocados
Salt
Pepper

Mix the flavored gelatin with boiling water, cool slightly, and add vegetables, except avocados. Mix room-temperature cheese with mayonnaise. Mash avocados with a fork and add to cheese and mayonnaise. Then combine all ingredients and pour into a shallow refrigerator dish. Cover and chill until set. Be sure vegetables do not contain excess moisture and do not put too much water in gelatin. Cut into squares and serve on lettuce leaves with a dollop of mayonnaise. Serves 12.

Mrs. John H. Yochem (Phyllis Nigh)

Cucumber Mold

1 3-ounce package lime-flavored
   gelatin
¾ cup boiling water
1 large cucumber, minced
1 medium onion, minced

1 cup cottage cheese
1 cup mayonnaise
1 tablespoon lemon juice
1/3 cup chopped pecans (optional)

Dissolve gelatin in boiling water; chill until syrupy. Whip. Gently add remaining ingredients. Chill until firm. Serves 10 to 12.

Mrs. Lowell Kepp (Betty Ellis)

Dressings

Fruit Salad Dressing*

1 cup sour cream
1 7-ounce jar Kraft brand
   Marshmallow Creme

3 tablespoons créme de menthe
   (or more)

Mix together and serve over fruit salad. Makes 2 cups.

Mrs. Gerald Heinzelmann (Carolyn Jones)

Citrus Dressing

1½ cups sugar
½ cup prepared mustard
Juice of 1 lemon
2 cups vinegar

1 cup water
1½ teaspoons salt
2 cloves garlic
1 cup corn oil

Mix all ingredients except oil. Beat thoroughly and slowly add oil last. Keeps indefinitely in refrigerator. Makes 1 quart.

Mrs. George Taggart (Ethleen Reimers)

Poppy Seed Dressing with Honey

2/3 cup honey
1 teaspoon salt
2/3 cup vinegar
1 sliver onion
½ clove garlic

5 tablespoons poppy seed
1 tablespoon dry mustard
2½ cups salad oil
½ teaspoon paprika

Mix all ingredients in an electric blender until smooth. Makes 1 quart. Serve on fresh fruit salad and on citrus and avocado.

Mrs. Kenneth McKamey (Hattie Bell Colston)

Onion-Poppy Seed Dressing

¾ cup sugar
1/3 cup vinegar
1 teaspoon salt
¼ cup grated onion

1 teaspoon dry mustard (optional)
1 cup salad oil
2 tablespoons poppy seeds

Mix first 5 ingredients thoroughly. Slowly add salad oil and mix very well. Add poppy seeds to mixture and beat thoroughly. Refrigerate and mix by shaking. Makes about 1½ cups.

Mrs. Donald Everett Jackson (Patricia Ann Alexander)

Hot Sauce for Avocados

2 tablespoons butter	2 tablespoons catsup
2 tablespoons Worcestershire sauce	1 tablespoon sugar
2 tablespoons vinegar	Salt
	Coarsely ground pepper

Heat all ingredients together in the top of a double boiler until very hot. Serve in gravy boat for guests to spoon over halved, seeded avocados. Makes 1 cup.

Mrs. Emil Tejml (Sue Rosson)

Tarragon-Anchovy Dressing

8 to 10 anchovy filets	1 tablespoon crumbled tarragon
1 green onion, minced	soaked in vinegar, then
1/4 cup minced chives	strained (or 2 tablespoons
1/4 cup minced parsley	minced fresh tarragon)
1/4 cup tarragon vinegar	3 cups mayonnaise

Make a paste of the anchovy filets and mix well with all other ingredients. Chill before use. Serve on green salad. Makes about 1 quart.

Miss Coleene McCracken

Curry Salad Dressing

Juice of 1/2 lemon	Salt
1 tablespoon dry minced onion (2 tablespoons, if fresh)	Pepper
2 tablespoons minced parsley	1 tablespoon wine vinegar
1/2 teaspoon curry powder (or more)	1/2 cup mayonnaise
2 to 3 dashes garlic powder	Buttermilk (enough to thin to desired consistency)

Mix all ingredients in a jar and age for 2 hours in the refrigerator. Serve on a green salad sprinkled with toasted sesame seeds. Also good on leftover cold broccoli. Makes about 1 cup.

Mrs. Dudley A. Chatham (Melba Welsh)

Heavenly Dressing*

½ cup salad oil
3 tablespoons vinegar
1 tablespoon prepared
  horseradish
Dash pepper

1½ teaspoons salt
1½ teaspoons Worcestershire
  sauce
2 dashes Tabasco brand
  pepper sauce

Combine all ingredients in a covered jar. Chill. Shake well before using. Serve on green salad. Makes about 1 cup.

Mrs. Charles DeCou (Martha McKamey)

Green Salad Dressing

1 teaspoon salt
1 egg
1 teaspoon sugar
Dash Tabasco brand pepper
  sauce

3 tablespoons vinegar
1 clove garlic
1 cup chives (or green onion tops)
1 cup parsley
¾ cup salad oil

Put all ingredients except salad oil into blender and blend a few seconds. Add salad oil and blend until dressing is smooth. Makes 1 pint. Serve on green salads.

Mrs. James C. Sharp, Jr. (Amber DeForest)

Roquefort Dressing*

1 pint mayonnaise
1 12-ounce carton small curd
  cottage cheese
1 cup sour cream
¼ teaspoon onion salt

¼ teaspoon sugar
¼ teaspoon salt
⅛ teaspoon garlic powder
6 to 8 ounces Roquefort cheese

Blend all ingredients, except Roquefort cheese, in an electric blender until smooth. Add crumbled cheese and blend briefly. Crumble additional cheese over salad if desired. Makes 5½ cups.

This dressing is thick enough to be used as a dip for chips or raw vegetables.

Mrs. W. Richard McCracken (Lucy McFadyen)

Roquefort-French Salad Dressing*

1 egg   3 ounces Roquefort cheese
1 clove garlic   1 cup corn oil
1 teaspoon salt   ¼ cup wine vinegar

Pour all ingredients into blender and mix. Then store in refrigerator. Makes about 1½ cups.

Mrs. George Taggart (Ethleen Reimers)

Romano Cheese Salad Dressing

6 ounces Romano cheese, grated   ¼ cup cider vinegar
1 cup salad oil   ½ teaspoon salt
¼ cup wine vinegar   ⅛ teaspoon pepper

Fill jar with freshly grated Romano cheese. Pour in oil and vinegars. Add salt and pepper. Shake and let stand for 24 hours before using. Keeps indefinitely. Serve on green salad. Makes 1 pint.

Mrs. Jack Best (Betty Reno)

Renee's Salad Dressing

¾ cup salad oil   1½ teaspoons salt
1 tablespoon lemon juice   ½ teaspoon mustard seed
1 tablespoon vinegar   ½ teaspoon celery seed
1½ teaspoons minced onion   ¼ teaspoon thyme
1½ teaspoons minced parsley   1 clove garlic, minced
1½ teaspoons sugar   ¼ cup heavy cream

Mix all ingredients but cream and refrigerate overnight. Add cream, mix again, and serve over lettuce. Makes about 1 cup.

Mrs. Lev H. Prichard, III (Ella Wall)

Salad recipes found in Chapter 1. MEXICAN FOOD:

Guacamole Salad   *Taco Salad*
Mexican Chef Salad

Eggs, Cheese, Grains, and Pasta

7. EGGS, CHEESE, GRAINS, and PASTA

Most of the time, when a South Texan cooks eggs, cheese, or rice, she borrows the methods and seasonings of Mexico. But she can cook the classic dishes as well, and often does, though she may add an extra dash of pepper to "properly" season them. Rice is a major substitute for potatoes, since Texas rice producing country begins only 100 miles Northeast, and recipes abound, from the simplest to the most elegant.

Eggs

Eggs Benedict

4 slices Canadian bacon	4 eggs
2 English muffins	Hollandaise sauce
Butter	Dash cayenne pepper

Fry Canadian bacon; drain. Split muffins and toast. Butter muffins. Meanwhile, poach eggs for 4 minutes. Arrange muffins on plate; top them with bacon, then poached eggs. Spoon Hollandaise sauce over eggs. Sprinkle with cayenne pepper for color. Serve hot. Serves 4.

Mrs. Earl Sams Lightner (Robin Holmes)

Omelette Basquaise

1 bell pepper, chopped	3 tablespoons margarine or
½ serrano pepper, minced	olive oil
(optional)	½ cup chopped cooked ham
1 onion, chopped	Salt
1 clove garlic, minced	Pepper
3 tomatoes, peeled and seeded	6 eggs, beaten

Sauté onion, garlic, and peppers in oil for a few minutes. Add tomatoes and reduce heat. Cover and simmer a few minutes. Add ham and salt and pepper to taste. Simmer uncovered until tomatoes have cooked to mushiness and peppers and onions are done. Use as filling for 1 large or 3 smaller omelets. Serves 3.

Mrs. Jack M. Painter (Darlene Downer)

Herbed Eggs

8 eggs
½ cup sour cream
2 tablespoons butter
2 to 3 green onions, including
tops, chopped

Chopped parsley
Oregano
Garlic salt
Seasoned salt

Put eggs and sour cream in blender and blend until frothy. Melt butter in skillet and add egg mixture. Add herbs and seasonings and soft scramble. Serves 4.

Other herb variations could include any of the following: sweet basil, tarragon, chives, or Beau Monde brand seasoning.

Mrs. Max J. Luther, III (Maxine Jenkins)

Baked Eggs for Brunch

1 tablespoon butter
2 slices Swiss cheese
2 eggs
Salt

Pepper
2 tablespoons heavy cream
1 tablespoon dry white wine

Butter an individual ramekin with butter. Line the ramekin with Swiss cheese, covering bottom and sides. Drop eggs on cheese. Season with salt and pepper. Pour wine and cream over eggs. Bake 12 to 15 minutes at 300 degrees. Stir as you eat it. Serves 1.

Mrs. Jack M. Painter (Darlene Downer)

Deviled Eggs with Ham

8 hard-cooked eggs
1 2¼-ounce can deviled ham
2 green onions, minced
½ teaspoon prepared mustard
2 tablespoons pickle relish

Salt
Pepper
Mayonnaise
Paprika

Cut eggs in half and remove yolks. Mash yolks with fork. Add all remaining ingredients except mayonnaise and paprika. Add enough mayonnaise to make mixture gooey but not runny. Fill egg whites. Sprinkle with paprika. Makes 16.

Mrs. Earl Sams Lightner (Robin Holmes)

Deviled Eggs

12 hard-cooked eggs
1 cup mayonnaise
½ cup hot prepared mustard

1 teaspoon salt
1 teaspoon pepper
Paprika

Cut eggs in half, lengthwise. Place yolks in bowl. Mix remaining ingredients, except paprika. Place mixture back into egg whites. Sprinkle paprika on top. Makes 24.

Mrs. Robert C. Wood (Helen Heaney)

Toasted Cheese and Egg Cups

6 slices bread
2 tablespoons butter, melted
6 eggs, beaten
1 teaspoon salt (or less)
¼ teaspoon dry mustard
Dash Worcestershire sauce

Few grains cayenne pepper
¼ cup milk
Dash Tabasco brand pepper sauce
½ cup grated sharp Cheddar
  cheese

Remove crusts from bread. Brush both sides of each slice with melted butter. Gently press slices into muffin tin. Combine beaten eggs with remaining ingredients, except cheese. Stir and pour into bread cups. Sprinkle cheese in each cup. Bake at 350 degrees for 30 minutes or until egg mixture is set. Serves 6.

Mrs. John Charles Abbott (Jane Belfour)

Cheese
Quiche Lorraine

1 unbaked pie crust
8 green onions, minced
8 slices fried bacon, crumbled
1 cup grated Swiss cheese

3 eggs
1½ cups cream or milk
Salt
Pepper

In the bottom of a pie crust, put onions, bacon, and cheese. Beat eggs and add cream, salt, and pepper. Pour over the mixture in the pie crust. Bake 50 to 60 minutes at 350 degrees. Serve hot or cold.

Chopped ham or canned white crab meat may be substituted for the bacon. Cheddar instead of Swiss cheese is another variation.

Mrs. Harold Pettus (Genevieve Perry)

 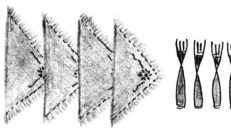

Gateau Fromage
CHEESE PIE

1 unbaked pie crust	1 egg
8 ounces Cheddar cheese, grated	¾ cup milk
4 to 5 slices bacon	¼ teaspoon salt
1 cup onion rings	⅛ teaspoon pepper

Fill pie crust with cheese. Fry bacon until crisp; drain and crumble. Sauté onion rings in bacon drippings; drain. Place bacon and onion on top of cheese and freeze at least 2 hours. Beat egg and add milk, salt, and pepper. Sprinkle over frozen pie and shake pie pan to mix ingredients. Bake at 350 degrees for 25 minutes. Serve like *Quiche Lorraine* as an *hors d'oeuvre* or a main dish.

Mrs. J. Michael Mahaffey (Lynn Smith)

Cheese Soufflé

2 tablespoons butter	¼ teaspoon paprika
3 tablespoons flour	1 cup milk
1 teaspoon salt	1 cup grated American cheese
¼ teaspoon mustard	3 eggs, separated

Melt butter over low heat; add flour and stir to make a smooth paste. Stir in seasonings. Add milk slowly, stirring constantly until sauce is thick. Add cheese and cook until smooth. Add beaten egg yolks. Set aside to cool slightly. Beat egg whites until dry and stiff; fold into cheese sauce. Pour into greased casserole. Place casserole in a shallow pan of hot water. Bake at 325 degrees for about 45 minutes or until top is firm to touch and nicely browned. Serve immediately. Serves 3.

Mrs. A. C. Skinner (Marshall Elmore)

Tomato-Cheese Soufflé

1 can condensed tomato soup
1 cup grated sharp Cheddar
  cheese
1 tablespoon sugar

⅛ teaspoon pepper
¼ cup diced stuffed olives
  (optional)
4 eggs, separated

Melt cheese in soup. Add sugar, pepper, and olives. Cool slightly. Add beaten egg yolks. Fold in egg whites that have been beaten until stiff but not dry. Pour into ungreased 1½-quart casserole or soufflé dish. Bake 40 minutes at 325 degrees. Do not open oven during baking. Serve at once. Serves 4.

Mrs. Austin Davies (Kathy Jones)

Libby's Cheese Casserole

6 slices bread, crusts removed
3 eggs, beaten
1 cup milk
Pinch dry mustard

1 rounded cup grated sharp
  Cheddar cheese
½ teaspoon seasoned salt

Line bottom of 1½-quart buttered baking dish with bread that has been cut in quarters. Beat eggs and add milk, mustard, cheese, and salt. Pour the mixture over bread and refrigerate for several hours. Bake at 350 degrees for about 40 minutes. Serves 2 or 3.

Mrs. Tom McArdle (Marion Hall)

Fail-Safe Rarebit

1 tablespoon butter
1 teaspoon corn starch
½ cup half and half (or more)
8 ounces sharp Cheddar cheese,
  cubed

¼ teaspoon dry mustard
Pinch paprika
Few grains baking soda
Few grains cayenne pepper
2 to 3 drops Worcestershire sauce

Melt butter over low heat; blend in corn starch. Stir in half and half and cheese, stirring until cheese is melted. Remove from heat and add remaining ingredients. Serve immediately on toast or unsalted crackers. Garnish the rarebit with tomato slices and crisp bacon. Serves 4.

Mrs. John Charles Abbott (Jane Belfour)

Rice

Green Rice Delight

2/3 cup cooking oil
2 eggs
4 cups cooked rice
1 5-1/3-ounce can evaporated
  milk
1½ cups grated sharp Cheddar
  cheese
2 3-ounce cans mushrooms
  (optional)

2 cans condensed cream of
  mushroom soup
1 large onion, chopped
1 10-ounce package frozen
  chopped broccoli, cooked and
  drained
Salt
Pepper

Add oil to beaten eggs. Combine all ingredients. Bake in greased 3-quart baking dish for 1 hour at 350 degrees. Casserole may be frozen before or after baking. Serves 12.

Mrs. Lowell Kepp (Betty Ellis)

Holiday Pilaf

¼ cup butter
1 cup diced celery
½ cup coarsely chopped Brazil
  nuts or almonds
3 tablespoons minced onion
2 beef bouillon cubes
½ teaspoon salt
¼ teaspoon Tabasco brand
  pepper sauce

1 16-ounce can green peas,
  drained (reserve liquid)
1 3-ounce can sliced mushrooms,
  drained (reserve liquid)
10 to 12 pitted ripe olives, sliced
2 tablespoons raisins
2 cups Minute brand pre-cooked
  rice

In a large skillet, melt butter and sauté celery, nuts, and onion 5 minutes. Add bouillon cubes, salt, and Tabasco. Add water to liquid from green peas and mushrooms to measure 2 cups. Add to mixture in skillet along with peas, mushrooms, olives, and raisins. Bring mixture to a boil; add 2 cups rice; toss to moisten. Cover. Remove from heat and let stand as directed on rice package. Serves 6 to 8. Freezes well.

Mrs. Max J. Luther, III (Maxine Jenkins)

Fried Rice

6 tablespoons cooking oil
2 eggs
1 teaspoon salt
2 green onions
½ cup diced raw shrimp
  (or more)
4 cups cold cooked rice

½ cup cooked green peas
¼ cup bamboo shoots
½ cup diced boiled ham
½ cup diced cooked chicken
½ cup chopped roast beef
2 tablespoons soy sauce
Chopped scallions

Heat 2 tablespoons oil. Beat eggs with ½ teaspoon salt and scramble in oil until firm, breaking into small pieces. Remove and reserve. Heat remaining oil. Add onions, shrimp, and remaining salt. Stir until shrimp turns pink. Break up the lumps of cold cooked rice and add to the shrimp. Stir until rice is heated and the grains of rice separate. Make a hole in the center of the rice. Add all ingredients except soy sauce and scallions. Stir until thoroughly heated and mixed. Sprinkle soy sauce over rice and mix. Salt and pepper to taste. Garnish with chopped scallions. Serves 4.

Mrs. Lowell Kepp (Betty Ellis)

Golden Risotto

½ cup chopped onion
¼ cup margarine
1 cup diced cooked chicken
1 cup cooked ham strips
1 cup diced cooked roast
2 cups bouillon

1 4-ounce can mushrooms
1/8 teaspoon crushed saffron
1-1/3 cups Minute brand
  pre-cooked rice
¼ cup grated Parmesan cheese

Sauté onion in margarine. Add meats, bouillon, and mushrooms and bring to a boil. Add saffron, rice, and cheese and bring to a boil. Reduce heat and simmer 5 minutes. Serves 6. This freezes well. Defrost, add a little bouillon, and heat in skillet.

Mrs. A. Jackson Ashmore (Gay Griffith)

The easiest, most foolproof method of cooking rice is to bake ½ cup rice and 1 can condensed consommé in a covered 1½-quart casserole at 350 degrees for about 1 hour.

Rice-Onion Dish*

½ cup melted butter
1 cup rice
1 3-ounce can mushrooms
1 can condensed onion soup

1 8½-ounce can water
    chestnuts, sliced
1 soup can water
Salt

Combine all ingredients in a 2-quart casserole and bake for 45 minutes to 1 hour at 350 degrees. Serves 4 to 6.

Mrs. John F. Cram (Janet Tyson)

Baked Rice

¼ cup minced onion
¼ cup minced bell pepper
½ cup sliced mushrooms
   (optional)

¼ cup slivered blanched almonds
3 cans condensed consommé
1½ cups converted rice

Sauté onion, pepper, and mushrooms in butter in a flame-proof 3-quart casserole until tender. Add rice and consommé and bake covered at 350 degrees for 45 minutes. Add almonds and cook 30 minutes longer or until rice has absorbed all liquid.

Mrs. William N. Woolsey (Sandra Callaway)

Wild Rice

Kay's Wild Rice Casserole

4 green onions
1 4-ounce can chopped
   mushrooms
1 6-ounce box long grain and
   wild rice

½ cup butter
1 can condensed beef broth
2 cups water

Chop green onions, including tops. Sauté onions, mushrooms, and rice in melted butter until onions and rice are transluscent. Stir in seasonings from the box of rice mix. Transfer to a 1½-quart casserole. Add broth and water. Cover and bake at 325 degrees for 1 hour or until liquid is absorbed. Serves 6.

Mrs. Charles Canfield (Patricia Kitchen)

Wild Rice and Cheese

½ cup milk
1 can condensed cream of
  mushroom soup
1-inch-thick slice American
  cheese

1/3 cup long grain rice, cooked
1/3 cup wild rice, cooked
3 ounces fresh mushrooms, sliced
2 slices bacon, fried and crumbled

Blend milk into soup. Cube cheese. Add cheese, rice, and mushrooms to soup mixture. Blend well. Add bacon. Pour into a 1-quart baking dish. Bake at 300 degrees for 45 minutes. Serves 4.

Mrs. A. Jackson Ashmore (Gay Griffith)

Wild Rice

1½ cups wild rice
4 cans condensed beef broth
1 cup chopped onion
1 cup sliced mushrooms

¼ cup butter
1 cup heavy cream
Salt
Pepper

Wash rice thoroughly. Simmer in broth until most of liquid is absorbed. Sauté onions and mushrooms in melted butter. Add cream, salt, and pepper. Mix with rice; put in buttered 2-quart casserole. Bake at 350 degrees for 20 minutes. Serves 6 to 8.

Mrs. H. William Volk, Jr. (LaVerne Ryan)

Grits

Grits Casserole

1½ cups grits
6 cups water
½ cup margarine
1 1-pound box Old English
  brand process cheese
3 eggs, beaten

1 teaspoon salt
½ teaspoon garlic salt
1 tablespoon seasoned salt
2/3 teaspoon Tabasco brand
  pepper sauce
Paprika

Cook grits in 6 cups unsalted boiling water for 5 minutes or until thick. Remove from heat; add margarine and cheese and stir until both are melted. Add eggs and all seasonings except paprika and mix well. Pour into 3-quart casserole and sprinkle paprika on top. Bake at 350 degrees for 1 hour. Serves 12.

Mrs. Robert B. Wallace (Beverley Bird)

Pasta

Spaghetti Carbonara

1 pound spaghetti	¾ cup grated Parmesan cheese
4 ounces hog jowl, cut in	¼ cup heavy cream
1-inch pieces*	½ teaspoon salt
1 tablespoon cooking oil	1 teaspoon freshly ground pepper
4 eggs	¼ cup butter

Cook the spaghetti in a large amount of rapidly boiling salted water until barely tender. Drain. Fry the hog jowl with the oil in a skillet over high heat until crisp and brown. Beat the eggs in a bowl with the cheese, salt, pepper, and cream. Melt the butter in a heavy sauce pan over medium heat; when it turns dark gold (almost nut-colored), begin to beat in the egg mixture gradually. Stir quickly. When mixture begins to thicken, add the spaghetti and the fried hog jowl. Mix very quickly and serve at once. It is important to have the spaghetti cooked and drained when the eggs just begin to thicken. Eggs must not be allowed to overcook and should be moist. Serves 6.

*Parboiled salt pork or bacon, fried crisp, as above, may be substituted for the hog jowl.

Mrs. Charles Weathered, Jr. (Jane McGee)

Sopa de Fideo
DRY VERMICELLI SOUP

8 ounces vermicelli	2 medium tomatoes, quartered
Bacon drippings to cover bottom	1 to 2 chicken bouillon cubes
of skillet (about 1/3 cup)	Salt
½ medium onion, chopped	Pepper
1 clove garlic, minced	2 cups water

Fry vermicelli in bacon drippings until lightly browned, stirring constantly to prevent burning. Add remaining ingredients and simmer, covered, until dry, about 20 to 30 minutes. Dish can be served with a sprinkling of grated cheese on top. Serves 4 to 6. This is a good meatless entrée as well as an unusual substitute for potatoes or rice.

Mrs. Thomas W. Marshall (Florence Deutz)

Noodles Antin

1 8-ounce package narrow
  noodles
1 13¾-ounce can chicken broth
1 egg, beaten
1½ cups creamed cottage cheese
1 cup evaporated milk
1 teaspoon salt

Pepper
Worcestershire sauce
Tabasco brand pepper sauce
¼ cup chopped green onion
  (or ½ clove garlic, chopped)
¼ to ½ cup chopped parsley
Grated Parmesan cheese

Cook noodles in broth and a little water. Mix all remaining ingredients except Parmesan cheese. Add drained noodles. Bake in 1½-quart casserole at 325 degrees for 30 minutes. Sprinkle liberally with Parmesan cheese and bake a little longer. Serves 6 to 8.

Mrs. H. William Volk, Jr. (LaVerne Ryan)

Noodles Romanoff

3 cups noodles, green or plain
2 cups creamed cottage cheese
2 cups sour cream
½ cup chopped onion
½ teaspoon garlic powder

4 teaspoons Worcestershire sauce
½ cup grated Parmesan cheese
½ cup stale bread crumbs
2 teaspoons seasoned salt

Cook noodles and drain. Add remaining ingredients. Put in a greased 3-quart baking dish; sprinkle with paprika. Bake 45 minutes at 350 degrees. May be made the day before. Serves 6.

Mrs. Charles DeCou (Martha McKamey)

Egg, cheese, and rice recipes found in Chapter 1. MEXICAN FOOD:

Border-Style Eggs
Huevos Rancheros
Jalapeño Pie
Chili Soufflé

Chili con Queso
Cindy Ryder's White Smash
Green Chili Enchiladas
Spanish Rice

Seafood

8. SEAFOOD

Corpus Christi is the heart of the Texas fishing industry. Party fishing boats and commercial shrimp boats dock in the bay in the downtown area, and children catch crabs and small fish from the shore. Aransas Pass, 20 miles to the north, boasts the state's largest shrimp boat fleet. Across the harbor, on Mustang Island, is Port Aransas where the game fishing boats leave for Gulf waters in search of tarpon, marlin, mackerel. The Laguna Madre, which separates Corpus Christi and indeed the entire lower Texas coast from Padre Island, yields flounder, redfish, pompano, and bass.

Crab

Vol au Vent

1 cup sliced fresh mushrooms	½ teaspoon salt
2 tablespoons minced onion	¼ teaspoon pepper
1 teaspoon dried parsley	¼ teaspoon paprika
¼ cup butter	½ cup dry white wine
3 tablespoons flour	2 cups cooked king crab, diced
1½ cups milk	12 flaky pastry shells

Sauté mushrooms, onion, and parsley in butter. Add flour and cook until bubbly. Slowly add milk, salt, pepper, and paprika. Simmer about 20 minutes; add wine and crab and cook another 20 minutes. Serve in flaky pastry shells or over rice. White lump crab meat can be used, but the king crab is prettier. Serves 12.

Mrs. William N. Woolsey (Sandra Callaway)

Crab Meat au Gratin

½ cup butter	2 egg yolks
½ cup chopped green onion	½ teaspoon salt (or less)
½ cup chopped celery	¼ teaspoon cayenne pepper
6 tablespoons flour	¼ teaspoon black pepper
1 5-1/3-ounce can evaporated milk	1 pound white lump crab meat
	½ cup grated American cheese

Sauté onions and celery in butter in a heavy skillet. Add flour gradually and then add milk mixed with beaten egg yolks. Add salt and pepper, mix with crab meat, and put in buttered ramekins or casserole. Top with grated cheese and bake at 350 degrees until brown. Serves 4.

Mrs. Vernon Medlin (Mamie Smith)

Crab Lorenzo

1 4-ounce can sliced mushrooms	1 pound lump crab meat
1/3 cup butter	1/4 cup dry vermouth or Sherry
2 tablespoons flour	(optional)
1 cup milk	Toast rounds

Sauté mushrooms in 2 teaspoons butter. Make a medium white sauce with remaining butter, flour, and milk. When the sauce has thickened, add crab meat and wine. Generously cover toast rounds with crab meat mixture and top with Hollandaise sauce. Broil until bubbly and slightly browned. Serves 6.

HOLLANDAISE SAUCE:

4 egg yolks	Paprika
3 tablespoons lemon juice	1/2 cup soft butter
1/2 teaspoon salt	1/2 cup boiling water

Blend all ingredients except water until well mixed. Add water. Cook in a double boiler until sauce reaches the consistency of custard. Serve over Crab Lorenzo.

Mrs. Gerald Heinzelmann (Carolyn Jones)

Mother's Crab Dish

1/2 cup margarine	Dash Tabasco brand pepper
2 onions, chopped	sauce
4 cloves garlic, chopped	Salt
1 bell pepper, chopped	Coarsely ground pepper
2 tablespoons flour	8 ounces Velveeta brand
1 13-ounce can evaporated milk	process cheese
1 tablespoon Worcestershire	1 pound fresh crab meat
sauce	Cooked rice
1 teaspoon curry powder	

Fry onion, garlic, and bell pepper in margarine until soft. Add flour and blend. Stir in milk and season with Worcestershire sauce, Tabasco, salt, pepper, and curry powder. Add cheese and melt; then add crab meat. Serve over rice. Serves 6.

Mrs. Austin Davies (Kathy Jones)

Crab Meat Lonnie

1 medium onion, sliced in rings
¼ cup butter
1 pound lump crab meat

Pepper
¼ cup dry Sherry

Sauté onion rings in butter; add crab meat and lots of pepper. Add Sherry, heat, and serve topped with Hollandaise sauce. Serves 4.

Mrs. Charles K. McCauley (Claire Jo Cummings)

Best Stuffed Crabs Ever

¼ cup butter
¼ bell pepper, diced
1 onion, diced
1 cup diced celery
8 ounces lump crab meat
1 tablespoon Worcestershire sauce
1 tablespoon catsup

Dash Tabasco brand pepper sauce
1 cup heavy cream
1 cup bread crumbs
Paprika
Salt
Pepper

Sauté pepper, onion, and celery in butter. Combine remaining ingredients; then add pepper, onion, and celery. Bake in crab shells at 350 degrees for 30 to 40 minutes. Serves 4.

Mrs. Earl Sams Lightner (Robin Holmes)

Curried Crab in Shells

¼ cup butter
2 tablespoons flour
1 cup milk
1 teaspoon salt
1 teaspoon dry mustard
¼ teaspoon pepper

1 tablespoon curry powder
½ small bell pepper
1 teaspoon Worcestershire sauce
1 pound fresh backfin lump crab meat
Buttered bread crumbs

Make a white sauce using the butter, flour, and milk. Blend in seasonings when thickened. Add bell pepper, Worcestershire sauce, and crab meat and cook briefly. Fill shells or ramekins and top with buttered bread crumbs. Brown crab mixture in a preheated 400-degree oven. Stuffed shells may be frozen before baking. Thaw at room temperature 1 hour before baking.

Mrs. Williams C. Cunningham (Nancy Nixon)

Crab Meat Dewey

¼ cup butter
¼ cup flour
1 chicken bouillon cube
1 cup milk
1 cup heavy cream
1 4-ounce can sliced mushrooms
  undrained

1 pound lump crab meat
3 egg yolks, beaten
Salt
Cayenne pepper
Shallots (or parsley)
1 small loaf unsliced bread
Melted butter

Melt butter in top of a double boiler. Blend in flour and add bouillon cube, milk, cream, and mushrooms. Stir constantly until thick. Add crab meat and heat well. Add small amount of crab mixture to egg yolks. Stir vigorously. Stir eggs quickly into the mixture in the double boiler. Cook 3 to 4 minutes. Season with salt and pepper. Serve on croustades* and sprinkle with parsley or shallots. Serves 4.

*To make croustades, cut crust off a loaf of unsliced bread. Cut into 4 sections and scoop out centers. Brush inside and out with melted butter before toasting slowly in the oven. Fill with crab meat.

Mrs. John F. Cram (Janet Tyson)

Crab Casserole*

1 10-ounce package frozen
  broccoli spears
½ cup grated sharp Cheddar
  cheese
6 tablespoons butter
2 tablespoons minced onion

2 tablespoons flour
½ teaspoon salt
1 cup milk
1 tablespoon lemon juice
1 cup crab meat
½ cup soft bread crumbs

Cook broccoli according to package directions. Arrange in a greased 1-quart casserole and sprinkle with cheese. Melt ¼ cup butter and sauté onion until golden. Stir in flour and salt. Gradually stir in milk; cook, stirring constantly, over low heat until thickened. Stir in lemon juice; add crab meat. Pour mixture over broccoli. Mix remaining butter with bread crumbs and sprinkle over crab mixture. Bake at 350 degrees for 30 minutes. Serves 4.

Mrs. Robert C. Wolter (Frances Overton)

Crab Meat and Artichoke Casserole

3 tablespoons margarine
3 tablespoons flour
1 cup milk
1 teaspoon Worcestershire
   sauce
¼ teaspoon dry mustard
3 to 4 drops Tabasco brand
   pepper sauce
½ teaspoon salt

¼ teaspoon pepper
1 16-ounce can artichoke
   hearts, drained
1 pound fresh crab meat
¼ cup dry Sherry
4 hard-cooked eggs, chopped
½ cup grated Parmesan cheese
½ cup buttered fine bread crumbs

Make a white sauce with margarine, flour, and milk. Add Worcestershire sauce, mustard, Tabasco, salt, and pepper. Mix artichokes, crab meat, Sherry, and eggs and add to sauce. Pour mixture into a greased 1½-quart casserole. Sprinkle top with mixed bread crumbs and cheese. Bake 45 minutes to 1 hour at 350 degrees. Serves 6.

Mrs. Donald McClure (Sally Garrett)

Frog Legs

Frog Legs Provençale

10 jumbo frog legs
Milk
Seasoned flour
Cooking oil

2 tablespoons butter
1 clove garlic, minced
Juice of ½ lemon
Minced parsley

Cover frog legs with water and soak at least 2 hours. Drain on paper towel. Dip in milk and coat with flour. Cook frog legs in hot oil until golden brown, turning to cook both sides, 6 to 8 minutes. Transfer to a hot platter and pour off oil. Add butter to the skillet in which frog legs were cooked and sauté until golden brown. Add garlic and pour over frog legs. Sprinkle frog legs with lemon juice and parsley and serve immediately. Serves 4.

Mrs. W. Richard McCracken (Lucy McFadyen)

Lobster

Grilled Lobster

2/3 cup cooking oil
1/2 cup Sauterne
1/2 cup soy sauce
2 cloves garlic, minced
1/2 teaspoon ginger

1/2 teaspoon paprika
Dash pepper
1/4 cup lemon juice
6 to 8 lobster tails

Combine first 8 ingredients and let stand 1 hour. Cut underside membrane of lobster tails around edges and remove. Spoon sauce over the lobsters and let them marinate for 2 to 4 hours. Broil with the meat side up over hot coals for 5 minutes; then turn and broil 5 minutes more. Heat remaining sauce and serve with the lobsters. Serves 6 to 8.

Mrs. A. Jackson Ashmore (Gay Griffith)

Oysters

Scalloped Oysters

1 pint oysters
Crushed crackers
Butter
2 eggs, beaten

1/8 teaspoon baking powder
2/3 cup half and half
Salt
Pepper

Drain oysters, reserving liquor. Rinse oysters well. Squeeze liquor through a linen towel to clean. Grease ramekins or a shallow casserole generously with butter. Put a 1/2-inch thick layer of cracker crumbs on bottom. Layer oysters on crackers and salt lightly. Pepper generously. Cover with thin pats of butter. Sprinkle with cracker crumbs.

Put oyster liquor, eggs, baking powder, and half and half in a quart jar. Put top on and shake. Pour enough mixture over the oysters so that you can see the liquid, but it doesn't cover the top of crackers. Put a pat of butter on top. Bake about 20 to 25 minutes at 400 degrees. In ramekins, this is a good first course and serves 6. Serves 2 or 3 as a main dish.

Mrs. Max J. Luther, III (Maxine Jenkins)

Deviled Oysters

¼ cup butter
1 tablespoon cooking oil
1 medium onion, minced
1 pint oysters, cleaned,
  drained, and halved
1 cup coarse bread crumbs

Juice of 1 lemon
1 tablespoon Worcestershire
  sauce
½ teaspoon salt
Tabasco brand pepper sauce
  (or chili pequin)

Melt butter with the cooking oil in a large skillet. Add minced onion and cook until soft. Add oysters, bread crumbs, lemon juice, Worcestershire sauce, salt, and Tabasco sauce. Mix well in the skillet. Cook over low heat until edges of oysters curl. Put oyster mixture in buttered oyster shells or ramekins, cover with additional bread crumbs, dot with butter, and bake at 350 degrees until thoroughly heated and browned on top. Serves 4. This may be prepared ahead and refrigerated before baking.

Mrs. A. C. Skinner (Marshall Elmore)

Sea Heiress Oysters

1 clove garlic
½ cup olive oil
48 large oysters
¾ cup grated Parmesan cheese
½ cup seasoned bread crumbs
Salt

Pepper
Monosodium glutamate
Ground thyme
Lemon juice
Worcestershire sauce

Mince garlic and soak in olive oil about 30 minutes. Rinse oysters to remove sand and grit; drain. Dip them in oil and garlic; then remove to paper towels to drain. Mix cheese and bread crumbs and toss the oysters in the crumb mixture. Put on greased oven-to-table platter in a single layer and season with salt, pepper, monosodium glutamate, and thyme. Sprinkle with lemon juice, Worcestershire, and more cheese. Bake at 450 degrees until browned. Serves 6 to 8.

This can also be prepared in individual ramekins and served as an appetizer. In this case, cooking time should be extended slightly.

Mrs. Joe P. Nelson (Harriet Hornish)

Scallops

Easy Scallop Casserole*

1 tablespoon butter
¼ cup chopped onion
1 can condensed cream of
   shrimp soup

1 pound fresh scallops, sliced
1 tablespoon dry Sherry
Toasted bread crumbs
Grated mellow Cheddar cheese

Melt butter in skillet, add onion, and sauté gently. Add shrimp soup and scallops and cook a few minutes. Stir in the Sherry. Put into a 1-quart casserole dish; top with toasted bread crumbs and grated cheese. Bake at 350 degrees for 20 minutes. Serves 4.

Mrs. James C. Freeman (Cornelia Herz)

Shrimp

Simple Shrimp*

12 shrimp
Salt
Cayenne pepper

1 tablespoon margarine
2 tablespoons dry vermouth
1 tablespoon lemon juice

Shell and devein shrimp. Dry on paper towels. Season with salt and cayenne pepper. Sauté shrimp in melted margarine on both sides. Add vermouth and lemon juice. Reduce sauce over highest heat until there is only a small amount left. Serves 1.

Mrs. Jack M. Painter (Darlene Downer)

Lemony Barbecued Shrimp*

½ cup butter
2 tablespoons Worcestershire
   sauce

2 tablespoons lemon juice
2 pounds shelled, drained shrimp

Melt butter; add lemon juice and Worcestershire sauce. Add shrimp to marinate 2 hours before time to cook. Do not refrigerate. Put shrimp on a small grill for 2 to 5 minutes (according to size), basting with the butter mixture. The shrimp will be opaque and pink when done. Good served with baked rice and tossed salad. Serves 4 to 6.

Mrs. William N. Woolsey (Sandra Callaway)

Joan's Shrimp

½ cup cooking oil
2 cloves garlic
1½ cups Chianti or Burgundy
1 teaspoon salt
1 teaspoon dry mustard

1 teaspoon oregano
Pepper
2 pounds shelled and deveined
   shrimp (leave tails on)

Mix oil, garlic, wine, salt, dry mustard, oregano, and pepper in pan and heat. Pour over shrimp and marinate in refrigerator. Return to room temperature when ready to use. Broil 6 to 8 inches from flame until pink and opaque. Serves 4 to 6.

Mrs. James W. Cottingham (Linda Yancy)

Plantation Fried Shrimp

1 pound shrimp, shelled with
   tails left on
Salt

Pepper
2 egg whites
Cracker crumbs

Butterfly shrimp if desired. Sprinkle with salt and pepper. Beat egg whites until stiff. Dip shrimp into egg whites, then into crumbs. Repeat if shrimp are not coated the first time. Fry shrimp in deep fat until lightly browned. Serves 4.

Mrs. Maurice Priday (Joan McCroskey)

Shrimp Puff*

½ cup water
Salt
4 slices bread, crusts removed
2 eggs, beaten

½ cup mayonnaise
1 pound shrimp, shelled
Cracker crumbs
Butter

Place all ingredients except cracker crumbs and butter in a 1-quart casserole. Stir until bread comes apart and mixture is well blended. Sprinkle with crumbs. Dot with butter. Bake at 350 degrees for 30 minutes.

Mrs. Jack Best (Betty Reno)

Jackie's Shrimp

3 *pounds shrimp, cleaned*
Seasoned flour
1/2 *cup butter*
3 *large cloves garlic, minced*
1/2 *cup chopped green onion*
   (tops and all)

1/2 *cup chopped parsley*
1 *cup catsup*
1 *tablespoon Worcestershire*
   sauce
Tabasco brand pepper sauce
1 *cup dry Sherry*

Shake shrimp in seasoned flour. Place butter in a skillet and Sauté garlic with floured shrimp on both sides until barely yellow. Arrange cooked shrimp in an oven-to-table casserole and sprinkle the parsley and green onion over the top. Heat the catsup, Worcestershire sauce, Tabasco, and Sherry together in the skillet in which the shrimp was cooked until slightly thickened; then pour over shrimp. Place in a 350-degree oven until hot and bubbly. Do not overcook. Serves 6 to 8.

This may be made ahead of time and heated at the last minute. For *hors d'oeuvres*, serve with toothpicks.

Mrs. Gerald Heinzelmann (Carolyn Jones)

Wild Rice and Shrimp Casserole

1 6-ounce box long grain and
   wild rice
1 can condensed cream of
   mushroom soup
2 tablespoons chopped bell
   pepper (optional)
2 tablespoons chopped onion
2 tablespoons melted butter

1 tablespoon lemon juice
1/2 teaspoon Worcestershire
   sauce
1/2 teaspoon dry mustard
1/4 teaspoon pepper
1/2 cup grated Cheddar cheese
1 pound shrimp, cleaned and
   drained

Cook rice according to package directions. Mix all ingredients thoroughly. Pour into a greased 1½-quart casserole and bake at 375 degrees for 30 to 35 minutes. Serves 4.

Mrs. Lowell Kepp (Betty Ellis)

Shrimp Casserole

2 cups cooked rice
1 cup condensed cream of
  mushroom soup
1 pound cooked shrimp
½ cup cubed Cheddar cheese
2 tablespoons butter
3 tablespoons chopped onion

2 tablespoons chopped bell
  pepper
1 tablespoon lemon juice
½ teaspoon Worcestershire sauce
½ teaspoon prepared mustard
¼ teaspoon pepper

Combine all ingredients in greased 1½-quart casserole. Mix well and bake uncovered at 375 degrees for 40 minutes. Serves 4.

Mrs. Jack Best (Betty Reno)

Shrimp and Egg Casserole

½ cup butter
5 tablespoons flour
2 cups milk
4 ounces sharp Cheddar cheese
1 tablespoon catsup
½ teaspoon dry mustard
1½ teaspoons seasoned salt
½ teaspoon garlic powder
¼ teaspoon paprika
1 tablespoon chopped parsley

¼ cup dry Sherry
1½ teaspoons Worcestershire
  sauce
Salt
Pepper
1 pound shrimp, shelled and
  cooked
6 deviled eggs
¾ cup finely crushed saltine
  crackers

Make a white sauce using ¼ cup butter, flour, and milk. Add cheese and cook until melted. Add catsup, seasonings, and shrimp. In a casserole, alternate layers of deviled eggs and of shrimp mixture. Melt remaining butter and mix with cracker crumbs; sprinkle over top of casserole. Heat at 350 degrees until bubbly. Serves 6 to 8.

DEVILED EGGS:

6 hard-cooked eggs
¼ cup mayonnaise
½ teaspoon dry mustard

Dash Tabasco brand pepper sauce
Salt
Pepper

Cut eggs in half; mix the yolks with remaining ingredients and stuff into the egg whites.

Mrs. James C. Freeman (Cornelia Herz)

Jambalaya

2 onions, chopped
1/4 cup butter
1 28-ounce can tomatoes
1/2 6-ounce can tomato paste
2 cloves garlic, chopped
2 ribs celery, chopped
1/4 bell pepper, chopped
1 teaspoon chopped parsley
1/2 teaspoon thyme

3 cloves, chopped
1 pound boiled ham, diced
2 pounds shrimp, shelled and
  boiled
3 cups cooked rice
Salt
Cayenne pepper
Black pepper

Sauté onions in butter 5 minutes. Add tomatoes and tomato paste and cook 5 minutes, stirring constantly. Add garlic, celery, bell pepper, parsley, thyme, and cloves. Cook 30 minutes, stirring frequently. Stir in ham and cook 5 minutes. Stir in shrimp and cook 5 minutes longer. Stir in rice, season to taste, and simmer 30 minutes, stirring often. Serves 6 to 8.

Mrs. George Taggart (Ethleen Reimers)

Shrimp Creole

1 heaping tablespoon shortening
1 tablespoon flour
2 onions, minced
2 cloves garlic, minced
1 large bell pepper, minced
2 teaspoons parsley, minced
1 28-ounce can tomatoes

Cayenne pepper
Salt
Bay leaves
Celery seeds
1/4 teaspoon powdered thyme
2 pounds shelled shrimp

Make a rich roux with shortening and flour. Add onion, garlic, bell pepper, and parsley; stir until onion browns slightly; then add tomatoes. Season highly with cayenne pepper, salt, bay leaves, celery seeds, and thyme. Add shrimp, cover, and cook slowly for 1 hour, preferably in an iron pot or heavy dutch oven with a tight fitting lid. Do not add water. Serve over rice. Serves 6.

Mrs. Fred L. Crook, Jr. (Gibbs Beasley)

Curried Shrimp*

¼ cup butter	1 cup milk
3 tablespoons diced onion	½ cup chicken broth
3 tablespoons diced apple	3 cups cooked diced shrimp
2 tablespoons flour	(or more)
2 teaspoons curry powder	

Sauté onion and apple in butter; mix flour and curry and stir into butter slowly. Add milk and broth and cook until slightly thick. Add shrimp and serve hot over rice. Suggested condiments: chopped salted peanuts, chopped banana, toasted coconut, chutney. Serves 6.

Mrs. William N. Woolsey (Sandra Callaway)

Ella Lee's Shrimp con Queso*

1 6-ounce roll jalapeño cheese	2 cups cleaned boiled shrimp
1 can condensed cream of	1 4-ounce jar pimientos
mushroom soup	1 to 2 teaspoons minced parsley
1 8-ounce can mushroom	
pieces, drained	

Heat cheese and soup in top of a double boiler until cheese is melted and sauce is smooth. Add other ingredients and blend until desired consistency is reached. Serve over rice. Serves 4.

Mrs. Lawrence Riley Williams (Ann Reading Parsley)

Shrimp Wiggle

1 pound shrimp	⅛ teaspoon Worcestershire sauce
¼ cup butter	¼ teaspoon dry mustard
¼ cup flour	1 tablespoon soy sauce
2 cups milk	1 10-ounce package frozen peas,
1 teaspoon salt	cooked
Pepper	Canned Chinese noodles

Cook and clean shrimp. Make white sauce with butter, flour, milk, salt, and pepper. Add Worcestershire sauce, mustard, and soy sauce. Add shrimp and peas and heat through. Serve on canned Chinese noodles. Serves 4.

Mrs. A. C. Gilmore (Clydell Hollon)

Gulf Coast Casserole

¾ cup ripe olives
2 4½-ounce cans medium-size
 deveined shrimp (or
 equivalent of fresh shrimp)
1 cup rice
1 can condensed consommé
2 teaspoons instant minced
 onion

1 cup water
1 tablespoon lemon juice
½ teaspoon Worcestershire sauce
¼ teaspoon salt
⅛ teaspoon garlic powder
1½ cups diced American cheese
1 10-ounce package frozen
 green peas

Quarter ripe olives. Drain shrimp well. Combine olives, shrimp, rice, and consommé in a 1½-quart casserole. Combine water, onion, lemon juice, Worcestershire sauce, salt, and garlic powder. Stir into casserole with ½ cup cheese cubes. Cover and bake in a 350-degree oven for 1 hour. Uncover and stir in remaining cheese and uncooked peas. Bake uncovered 10 minutes. Serves 4 to 5.

Mrs. Lowell Kepp (Betty Ellis)

Mixed Shellfish

Seafood Aransas

6 tablespoons margarine
½ cup fresh mushrooms, sliced
3 tablespoons flour
¼ teaspoon paprika
3 cups milk
Dash Worcestershire sauce
Dash Tabasco brand pepper
 sauce

½ teaspoon salt
1 tablespoon dry Sherry
½ cup grated Swiss cheese
3 cups seafood (crab, cooked
 shrimp, etc.)
¼ cup roasted, slivered almonds
 (optional)
1 tablespoon minced parsley

Melt 3 tablespoons margarine in top of double boiler or chafing dish. Add mushrooms and cook until margarine is absorbed. Remove mushrooms and set aside. Make white sauce with remaining margarine, flour, paprika, and milk. Add Worcestershire sauce, Tabasco, salt, Sherry, and cheese and cook until blended. Add seafood, mushrooms, and almonds and cook until heated through. Sprinkle parsley on top. Serve on toast or in individual pastry shells. Serves 8.

Mrs. Lev H. Prichard, III (Ella Wall)

Shellfish Casserole

7 tablespoons butter
¼ cup flour
1½ cups milk
½ teaspoon salt
¼ teaspoon dill weed
⅛ teaspoon pepper
⅛ teaspoon dry mustard
Pinch thyme
2½ cups grated mellow
  Cheddar cheese
2 egg yolks, lightly beaten

8 ounces mushrooms, thinly
  sliced
1 pound shrimp, cooked in 2
  cups water and 1 tablespoon
  vinegar (or 2 5-ounce packages
  frozen shrimp)
1 pound crab meat (or 3 6-ounce
  packages frozen, flaked)
1 pound fresh lobster meat (or
  2 5-ounce cans)
Juice of 1 lemon (or ½ cup
  dry Sherry)

Using a double boiler, make white sauce with ¼ cup butter, flour, and milk. Season with salt, dill, pepper, dry mustard, and thyme. Add 2 cups grated cheese. Mix well and cook until the cheese melts. Add egg yolks and cook 5 minutes. Keep warm over barely simmering water. Heat remaining butter in skillet and sauté mushrooms until golden. Drain on paper towel and add to cheese sauce. Mix together seafood and sauce. Reheat gently. The dish can be held at this point 15 to 20 minutes. Before serving, stir in lemon juice or Sherry and pour into a 3-quart casserole. Sprinkle remaining cheese over seafood. Place under broiler until top is golden or serve in a chafing dish. Serves 8.

Mrs. Gary Dukes (Bonnie Jean Cameron)

Fish

Baked Fish Veracruz

2 tablespoons corn oil
1 tablespoon flour
12 fish filets
2 onions, sliced thin

3 lemons, sliced thin
8 sprigs parsley, minced
½ cup catsup
½ cup Worcestershire sauce

Layer half the ingredients in the order listed. Repeat. Cook uncovered at 325 degrees for 1 hour. Serves 6.

Mrs. Gordon Heaney (Elizabeth Van Westrum)

Baked Fish for Lazy Fishermen*

1 potato, sliced
1 onion, sliced
3 to 4 ribs celery, sliced
4 fish filets or scaled whole fish
  (minus the head)
Salt
Pepper
1 can condensed cream of
  mushroom or celery soup
¾ cup dry white wine

Grease a casserole and cover the bottom with potato slices. Then place a layer of celery and onion mixed together. Top with the fish. Season with salt and pepper. Pour the soup mixed with wine over all. Bake at 350 degrees for 1 hour.

Mrs. James W. Cottingham (Linda Yancy)

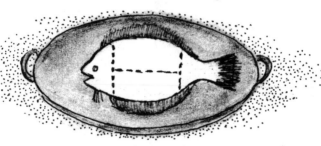

Stuffed Flounder

1 large flounder or individual
  small flounders
1 onion, chopped
1 bell pepper, chopped
Butter
1 cup soft bread crumbs
1 6½-ounce can crab meat
Salt
White pepper
Paprika
Lemon juice

If using 1 large fish, split as illustrated; then cut with sharp knife along the bone almost to the sides to make a pouch. If using small fish, split from the side along the bone. Sauté onion and bell pepper in 2 tablespoons butter. Mix in bread crumbs and crab meat. Season with salt and white pepper. Stuff fish and place in a well buttered shallow baking pan. Sprinkle with paprika. Broil several inches from heat, basting frequently with melted butter and lemon juice. Serves 4.

Mrs. Max J. Luther, III (Maxine Jenkins)

Easy Elegant Baked Fish*

1 3- to 4-pound fish
Butter
Salt
Cayenne pepper

Lemon wedges
Parsley
Shrimp (optional)
Capers (optional)

Clean, scale, wash, and dry fish. You may cut off head if desired. Put generous amount of butter in cavity; spread more butter on outside. Sprinkle with a little salt and cayenne pepper. Place in generously buttered shallow casserole and cover with well-buttered brown paper cut the shape of the casserole. Bake 400 degrees about 10 minutes per pound, or about 20 minutes for filets. To serve, garnish with lemon wedges and parsley. To be really elegant, surround fish with hot boiled shrimp and a sprinkling of capers. Sheepshead is especially good prepared this way, but redfish or snapper is fine. You may also use several small whole trout instead, or even filets, but 1 big fish is prettier.

Mrs. Max J. Luther, III (Maxine Jenkins)

King Fish in Creole Sauce

½ onion, chopped (or more)
2 cloves garlic, pressed
1 large bell pepper, sliced
1 1-inch-long chili serrano,
   minced
2 tablespoons bacon drippings

1 8-ounce can tomato sauce
½ cup water
½ teaspoon spaghetti seasoning
Celery salt
1 king fish

Sauté onion, garlic, bell pepper, and chili in hot drippings until onions are soft. Add tomato sauce, water, and seasonings and simmer, covered, about 20 minutes. Fillet king fish; cut meat in chunks. Add king fish to the sauce, cover, and steam 2 minutes. Serve fish with the sauce plain or over rice. Serves 6.

Mrs. Dudley A. Chatham (Melba Welsh)

Succulent Baked Fish

2 pounds fish filets
Salt
Lemon slices
1 large onion, minced
1 clove garlic, minced
1/2 bell pepper, chopped

2 tomatoes, peeled and cut in
  eighths
Pepper
1/2 to 1 teaspoon oregano
1/2 cup dry white wine
1/2 cup cooking oil

Preheat oven to 400 degrees. Separate fish filets, preferably ·king fish. Salt filets and roll each around a slice of lemon. Spread onion, garlic, and bell pepper in a greased baking dish. Add fish rolls, tomato wedges, more salt, pepper, oregano, white wine, and cooking oil. Bake 45 minutes to 1 hour, basting every 15 minutes. Fish can be marinated in a French oil dressing for a few hours before preparing. Serve with tartar sauce. Serves 4 to 6.

Mrs. Robert Biel (Corinne Vauter)

Baked Flounder in Cream Sauce

1 pound flounder filets
1 tablespoon minced parsley
  stems
1 large rib celery, minced
1 large carrot, minced
1/2 medium onion, minced
Butter
Salt

Pepper
1/2 cup dry vermouth
  (or white wine)
Water
2 tablespoons flour
1/2 cup heavy cream
1 cup rice, cooked

Sauté vegetables in sauce pan in 2 tablespoons of butter over low heat for 8 to 10 minutes. Place filets in a circle in a glass pie pan with tails hanging out of pan. Spoon all but 1 tablespoon of the vegetable mixture over filets. Salt and pepper. Dot with butter. Fold tails over the vegetable mixture. Add vermouth and water to cover 2/3 fish. Cover with foil. Bake 15 minutes at 350 degrees. Add 2 tablespoons melted butter, salt, pepper, and flour to 1 tablespoon vegetable mixture left in sauce pan. Bubble 1 to 2 minutes to make roux. Add liquid from fish casserole to roux and boil down. Add cream and simmer 2 to 3 minutes. Mound cooked rice between filets and cover all with sauce. Serve at once. Serves 4.

Mrs. Emil Tejml (Sue Rosson)

Cold Poached Fish

1 onion, chopped
¼ cup chopped celery leaves or
　celery
1 flounder, redfish, or red
　snapper

1 cup dry white wine or
　vermouth
1 tablespoon salt
1 teaspoon pepper
Fish stock (or water)

Put chopped vegetables in a large skillet and place the fish on top. Add wine, salt, pepper, and enough fish stock or water to cover the fish. Bring to a boil and simmer until fish is done at its thickest part. Cool the fish in the poaching liquid. If desired, remove the skin while the fish is warm. Carefully remove the fish from the liquid and place on a platter. Chill. Garnish with hard-cooked egg quarters, tomato quarters, marinated cucumber, and artichoke hearts, parsley, or lettuce. Serve as a main dish for a summer supper with hot hush puppies or corn dodgers and a hot vegetable. Be sure to serve a cold sauce with the fish, such as homemade mayonnaise, a good Green Goddess dressing, or remoulade. Serves 4. Leftover fish may be used as fish salad or in fish au gratin.

Mrs. Jack M. Painter (Darlene Downer)

Fish au Gratin

¼ cup minced onion
3 tablespoons margarine
3 tablespoons flour
¼ cup dry white wine or
　vermouth
¾ cup fish stock (or milk)

½ cup heavy cream
Salt
Pepper
1½ cups cooked flaked fish
¼ to ½ cup grated Swiss cheese

Sauté onion in margarine; add flour and cook 2 minutes or until bubbly and cooked through. Add fish stock, wine, cream, salt, and pepper. Cook until smooth and thickened. Add fish. Pour into buttered shells or ramekins and top with cheese. Bake at 400 degrees for about 15 minutes, or until hot and browned. Serves 6.

The filled ramekins may be frozen. Thaw before baking. Serve for lunch or as a first course.

Mrs. Jack M. Painter (Darlene Downer)

Poultry

9. POULTRY

The virtue of poultry is that it can be prepared so many ways, and Corpus Christians' collections of poultry recipes are truly eclectic. From around the world — French crepes to Indian curry — as well as such Southern basics as fried chicken with cream gravy and chicken and dumplings, Corpus Christians prepare and serve poultry that rates as company fare.

Chicken

Chicken Rosemary

2 teaspoons crushed rosemary	2 to 4 green onions, chopped
½ cup flour	1 clove garlic, chopped
8 whole chicken breasts	1½ cups dry white wine
1 cup butter	1 8-ounce carton sour cream

Mix rosemary and flour in sack. Add chicken and shake to coat. Heat butter in heavy skillet. Brown chicken. Remove chicken to shallow baking dish and brown onion and garlic in skillet. Add wine. Pour the mixture over chicken. Bake at 350 degrees for 1 to 1½ hours, basting every 20 minutes. When done, spoon sour cream over chicken and return to oven for 3 to 5 minutes. Serves 8.

Mrs. William Hall Keys (Rose Mary Blackshear)

Mandarin Orange Chicken

2 11-ounce cans mandarin oranges	1 cup tomato sauce
½ cup dry white wine	1 clove garlic, minced
½ cup melted butter	½ teaspoon ground ginger
2 tablespoons soy sauce	3 2-pound chickens, quartered

Drain oranges, reserving syrup. Combine wine, butter, and soy sauce. Marinate chicken in the sauce for 3 hours in refrigerator. Season chickens and bake or broil as preferred. Add to marinade orange syrup, tomato sauce, garlic, and ginger. Heat and use to baste chickens. Add orange segments to sauce 5 minutes before serving. Spoon generous amounts of sauce on each portion. Serves 6.

Mrs. Joseph W. Holt (Shirley Dawson)

Baked Chicken Breasts*

4 whole chicken breasts   Pepper
Salt   Skim milk

Place chicken skin side up in shallow baking dish. Salt and pepper to taste. Pour skim milk over this until breasts are about 2/3 covered. Bake at 350 degrees for about 1 hour. Add more milk if original cooks away. Serves 4. For family, legs may be used instead of breasts.

Mrs. E. Jackson Giles (Mary Kathryn Garrett)

Sherried Chicken

12 chicken thighs   3 cans condensed cream of
12 chicken legs   mushroom soup
6 whole chicken breasts   1½ soup cans dry Sherry
Butter   1 4-ounce can mushrooms

Rub chicken with butter, place in shallow roasting pan, and bake at 400 degrees until browned. Cover chicken with undiluted soup, then Sherry; cover and bake 1 hour 30 minutes at 325 degrees. To serve, remove chicken to serving platter and serve sauce separately. Serves 12. Excellent with wild rice.

Mrs. Terry Hart (Lois Young)

Chicken Parmesan

2 2- to 2½-pound chickens   1 clove garlic, pressed
2 cups bread crumbs   1½ teaspoons salt
¾ cup grated Parmesan cheese Pepper
¼ cup chopped parsley   1 cup melted butter

Dip chicken in butter, then in a mixture of remaining ingredients. Place chicken in shallow open roasting pan and pour remaining butter over the pieces. Bake 1 hour at 350 degrees. Do not turn. Serves 6. Boned chicken breasts may be used in place of the whole chicken.

Mrs. Jack Best (Betty Reno)

Lib MacMillan's Chicken with Salad

½ to ¾ inch salt
¾ cup olive oil
¾ cup lemon juice
½ teaspoon freshly ground
  pepper
½ teaspoon paprika

4 to 5 cloves garlic, split
2 2- to 2½-pound chickens,
  quartered
Lettuce
Spinach

In a pint Mason jar place salt, olive oil, lemon juice, black pepper, paprika, and garlic. Shake and refrigerate several hours. Place chickens in broiler pan and cover with marinade. After 1 hour, pour off excess marinade and reserve. Broil chicken as far away from heat as possible, basting with marinade occasionally. When chicken is done, remove to a platter and add remaining marinade to that in broiler, scraping the bits off the bottom of the pan. Pour hot marinade over a large bowl of lettuce and spinach. Toss. Serve chicken with the wilted lettuce and spinach and crusty French bread.

Mrs. J. Franklin Critz (Isabelle Pattee)

Quarter a 2-pound chicken; moisten well with water; coat with seasoned salt. Broil over charcoal.

Barbecued Chicken

½ cup cooking oil
¾ cup lemon juice
¼ cup water
3 tablespoons sugar
1½ tablespoons salt

2 teaspoons Tabasco brand
  pepper sauce (or more)
2 teaspoons Worcestershire sauce
2 2-pound chickens, cut up

Combine all ingredients except chicken in a sauce pan. Heat to boiling. Keep hot while basting chickens. Mix thoroughly before each basting. Brush or dip each chicken part in the sauce immediately before placing on the grate over hot charcoal. Cook slowly until tender, turning frequently, and basting each time. Adding apple wood or any other handy hardwood to the charcoal enhances the flavor. Serves 6.

Mrs. William H. Berry, Jr. (Ann Wiley)

Oven Barbecued Chicken

1 2- to 2½-pound chicken
¼ cup butter
¼ cup lemon juice
¼ cup vinegar
1 tablespoon sugar
1 tablespoon prepared mustard

1/3 cup Worcestershire sauce
Salt
Pepper
Tabasco brand pepper sauce
Catsup (optional)

Cut up chicken and brown in a skillet. Make a sauce of remaining ingredients except catsup. Pour the sauce over chicken. Cook uncovered at 350 degrees for 30 minutes. Add catsup if desired, cover, and cook about 15 minutes longer. Serves 4.

Mrs. Marshall P. Graham (Louise Bryson)

Almond Chicken

2 chickens, boned and skinned
3 tablespoons oil
½ cup thinly sliced onion
1 cup thinly sliced celery
1 8-ounce can water chestnuts, sliced
1 6-ounce can bamboo shoots
2 cups chicken broth
2 tablespoons soy sauce

2 teaspoons monosodium glutamate
1 8-ounce package frozen snow pea pods
2 to 3 tablespoons corn starch
2 tablespoons water
Salt
½ cup toasted almonds

Cut chicken into ¼-inch slices. Sauté in hot oil 3 minutes. Add onion and celery. Cook 5 minutes. Add water chestnuts, bamboo shoots, chicken broth, soy sauce, and monosodium glutamate. Cover and simmer 3 minutes. Add pea pods and simmer 2 minutes. Blend corn starch and water; add and cook until thickened. Salt to taste and sprinkle with toasted almonds. Serve with rice. Serves 6.

Ingredients can be assembled ahead of time and the chicken cooked in front of guests in a chafing dish. Do not use water pan for sautéeing chicken, onion, and celery.

Mrs. W. Richard McCracken (Lucy McFadyen)

Hawaiian Luau Chicken

1 5-pound stewing hen
2 cups water
1/3 cup chopped onion
1/3 cup chopped bell pepper
2 cups slivered celery
1 8-ounce can water
  chestnuts, sliced
½ cup chicken fat
¼ cup flour

1 tablespoon salt
2 cups chicken broth
1 3-ounce package slivered
  almonds
2 tablespoons butter
1 6-ounce can bamboo shoots
1 4-ounce jar pimiento
1½ cups pitted ripe olives, sliced
2 cups grated Cheddar cheese

Simmer hen in water until tender; cool in broth; remove skin and bones from chicken; reserve broth and fat.

Sauté onion, bell pepper, celery, and water chestnuts in ¼ cup chicken fat until wilted and clear.

In a dutch oven, melt ¼ cup chicken fat, stir in flour to make a roux, add salt and reserved broth, and cook until thick. Add chicken pieces and sautéed vegetables. Heat until steaming. (You may do this ahead of time; simply reheat and complete at serving time.)

Brown almonds in butter. Just before serving, stir almonds, olives, bamboo shoots, pimiento, and cheese into hot chicken mixture and heat until cheese melts. Serve over rice with side dishes of shredded coconut, diced bell pepper, chopped peanuts, and chutney. Serves 12.

Mrs. Lev H. Prichard, III (Ella Wall)

Chicken Breasts with Wild Rice*

3 to 4 slices bacon
1 6-ounce box long grain and
  wild rice
4 whole skinned chicken breasts

1 can condensed golden
  mushroom soup
¾ cup water

Place bacon on bottom of a shallow 2-quart baking dish. Place rice over bacon. Reserve package of seasonings. Place chicken on rice, bone down. Pour soup over the chicken, then add water. Top with package of seasonings. Cover and cook at 350 degrees for 1 to 1½ hours. Check toward the end to be sure rice has cooked but is not too dry. Serves 4.

Mrs. Lawrence Riley Williams (Ann Reading Parsley)

Chicken Curry

6 *whole chicken breasts, boned*	1 *teaspoon salt*
Flour	½ *teaspoon ground ginger*
½ *cup cooking oil*	¼ *teaspoon cinnamon*
¼ *cup butter*	¼ *teaspoon onion salt*
1 *large onion, chopped*	¼ *teaspoon pepper*
2 *cloves garlic, minced*	3 *cups chicken broth*
2 *tablespoons curry powder*	2 *tablespoons lime juice*

Flour chicken; heat oil in dutch oven and brown chicken. Remove chicken; drain off oil. Heat butter in same pan; sauté onion and garlic until lightly browned. Combine seasonings, stir into onion mix, and cook 2 to 3 minutes, stirring constantly. Add chicken broth and chicken. Cover and simmer 30 minutes or until chicken is tender. Remove chicken and keep warm. Simmer sauce uncovered 10 to 15 minutes until thick; stir in lime juice. Return chicken to pan to heat through. Serve chicken on a bed of rice, smothered in sauce. Serve side dishes of chutney, coconut, plumped raisins, sieved hard-cooked egg, and finely chopped peanuts. Serves 6.

Mrs. Lev H. Prichard, III (Ella Wall)

Chicken and Dumplings

1 *3-pound chicken*	½ *teaspoon salt*
½ *cup milk*	2 *tablespoons vegetable oil*
1 *egg*	1 *to 1½ cups flour*
1 *teaspoon baking powder*	

Boil chicken until tender. While chicken is cooking, beat together milk, egg, baking powder, salt, and vegetable oil. Gradually add flour until mixture is the consistency of moist pastry dough. Roll the dough out thin and cut into 1- to 2-inch squares. When chicken is done, remove from broth. Bring broth back to a boil, drop the dumplings in the broth, and allow them to cook about 12 minutes or until done. While the dumplings cook, bone the chicken. Return the chicken meat to the cooked dumplings, heat through, and serve at once. Serves 8.

Mrs. Kenneth McKamey (Hattie Bell Colston)

Southern Fried Chicken

1 2 to 2½-pound chicken
Ice water
2 tablespoons salt
1 teaspoon pepper

2 cups flour
Cooking oil
½ cup butter

Several hours before cooking, cut chicken into 10 to 11 serving pieces, place in a bowl, cover with ice water with 1 tablespoon salt added, and refrigerate.

Mix remaining salt, pepper, and flour in a paper sack. Drain water off chicken but do not dry. Shake 3 or 4 pieces of chicken at a time in flour sack until all chicken is well floured. Reserve flour for gravy.

Put oil to depth of ¼ inch in electric skillet, add butter, and heat to 400 degrees. Put chicken in skillet skin side down, lower temperature to 375 degrees, and cook uncovered 25 minutes. Turn and cook 20 minutes on other side. Drain on paper towels while making cream gravy. Serves 3 to 4.

CREAM GRAVY:

2 tablespoons drippings from
  chicken, including crusty bits
2 tablespoons seasoned flour
½ cup water

1 cup milk
Salt
Pepper

After the chicken is fried, pour off all but about 2 tablespoons oil, leaving the crusty flour bits in the skillet. Set skillet at 300 degrees. Slowly stir in 2 tablespoons flour until most, but not all, grease has been absorbed and flour mixture is golden brown. (If you see at this stage that there is too much grease, gradually add more flour and increase liquids proportionately.) Pour in water; stir until smooth and thick. Add milk, lower temperature to bare simmer, cook to desired thickness, and adjust seasoning. Gravy should appear slightly curdled rather than like a white sauce. Serve over rice or mashed potatoes.

Mrs. Lev H. Prichard, III (Ella Wall)

Chicken Puff*

2 5-ounce cans boned chicken
3 cups soft bread crumbs
4 eggs
¾ cup cooked rice
1 teaspoon salt
½ teaspoon paprika
1 2-ounce jar pimiento

1 can condensed cream of
   chicken soup
1 cup milk
Grated Swiss cheese (optional)
1 can condensed cream of
   mushroom soup

Mix all ingredients except cheese and soup in a bowl. Pour into a greased 9-by-13-inch baking dish. Bake at 325 degrees for 45 minutes. Additional paprika and grated cheese may be sprinkled on top after 30 minutes if desired. Top with heated mushroom soup. Serves 6.

Mrs. Gerald A. Reeves (Lois Arnett)

Virginia Conolly's Chicken Casserole

1 5- to 6-pound hen
10 to 12 ounces narrow noodles
2 cans condensed cream of
   mushroom soup
1 2½-ounce jar dried beef,
   shredded
2 tablespoons minced parsley
1 8-ounce can mushroom stems
   and pieces

2 8½-ounce cans water
   chestnuts
1 6-ounce jar stuffed green
   olives, sliced
2 to 3 tablespoons chicken broth
1 tablespoon Worcestershire sauce
Freshly ground black pepper
Grated Cheddar cheese

Boil hen; skin and bone; cut meat in small pieces. Bring broth back to a boil and cook noodles until barely done. Drain. Mix all ingredients except cheese, draining liquid from mushrooms, water chestnuts, and olives. Bake in a 3-quart casserole at 325 degrees until mixture is heated through. Top with a layer of grated cheese and return casserole to oven until cheese is melted. Serves 12. The unbaked casserole freezes well.

Mrs. J. Rogers Rainey, Jr. (Kathleen Lutner)

Chicken à la King

¼ cup butter
¼ cup flour
½ cup chicken stock
½ cup heavy cream
1 3-ounce can mushrooms
1 2-ounce jar pimientos, minced

½ cup liquid from mushroom
   and pimiento cans
1 cup cooked chicken meat
Salt
Paprika

Melt butter and stir in flour. Add chicken stock, cream, and mushroom and pimiento juice. When sauce is smooth and thick, add mushrooms, pimientos, chicken, salt, and paprika and heat through. Do not stir much after adding chicken. Serve over toast points or in small pastry shells. Serves 4. This may be served from a chafing dish at a buffet.

Mrs. Ben Donnell (Elinor Drake)

Chicken Spaghetti

2 6-ounce cans tomato paste
2 tablespoons Worcestershire
   sauce
1 teaspoon Tabasco brand
   pepper sauce
1 teaspoon paprika
Salt
½ teaspoon black pepper
½ teaspoon cayenne pepper
1 teaspoon cumin
½ teaspoon chili powder
2 quarts chicken broth

1 5-pound hen, cooked and
   boned
4 large onions, chopped
8 ribs celery, chopped
2 bell peppers, chopped
4 cloves garlic, minced
1 cup butter
20 ounces spaghetti, cooked
1 16-ounce can green peas
   (optional)
2 cups canned chopped
   mushrooms
10 ounces Cheddar cheese, grated

Mix tomato paste, seasonings, broth, and cut-up chicken and simmer in an 8- to 10-quart soup kettle for 30 minutes. In a large skillet, sauté onion, celery, bell pepper, and garlic in melted butter until vegetables are soft. Add vegetables to the soup kettle. Add the cooked spaghetti, undrained peas, and mushrooms to the soup kettle and simmer 1 hour longer. Stir in grated cheese and cook until cheese melts. Pass grated Parmesan cheese to be sprinkled on top of the spaghetti. Serves 18. Freezes well.

Mrs. John F. Cram (Janet Tyson)

Chicketti for 20

2 4-pound hens
2 13¾-ounce cans chicken broth
6 tablespoons minced onion
6 tablespoons minced bell
pepper
1 rounded cup minced celery

1½ teaspoons paprika
¾ cup chopped pimiento
1 16-ounce package spaghetti
3 4½-ounce cans ripe olives,
chopped
3 cups grated Cheddar cheese

Boil hens in salt water until tender. Reserve stock. Cool; bone and cut into pieces. Add canned broth and water to stock to make 2½ quarts liquid. Combine with chicken in a large dutch oven. Heat to boiling point; add all ingredients except olives and cheese. Bake at 300 degrees for 1 hour or until spaghetti is done. Stir occasionally. Add more broth or water if needed. Fold in olives and half of cheese. Serve in large dish and sprinkle with remaining cheese.

Mrs. A. C. Gilmore (Clydell Hollon)

Chicken Tetrazzini

1 4- to 5-pound hen
3 slices bacon, diced
1 large onion, chopped
1 4-ounce can pimientos,
minced
1 can condensed cream of
mushroom soup

1 large bell pepper, sliced
1 4-ounce can mushrooms
1 pound long spaghetti
1 pound American cheese
Toasted almonds
Chopped parsley
Grated Parmesan cheese

Stew hen and reserve broth. Bone hen and dice the meat. Fry bacon until light brown; add onion and cook until onion is clear. Add pimientos, bell pepper, soup, and mushrooms. Add sufficient chicken broth to make a sauce. Simmer 15 minutes. Boil spaghetti in chicken broth 15 minutes. Combine sauce, spaghetti, cheese, and chicken. Cook until cheese is melted, adding more broth if necessary to keep tetrazzini moist. Serve topped with toasted almonds and chopped parsley and with a side dish of grated Parmesan cheese. Serves 10.

Mrs. J. Franklin Critz (Isabelle Pattee)

Chicken and Shrimp Bechamel

1½ pounds shelled shrimp
1 3- to 4-pound hen
1 tablespoon margarine or
   chicken fat
1 tablespoon flour
1 cup milk
2 cans condensed cream of
   chicken soup

Fresh dill, minced, or 1 teaspoon
   dried dill weed (optional)
3 egg yolks
1 3-ounce can mushrooms,
   drained
¼ cup dry Sherry

Boil shrimp; drain and set aside. Boil chicken; bone and cut meat into large pieces. Melt fat in sauce pan; blend in flour and cook until bubbly. Remove from heat; gradually stir in milk. Stir over medium heat until thickened. Add soup and dill if desired; heat, stirring often. Beat egg yolks with a fork; mix some of hot mixture with yolks; stir all back into soup mixture. Stir over low heat about 5 minutes or until thickened. Add mushrooms, shrimp, and chicken. Mix lightly and heat. Add Sherry. Serve plain or with hot biscuits or wild rice. Serves 6 to 8. For a crowd use a 12-pound turkey and triple or quadruple recipe.

Mrs. Gary Dukes (Bonnie Jean Cameron)

Chicken Asparagus Casserole

1 4- to 5-pound hen
1 can condensed cream of
   mushroom soup
1 can condensed cream of
   chicken soup
½ cup mayonnaise
1 14½-ounce can cut asparagus

½ cup toasted slivered almonds
1 3-ounce can sliced mushrooms,
   drained
1 4-ounce package fine noodles,
   cooked
1 cup grated American cheese

Cook and bone the hen. Heat the soups over low heat; stir in mayonnaise. Cover the bottom of a 3-quart casserole with half the chicken. Top with half of each of the following in the order listed: asparagus, almonds and mushrooms, noodles, sauce, and cheese. Repeat. Sprinkle with paprika if desired. Bake at 350 degrees for 45 minutes. Serves 8 to 10.

Mrs. Ronald B. Brin (Lora Lou McCardell)

Chicken Divan

1/3 cup butter
6 tablespoons flour
1 cup chicken stock
1 cup half and half
2 egg yolks
1/3 cup grated Parmesan cheese
1/2 cup dry Sherry

Salt
Pepper
2 10-ounce packages frozen
   broccoli spears, lightly cooked
4 whole chicken breasts, split,
   baked, and boned

Melt butter; add flour; cook. Add stock and cream and cook until thick. Beat egg yolks. Add a little sauce to yolks; then add yolk mixture to rest of sauce. Slowly add cheese and Sherry. Season with salt and pepper. Arrange broccoli in a shallow casserole with chicken across the top. Add the sauce. Bake in 325-degree oven about 20 to 30 minutes, or until mixture is bubbly.

Mrs. Gerald Heinzelmann (Carolyn Jones)

Myra's Chicken-Broccoli Casserole

2 cans condensed cream of
   chicken soup
1/2 cup mayonnaise or salad
   dressing
1/2 teaspoon curry powder
1 tablespoon lemon juice
Salt

Pepper
2 10-ounce packages frozen
   broccoli (or large bunch fresh)
3 whole chicken breasts
1 cup grated sharp Cheddar
   cheese

Make sauce of cream of chicken soup, mayonnaise, curry powder, lemon juice, salt, and pepper. Cook broccoli slightly; drain. Boil chicken until done; bone. Layer large pieces of cooked chicken, broccoli, and then sauce. Repeat. Top with grated cheese. Bake at 325 degrees about 30 minutes until ingredients are well blended and cheese melts. Serves 8 to 10.

Mrs. Sam L. Allen (Phyllis Coffee)

*Chicken Casserole**

1 6-ounce box long grain and
　wild rice
2 2½-pound fryers, cooked and
　boned
1 can condensed cream of
　celery soup
1 onion, minced
1 2-ounce jar pimiento

2 cups mayonnaise
1 8-ounce can water chestnuts,
　thinly sliced
2 16-ounce cans French-style
　green beans, drained
Paprika
Grated Parmesan cheese

Cook rice as directed on box. Add all ingredients except paprika and cheese and mix thoroughly. Pour into greased shallow 3-quart baking dish. Sprinkle with paprika and Parmesan cheese. Bake at 350 degrees until bubbly, about 30 to 40 minutes. Serves 12. Freezes well. When frozen, remove from freezer at least 4 hours before heating. Serve with mixed green salad and hot rolls or corn bread.

Mrs. George Taggart (Ethleen Reimers)

Company Chicken Dinner

1 2¼-pound fryer, cut up
¼ cup cooking oil
1 cup sliced onion
1 clove garlic, minced
1 cup rice
2½ teaspoons salt
¼ teaspoon pepper
1 teaspoon tarragon

⅛ teaspoon thyme
½ teaspoon marjoram
1 bay leaf
2 whole cloves
1¾ cups chicken broth
¼ cup blanched almonds
1 9-ounce package French-style
　frozen green beans, thawed

In a dutch oven, brown chicken in cooking oil. Add onion and garlic; cook 5 minutes longer, stirring constantly. Sprinkle rice, salt, pepper, and spices over chicken. Add broth, almonds, and beans. Cover pan tightly. Cook slowly until rice is tender and liquid absorbed, about 20 minutes. Remove bay leaf and cloves before serving. Serves 4.

Mrs. Joseph W. Holt (Shirley Dawson)

Chicken Crepes

CREPES:

1 cup water	½ teaspoon salt
1 cup milk	¼ cup butter, melted
1 cup flour	2 eggs, beaten

Mix water and milk with flour; add salt, melted butter, and well beaten eggs. Using 1 tablespoon batter for each crepe, cook as you would pancakes. Cook on each side until crepes are done but not brown. Crepes must be very thin.

CHICKEN FILLING:

1 3- to 4-pound hen	Pepper
1 4-ounce can green chilies, chopped	1 teaspoon chopped pimiento
	1 pound Swiss cheese, grated
1 tablespoon chopped onion	1 pint half and half
1 teaspoon salt	

Boil chicken until tender. Cool; skin and bone the chicken; cut the meat into small pieces. Mix the chicken with the green chilies, onion, salt, pepper, and pimiento. Add most of the grated cheese, reserving enough to sprinkle over the top. Place meat mixture on each crepe, roll into a cone, and place in a 7-by-11-inch baking dish. When dish is filled, sprinkle cheese on top, add cream, and bake at 350 degrees until bubbly. Makes about 20 crepes.

Mrs. Harold Pettus (Genevieve Perry)

Turkey

Marinade for Smoked Turkey

3 gallons water	1½ ounces saltpeter
2 pounds salt	(available at drug store)
2 pounds dark brown sugar	

Mix all ingredients together in a very large crock. Marinate a thawed turkey in the marinade, allowing 1 hour per pound. Weigh the turkey down with a plate or heavy lid to keep it completely submerged. Then pat the turkey dry, truss the wings and legs, and smoke according to the directions on your smoker.

Mrs. Gerald Heinzelmann (Carolyn Jones)

Turkey and Dressing

1 18- to 20-pound turkey   1 cup butter
Salt

Rub inside and outside of turkey with salt about 8 hours before roasting. Before roasting, rub outside with butter, stuff lightly with dressing, and roast at 300 degrees in "tent" of foil about 6 or 7 hours. Remove tent and brown at 425 degrees for 20 minutes.

DRESSING:

1 cup chopped onion	½ cup crumbled butter
1 cup chopped bell pepper	½ cup minced pecans
1 cup chopped celery	½ teaspoon poultry seasoning
6 hard-cooked eggs, chopped	Salt
2 recipes corn bread, crumbled	Pepper
6 pieces oven-dried white	1 cup stock from giblets
bread, crumbled	Drippings from turkey

Toss all ingredients except drippings lightly and use to stuff turkey. As turkey cooks, collect drippings from pan and spoon into cavity of turkey. Any leftover dressing can be placed in a skillet or shallow baking dish. Collect drippings from turkey, spoon over dressing, and bake the dressing at 350 degrees for 45 minutes.

Mrs. William Hall Keys (Rose Mary Blackshear)

Giblet Gravy

2 tablespoons turkey drippings	Salt
2 tablespoons flour	Pepper
1 cup broth reserved from	Giblets, minced
boiling giblets	1 hard-cooked egg, minced
1 cup milk	(optional)

Stir flour into hot drippings and cook until smooth. Stir in broth. When gravy is simmering, add milk. Season to taste. Stir in giblets or sprinkle on top of gravy along with egg if desired. Makes about 3 cups.

Mrs. Lev H. Prichard, III (Ella Wall)

Turkey Curry

½ cup margarine
½ cup flour
2 cups milk
2 cups turkey or chicken stock
Salt
3 tablespoons curry powder

2 tablespoons dry vermouth
(or water)
Dash ginger
3 to 4 cups cooked turkey meat
¼ cup raisins (optional)

Melt margarine and stir in flour. Slowly add milk and stock. Stir over low heat until thick and bubbly. Salt to taste. Make a paste of the curry powder, vermouth, and ginger and add to white sauce. Add turkey, then raisins. Heat thoroughly, but do not boil. Serve over dry rice with bowls of crumbled bacon, chopped green onion, chutney, sieved hard-cooked egg, chopped peanuts, or slivered almonds. Serves 8. Chicken may be substituted for the turkey.

Mrs. H. William Volk, Jr. (LaVerne Ryan)

Turketti

1¼ cups broken spaghetti
2 cups diced turkey
¼ cup diced pimiento
¼ cup diced onion
2 tablespoons chopped bell
pepper
½ cup turkey broth (or water)

1 can condensed cream of
mushroom soup
½ teaspoon salt
⅛ teaspoon pepper
1¾ cups grated sharp Cheddar
cheese

Cook spaghetti. Combine all remaining ingredients except cheese. Add the spaghetti and half the cheese. Toss lightly until well mixed. Sprinkle remaining cheese on top. Bake in a 1½-quart casserole for 45 minutes at 350 degrees. Serves 8. This can be prepared the day before and refrigerated until time to bake. If the recipe is doubled, allow 1 hour baking time.

Mrs. F. Elsea Peckenpaugh (Billie Stewart)

Cornish Game Hens
Glazed Cornish Game Hens

2 Cornish game hens
Salt
Paprika
2 chicken bouillon cubes
1 cup boiling water
1/3 cup Sauterne
¾ teaspoon instant minced
onion

½ teaspoon curry powder
Dash pepper
2 tablespoons butter
2 tablespoons flour
¼ cup water
1 3-ounce can sliced mushrooms,
drained

Sprinkle chicken with salt and paprika. Place in shallow baking dish. Dissolve bouillon in boiling water; add wine, instant onion, pepper, and curry powder. Pour over hens. Cover with foil and bake at 350 degrees for 2 hours. Melt butter in sauce pan, add flour, and cook until bubbly. Blend in water. Add pan juces. Stir over low heat until thickened. Add mushrooms and heat through. Pour sauce over chicken. Save some to pass. Serves 2.

Mrs. Willard Shuart (Marjorie Parris)

Stuffed Cornish Game Hens

1 small onion, chopped
2 ribs celery, chopped
¼ cup butter
½ pound lean ground beef

1 6-ounce box long grain and
wild rice, cooked
Dash cayenne pepper
6 Cornish game hens

Sauté onion and celery in melted butter until translucent. Remove from pan and reserve remaining butter. Sauté ground beef until brown; mix with onion, celery, cooked rice, and cayenne pepper. Stuff birds with the mixture and place on a broiler pan. Glaze birds with reserved butter. Cover with foil and bake at 350 degrees for 1 hour 30 minutes. Remove foil, baste with pan drippings, and cook birds about 15 minutes longer, or until brown. Serves 6.

Miss Nancy Bowen

Poultry recipes found in Chapter 1. MEXICAN FOOD:

Chicken Enchiladas
Marca's Enchiladas Suissas
Chicken Casserole Mexico

Chicken Tortilla Casserole
Creamed Chicken Tacos
Calabaza con Pollo

Meats

10. MEATS

South Texas is ranch country. The northern boundary of the world famous King Ranch abuts the city limits of Corpus Christi. Cattle grazed on Padre Island grasses long before the tourists discovered the pleasures of the long stretches of sandy beaches. This is the home of the outdoor barbecue. Since many South Texans raise and slaughter their own beef, they have learned how to turn the "less desirable" cuts like brisket, stew meat, and ground beef into dishes worthy of company.

Beef

Smoked Barbecued Beef

1 5-pound top round roast
1 tablespoon coarsely ground
   sage
1 teaspoon paprika
1 tablespoon ground summer
   savory
½ teaspoon chili powder
Bob's Barbecue Sauce

Rub the meat with seasonings, wrap, and place in refrigerator for a minimum of 2 hours before cooking. It is better to prepare the meat the preceding day. The meat should be cooked over low coals or off to 1 side where heat and smoke envelope it, never over open flames. After meat has browned and dried well, apply Bob's Barbecue Sauce with a brush. Repeat application of sauce at least 4 or 5 times during the cooking process. When turning the meat, use a spatula or tongs; do not use a fork for the juice will run out. Cooking time for a 5-pound roast is 4 to 5 hours. Serves 10 to 15.

BOB'S BARBECUE SAUCE:

½ cup butter
2 tablespoons lemon juice
5 tablespoons Worcestershire
   sauce
6 tablespoons catsup
2 tablespoons soy sauce
2 tablespoons clear
   French dressing
1 teaspoon salt
1 teaspoon Pickapeppa brand
   steak sauce or any spicy steak
   sauce

Place all ingredients in pan and heat until blended.

Mrs. Robert G. Kipp (Peggy Alcorn)

Barbecued Beef Tenderloin

½ cup margarine
2 tablespoons Worcestershire
  sauce
½ teaspoon Tabasco brand
  pepper sauce
2 tablespoons vinegar
Juice of ½ lime
3 to 4 cloves garlic, pressed

2 tablespoons olive oil
Dash cayenne pepper
1 teaspoon sugar
¼ cup catsup
2 tablespoons dry wine or beer
Salt
3- to 5-pound beef tenderloin

Melt margarine in sauce pan. Add remaining ingredients, except meat. Take meat out of refrigerator, wipe, baste with sauce, and let stand about 30 minutes. Sear over hot fire on grill. Move away from flame and hottest coals. Smoke with cover on grill for about 30 minutes. Serve with sauce. Serves 6 to 10.

Dr. Austin Davies

Place a rib roast in a preheated 375-degree oven. Roast 1 hour. Turn oven off. One hour before serving, turn oven to 375 degrees again. Do not open oven door at any time. Roast will be medium rare.

Standing Prime Rib*

4-rib roast
1 clove garlic
Pepper

Seasoned salt
Beau Monde brand seasoning

Cut garlic clove in half and rub the fat of the roast. Sprinkle pepper on the fat until it is covered; then sprinkle heavily with seasoned salt and Beau Monde. Rub the seasonings into the fat. Bake in pre-heated 325-degree oven in shallow roasting pan, letting the ribs form a rack for the meat; fat side will be up. Do not cover; do not add liquid; do not baste. Cook about 25 minutes per pound or until meat thermometer registers 155 degrees. A boned, rolled rib roast is easier to carve. Bake it on a rack and allow about 30 minutes per pound.

Mrs. Lev H. Prichard, III (Ella Wall)

Peppered Rib Eye of Beef*

6- to 8-pound rib eye roast   Lemon pepper to cover roast
2 tablespoons olive oil

Rub roast with olive oil and pat on pepper heavily. Insert meat thermometer into center of roast. Cook at 325 degrees about 1 hour 30 minutes until desired doneness, according to thermometer. Time will vary according to doneness desired and whether or not meat has been frozen.

This may also be done by the slow-cook method. Prepare meat as above, but you must use thermometer. Put roast in a 175-degree oven at about 3 p.m. It will be ready for dinner at 7:30 p.m. Check it every several hours. The temperature may be raised or lowered as dinner approaches so that desired doneness may be attained. You will find that your meat is very tender because you have not lost any of the juices. Serves 12 to 16.

Mrs. Jack Modesett, Jr. (Marcia Heyne)

To make wine gravy, mix corn starch with drippings. Add 3 parts of beef stock to 1 part dry red wine. Cook until gravy thickens. Salt to taste. Serve with roast.

Busy Day Brisket

4- to 5-pound boneless beef   Pepper
  brisket   Worcestershire sauce
1 envelope dry onion soup mix   Burgundy wine
Garlic powder

Place onion soup mix on large pieces of heavy foil. Rub both sides of meat with garlic powder, pepper, and Worcestershire sauce. Pour wine on both sides of beef. Seal foil and bake brisket at 300 degrees for about 6 hours. It is excellent sliced cold. Serves 8-10. Can be frozen.

Mrs. Charles Canfield (Patricia Kitchen)
Mrs. Joe P. Nelson (Harriet Hornish)

Mary Hutchens' Brisket*

5- to 6-pound boneless beef
 brisket

18-ounce bottle Cattlemen's
 brand barbecue sauce

Place the brisket in an open pan, fat side up. Pour sauce over the top and sides. Place in a 300-degree oven for 1 hour, then turn down to the lowest heat possible (140 to 175 degrees) and cook 10 to 12 hours. Serves 10-12.

This is great for an easy dinner served with beans, salad, and bread.

Mrs. William N. Woolsey (Sandra Callaway)

Roast Brisket

4- to 5-pound boneless beef
 brisket
2 tablespoons liquid smoke
1 teaspoon onion salt

1 teaspoon garlic salt
1 teaspoon celery salt
2 tablespoons Worcestershire
 sauce
Pepper

Rub liquid smoke and seasoned salts on meat, wrap tightly in foil, and refrigerate overnight on cookie sheet. The next morning, add Worcestershire sauce and freshly ground black pepper, place in 250-degree oven (in foil) for 5 hours. The secret of this moist brisket is to wrap the meat tightly, allowing no steam to escape. Serves 8-10.

Mrs. F. Elsea Peckenpaugh (Billie Stewart)
Mrs. Pete Baker (Susie Alderson)

Connie's Pot Roast*

4- to 5-pound pot roast
1 large onion, chopped
1 clove garlic, pressed
2 teaspoons salt
1/4 teaspoon pepper
1/4 teaspoon allspice

1/4 cup chopped parsley
1 beef bouillon cube
1/2 cup water
1/2 cup tomato juice
1 cup dry red wine

Put roast in pot. Add all other ingredients. Cover and bake at approximately 325 degrees until tender or for about 4 hours. Serves 6 to 8.

Mrs. Jack M. Painter (Darlene Downer)

Spanish Pot Roast

3- to 4-pound roast (rump or
  chuck)
1 3-ounce jar stuffed green
  olives

Cooking oil
Salt
Pepper
2 16-ounce cans stewed tomatoes

Take a knife and make deep slits in the roast. Stuff the olives down the slits lengthwise. Brown meat in cooking oil. Pour tomatoes over the roast and add salt and pepper. Cover. Simmer slowly on low heat about 2 hours or until roast is done to your liking. If liquid runs low, add a little water. Baste frequently. Serve with mashed potatoes and the gravy from the roast. When the roast is sliced, you'll have cross-sections of olives in the slices. Serves 6 to 8.

Mrs. Lawrence Riley Williams (Ann Reading Parsley)

Chinese Pot Roast Company Style

4-pound chuck roast
2 teaspoons garlic salt
1 teaspoon dry mustard
½ teaspoon pepper
2 tablespoons cooking oil
¾ cup water

¼ cup soy sauce
1 tablespoon vinegar
1 tablespoon honey
½ teaspoon ground ginger
2 tablespoons corn starch

Combine the garlic, mustard, and pepper and rub on both sides of the meat. Heat the oil in a pan, add meat, and brown on both sides. Combine water, soy sauce, honey, vinegar, and ground ginger. Pour over meat, cover, and simmer on low heat for 4 hours or in a 350-degree oven for 2 hours.

For gravy, skim fat from drippings. Blend corn starch in ½ cup cold water. Stir into drippings and continue stirring until thickened. If not thick enough, just add 2 tablespoons corn starch to ½ cup cold water all over again. If you want a sweeter gravy, then add a little more honey. Serve with fluffy mashed potatoes. Serves 8.

Mrs. James W. Cottingham (Linda Yancy)

Sauerbraten

6-pound beef rump (or venison)
5 cups vinegar
5 cups water
3 onions, sliced
1 lemon, sliced

12 whole cloves
6 bay leaves
6 whole black peppers
3 tablespoons salt

Place meat in large bowl; add other ingredients. Let stand for 36 hours in refrigerator, turning occasionally. Remove meat from marinade and brown in hot fat. Add 1 cup vinegar mixture, cover, and cook slowly atop stove for 2 hours or until tender. Add water, if necessary. Serves 12 to 16.

Mrs. Gerald A. Reeves (Lois Arnett)

Steaks Korean

¼ cup sesame seeds
Steak
½ cup soy sauce

½ cup onion juice
¼ cup sugar

Toast sesame seeds and pound slightly. Marinate steak in soy sauce, onion juice, and sugar for 1 hour or more; add sesame seeds. Broil to desired doneness.

Mrs. Edwin A. Durham, II (Kaye Tarrant)

J.R.'s Special Port Aransas Steak

4 choice round steaks, cut into
  strips
½ cup flour
1½ cups butter
2 tablespoons Worcestershire
  sauce

2 tablespoons A-1 brand
  steak sauce
2 4-ounce cans sliced mushrooms
½ cup water
½ cup dry Sherry (or dry
  white wine)

Dredge meat in flour; brown in butter; place in large oven casserole. Add remaining ingredients to butter in skillet, beat, and pour over meat. Cover with foil and cook for 1 hour 30 minutes at 350 degrees. This can be prepared the morning of the day you plan to serve. Serve on noodles with green salad. Serves 8.

Mrs. Richard King, III (Jimmie Rose Harrison)

Steak Diane

2 2-pound boneless sirloin steaks
2 tablespoons olive oil
1 teaspoon pepper
½ teaspoon salt
Pepper
¼ cup butter
2 tablespoons cooking oil

2 teaspoons dry mustard
Salt
1 tablespoon Worcestershire
    sauce
2 teaspoons lemon juice
2 tablespoons parsley

Place steaks between wax paper and pound to ½-inch thickness. Sprinkle olive oil on both sides of steaks and pepper generously. In large skillet, sauté the dry mustard and onions in 2 tablespoons of the butter and the cooking oil for 1 minute. Cook steaks in this for 2 minutes on each side, spooning juices once. Salt cooked meat. Put on platter and keep warm. Add 2 tablespoons butter, Worcestershire sauce, and lemon juice. Heat and pour over steaks. Sprinkle with parsley and serve with wild rice. Serves 4 to 6.

Mrs. Earl Sams Lightner (Robin Holmes)

Steak Kabobs

1 cup cooking oil
¾ cup soy sauce
½ cup vinegar
¼ cup prepared mustard
¼ cup Worcestershire sauce
1 onion, chopped
2 teaspoons pepper

2 cloves garlic
8 pounds steak, cubed
Onions, quartered
Bell peppers, quartered
Cherry tomatoes
Mushrooms

Mix first 8 ingredients well and pour over meat. Refrigerate at least overnight. (Naturally, sirloin is good, but this marinade tenderizes so even lean chuck or venison can be used). When ready to cook, arrange meat on skewers with pieces of onion, bell pepper, cherry tomatoes, and mushrooms. Broil on barbecue grill, basting frequently with marinade. Leftover marinade freezes well.

Kabobs are best served with rice, especially when you brown raw rice in butter and then cook in bouillon or beef stock.

Mrs. Max J. Luther, III (Maxine Jenkins)

Pepper Steak

1½-pound flank steak, cut into
  2-inch strips
½ teaspoon salt
1 cup diced onion
1 cup water
3 tablespoons soy sauce
1 clove garlic, minced

2 bell peppers, cut into 1-inch
  strips
2 tablespoons corn starch
¼ cup cold water
2 tomatoes, cut into eighths
  (optional)
3 to 4 cups cooked rice

Brown the meat in a lightly greased skillet. Sprinkle the salt on the meat as it is browning. Push meat to 1 side. Add onion; cook until tender. Add water, soy sauce, and garlic; cover and simmer for 10 minutes. Add bell peppers; cover and simmer for 5 more minutes. Blend corn starch with cold water; gradually stir into skillet. Cook, stirring constantly, until it boils. Boil and stir for about 1 minute. Add tomatoes; heat thoroughly. Serve immediately with hot rice. Serves 5 to 6.

Mrs. Robert C. Wolter (Frances Overton)

Lucy's Flank Steak

2- to 3-pound flank steak
Salt
Pepper
Flour
Cooking oil

¼ cup dry red wine
¾ cup water
Thyme
Oregano

Score meat; salt, pepper, and flour and brown in shallow cooking oil. Pour off oil; add red wine and water plus a pinch of thyme and oregano. Simmer for 1 hour 30 minutes, checking liquid often.

Miss Nancy Bowen

Marinade for Flank Steak

¼ cup soy sauce
2 tablespoons honey
2 tablespoons vinegar
½ teaspoon ground ginger

¼ teaspoon garlic powder
2 cloves garlic, pressed
¼ cup cooking oil

Combine ingredients and marinate steak for at least 5 hours, preferably overnight. The steak may then be barbecued, broiled, or pan fried.

Mrs. Lowell Kepp (Betty Ellis)

Easy Stew*

2 to 3 pounds stew meat
1 envelope dry onion soup mix
1 to 2 cans condensed golden
   mushroom soup
1 cup dry Sherry

1 16-ounce can whole new
   potatoes
1 16-ounce can onions
1 4-ounce can mushrooms

Place first 4 ingredients in heavy 3-quart casserole with lid. Bake covered in 250-degree oven for 2½ to 3 hours. After baking this long, add remaining ingredients. Recover and bake 1 hour longer at 350 degrees. Serves 4 to 6.

Mrs. Gerald Heinzelmann (Carolyn Jones)

Cowboy Stew

3 pounds beef (round steak,
   leftover roast, or uncooked
   Pike's Peak roast)
2 onions, diced
1 clove garlic, diced
2 quarts consommé (or beef
   broth)
½ fifth red cooking wine
1 tablespoon sugar

Salt
Pepper
1 tablespoon Kitchen Bouquet
   brand browning sauce
1 10-ounce package frozen mixed
   vegetables (optional)
Potatoes (optional)
Parsley (optional)

Cut beef into 3-inch cubes. If uncooked, dust with flour and brown in bacon drippings. Add onions and garlic and sauté. Add remaining ingredients and cook slowly for 2 to 3 hours, covered. Serves 6 to 8. The gravy is excellent served over homemade biscuits.

Mrs. Maurice Priday (Joan McCroskey)

Beef Stew Elaborate

2 pounds tenderloin, sirloin, or sirloin tip	1 pinch rosemary
	3/4 cup butter
Salt	1 bell pepper
Pepper	2 tomatoes
Flour	2 potatoes
2 tablespoons olive oil	1 tablespoon parsley
1 cup beef stock	6 small onions (or 1 cup
1 bay leaf	pearl onions)
1 clove garlic, chopped	2 cups dry red wine

Cut the meat into 1½-inch cubes and coat with flour seasoned with salt and pepper. Heat olive oil in a deep iron skillet or dutch oven. Brown meat slowly and add stock and seasonings. Cover tightly, turn meat often, and simmer for 10 minutes. In another skillet, melt the butter. Chop pepper coarsely, quarter tomatoes, and cut potatoes into large pieces. Combine these with the parsley and whole onions and brown in butter. Pour the vegetables over the meat, add wine, and simmer until meat is very tender, approximately 2 hours. Serves 6 to 8.

Mrs. John F. Cram (Janet Tyson)

Boeuf Bourguignon

6 medium onions, sliced in rings	1/4 teaspoon pepper
	1/2 teaspoon thyme
1/2 cup butter	1/2 teaspoon marjoram
3 pounds trimmed, cubed stew meat	2 cups beef broth or consommé
	1½ cups Burgundy
1 tablespoon flour	1 pound mushrooms
1 teaspoon salt	

Sauté onions in butter; add meat and brown. Add flour, salt, pepper, and spices. Stir until smooth. Add ½ cup broth and 1 cup wine. Simmer 3 hours. Add mushrooms; simmer 1 hour more. Add remainder of broth or wine as needed. Serve on rice. Serves 6.

Mrs. J. Michael Mahaffey (Lynn Smith)
Mrs. Charles DeCou (Martha McKamey)

Beef Tips Creole

3 pounds beef sirloin tips
3 tablespoons shortening
½ cup chopped onion
¼ cup chopped bell pepper
¼ cup chopped celery
¼ teaspoon salt
1 teaspoon parsley
½ teaspoon oregano

¼ teaspoon garlic powder
2 teaspoons gumbo filé
½ teaspoon sweet basil
¼ teaspoon chili powder
Dash nutmeg
1 16-ounce can tomatoes
1 cup water

Have butcher cut beef tips into 1-inch cubes. Sauté beef in shortening until it becomes a rich brown color. Add onions, celery, and bell pepper. Cook over medium heat for 20 minutes; stir. Add seasonings; cook 15 minutes more over low heat. Then add tomatoes and water and simmer about 1 hour or until meat is tender. Serve over rice. Freezes well. Serves 8.

Mrs. Jerry E. Fischer (Alice Ann Peters)

Beef Stroganoff

2 pounds sirloin (or filet)
¼ cup margarine
1 cup chopped onion
1 clove garlic, pressed
3 tablespoons flour
2 beef bouillon cubes
½ teaspoon salt

⅛ teaspoon pepper
1 tablespoon catsup
1 can condensed beef broth
½ cup Sauterne
1½ cups sour cream
1 4-ounce can sliced mushrooms

Cut sirloin into strips. Brown quickly in 1 tablespoon of the butter. Beef should be brown outside, rare inside. Melt remaining butter and sauté onion and garlic until onion is transparent. Remove from heat and add flour, catsup, salt, and pepper. Stir until smooth. Add bouillon cubes and broth gradually. Bring to a boil, stirring constantly. Simmer for 5 minutes. Add wine, sour cream, and mushrooms, then beef strips. Heat well. Serve on rice. Serves 6 to 8.

Mrs. Charles DeCou (Martha McKamey)

Hash

¼ cup drippings (or shortening) 1 cup gravy
1 medium onion, chopped Salt
2 cups boiled potatoes, diced Pepper
2 cups leftover roast, diced Paprika

Melt drippings in heavy skillet, preferably cast iron. Sauté onion until translucent. Stir in potatoes and roast and press down in skillet; pour gravy over. Cook covered over very low heat about 20 minutes; turn mixture and season to taste with salt, pepper, and paprika. Cook uncovered a few more minutes, until gravy is almost completely cooked down and potatoes begin to get crusty. Serves 4 to 6.

This makes a good Sunday night supper served on toast and topped with a poached egg and *picante* sauce.

Mrs. Lev H. Prichard, III (Ella Wall)

Ground Beef

Hamburger and Sour Cream Casserole

4 pounds ground beef Bay leaf
2 cloves garlic, chopped Cayenne pepper
2 medium onions, chopped 1 8-ounce package cream
4 6-ounce cans tomato paste cheese, softened
3 8-ounce cans tomato sauce 1 16-ounce carton sour cream
Salt 1 16-ounce carton cottage cheese
Pepper 1 bunch green onions, chopped
Basil 3 8-ounce packages noodles,
Oregano cooked

Brown meat and add garlic, onion, tomato paste, tomato sauce, and seasonings. Simmer for 1 hour. Mix together remaining ingredients thoroughly. Combine noodles, cheese mixture, and meat sauce. Put in greased casserole. (Can be frozen at this point, but if you do, don't add the sour cream until ready to cook.) Bake at 350 degrees for 1 hour. Serves 18.

Mrs. Richard King, III (Jimmie Rose Harrison)

Family Favorite Meat Loaf

1 pound ground beef
1 egg, lightly beaten
½ cup Progress brand seasoned
  bread crumbs
1 tablespoon instant minced
  onion
1 teaspoon salt

¼ teaspoon pepper
1 tablespoon Worcestershire
  sauce
Dash Tabasco brand pepper sauce
1 8-ounce can tomato sauce
Catsup

Stir egg into meat. Mix in dry ingredients. Add liquid ingredients except catsup. Shape into loaf and bake in shallow pan at 350 degrees for 40 to 45 minutes. Keep fat drained off. Spread the loaf with catsup the last 10 minutes of baking. Serves 4.

Mrs. Lev H. Prichard, III (Ella Wall)

Pizza Meat Loaf

2 pounds ground beef
1 cup cracker crumbs
½ cup chopped onion
½ cup chopped celery
2 eggs, beaten
½ cup grated Parmesan cheese
1½ teaspoons salt

1 teaspoon oregano
1 cup milk
1 15-ounce can pizza sauce
1 cup Mozzarella cheese, grated
1 4-ounce can mushrooms,
  drained
Bell pepper, sliced in rings

Mix first 9 ingredients and shape into loaf. Place in pan and bake for 1 hour at 350 degrees. Remove after 1 hour and pour off grease or move to another pan. Pour pizza sauce over meat loaf. Sprinkle with cheese; then add the mushrooms and bell pepper rings. Bake 15 minutes more. Serves 4 to 6. Excellent cold for sandwiches.

Mrs. Richard W. Sallee (Alice Heldenfels)

French Hamburger Steaks*

1 pound ground beef
¼ cup chopped green onion
¼ cup dry vermouth (or dry
    white wine)

¼ cup beef stock
Salt
Pepper

Form beef into 4 patties, handling as little as possible. Pan-broil hamburger steaks in skillet to desired state of doneness. Remove to heated platter. Sauté onion 2 to 3 minutes. Add vermouth and stock and reduce sauce to half over high heat. Salt and pepper steaks and sauce and pour sauce over steaks. Serves 4.

Mrs. Jack M. Painter (Darlene Downer)

Savory Lasagna

1 large onion, chopped
2 cloves garlic, minced
¼ cup olive oil
2 pounds ground beef
4 16-ounce cans tomatoes
2 6-ounce cans tomato paste
½ cup chopped celery
¼ cup chopped parsley
1½ teaspoons salt

2 teaspoons sugar
1 teaspoon basil
¼ teaspoon pepper
2 bay leaves
8 lasagna noodles, cooked
1½ pounds Ricotta cheese
4 eggs, beaten
Sliced Mozzarella cheese
Grated Parmesan cheese

Sauté onion and garlic in oil in a large kettle. Add beef to brown. Stir in vegetables and seasonings. Simmer, stirring occasionally, for 3 hours or more, until cooked down fairly thick. Chill overnight, then skim off hardened fat.

Break up the Ricotta cheese and mix it well with the eggs. In a greased 9-by-13-inch casserole, layer the cooked lasagna noodles and layer on half the Ricotta mixture. Top this with a layer of meat sauce and then a solid layer of Mozzarella cheese slices. Repeat these layers once more, ending with the Mozzarella. Sprinkle liberally with Parmesan. Heat until hot and bubbly in a 350-degree oven, approximately 30 minutes. To serve, cut into squares and pass an herbed tomato sauce as an accompaniment. Serves 6 to 8.

The meat sauce freezes well. It is also good served over spaghetti, adding mushrooms if desired.

Mrs. Gerald Heinzelmann (Carolyn Jones)

Green Chili Lasagna

1 16-ounce package medium
   noodles
1 teaspoon margarine
3 pounds lean ground beef
5 8-ounce cans tomato sauce
1 tablespoon sugar
2 teaspoons salt
1 teaspoon garlic salt
½ teaspoon pepper

2 cups large curd cottage cheese
1 8-ounce package cream cheese
   (softened)
1 cup sour cream
2 4-ounce cans green chilies,
   chopped
1 cup thinly sliced green onions,
   including tops
½ cup grated Parmesan cheese

Grease 2 9-by-13-inch baking dishes. Cook noodles according to directions. Drain and add teaspoon of margarine. Brown beef in small amount of fat. In a large sauce pan, combine tomato sauce, sugar, salts, and pepper. Add browned meat and simmer until meat is tender, about 30 minutes. Skim off fat. In a separate bowl, combine cottage cheese, cream cheese, sour cream, onions, and green chilies. Mix until smooth and creamy. Fill baking dishes in this order: Put ¼ cooked noodles in the bottom of each of the pans. Cover with ¼ meat sauce in each pan. Next, divide the cheese mixture between both pans — use all of it for 1 thick layer. Spread remaining noodles evenly over cheese. Use remaining meat sauce over noodles and finish with heavy coating of Parmesan cheese. Cover with foil and refrigerate. Before serving, heat in 350-degree oven for 45 minutes. Serves 24. Better if made day before.

Mrs. Ronald B. Brin (Lora Lou McCardell)

Manicotti

1 10-ounce package frozen
  chopped spinach, thawed
1 16-ounce carton cottage
  cheese
Salt
Pepper
1 cup grated Parmesan cheese
1 egg, beaten
2 tablespoons bread crumbs
8 ounces ground beef

2 tablespoons chopped onion
1 package Italian style
  spaghetti sauce mix
1 8-ounce can tomato sauce
1 2-ounce can mushroom stems
  and pieces
9 to 10 cooked manicotti tubes
1 8-ounce package sliced
  Mozzarella cheese

To make the stuffing, mix together the spinach, cottage cheese, salt, pepper, Parmesan cheese, egg, and bread crumbs. Set aside.

Sauté the ground beef and onion until beef is lightly browned. Combine spaghetti sauce mix and tomato sauce. Add sauce and mushrooms to meat and simmer 10 minutes. Set aside.

Pack the manicotti with the stuffing mixture. Place in a greased 7-by-11-inch baking dish. Pour the sauce over the stuffed manicotti and cover with Mozzarella. Bake at 350 degrees for 20 to 30 minutes. Serves 4.

Mrs. James Moore (Nancy Casmere)

Saucy Meat Balls

1 pound lean ground beef
1 teaspoon salt
Pepper
3 tablespoons minced parsley
2 tablespoons grated onion
1 teaspoon Worcestershire sauce
2 eggs, beaten
½ cup milk

1 cup soft bread crumbs
¼ cup cooking oil
1 cup catsup
2 tablespoons prepared mustard
1 tablespoon Worcestershire sauce
¼ cup vinegar
2/3 cup dry Sherry (or red wine)

Mix first 9 ingredients and shape into large or small meat balls. Let stand in refrigerator 1 hour. Brown on all sides in oil. Make sauce of remaining ingredients. Heat. Add to meat balls. Use as main course or as *hors d'oeuvres*.

Mrs. Emil Tejml (Sue Rosson)

Oniony Meat Balls

1 envelope dry onion soup mix	½ teaspoon oregano
1 cup water	½ teaspoon pepper
2 8-ounce cans tomato sauce	½ teaspoon thyme
½ teaspoon garlic salt	1 teaspoon dried parsley flakes
	1½ pounds lean ground beef

Mix onion soup mix with water and simmer. Pour 2 tablespoons of tomato sauce into a cup. To this, add the garlic salt, thyme, pepper, oregano, and parsley flakes. Stir well; then mix thoroughly with ground beef. Add remaining tomato sauce to the simmering onion soup.

Make beef mixture into meat balls the size of a fully rounded tablespoon. Place meat balls in a 2-quart casserole and cover with sauce. Bake covered at 350 degrees for 1 hour. Serve over rice. Serves 4 to 6.

This can be made early in the day and refrigerated.

Mrs. Charles Canfield (Patricia Kitchen)

Stuffed Cabbage Leaves

1 pound lean ground beef	1 egg, beaten
1 cup cooked rice	12 cabbage leaves
1 small onion, chopped	Bacon drippings
1 teaspoon caraway seed	2 8-ounce cans tomato sauce
1 teaspoon salt	¼ cup water
¼ teaspoon pepper	

Mix first 7 ingredients well. Trim thickest part of stem from cabbage leaves. Steam leaves very slightly. Divide meat into 12 portions and wrap each portion in a leaf; fasten with toothpicks only if necessary. Brown cabbage rolls slowly in bacon drippings. Add tomato sauce and water. Cover and cook slowly for 40 minutes. Serves 4 to 6.

This is a good way to utilize leftover rice. These also freeze well, but do not add the tomato sauce until just before heating to serve. This dish can also be heated successfully in the oven in a serving dish.

Mrs. Gerald Heinzelmann (Carolyn Jones)

Stuffed Peppers Italiano

8 bell peppers
1 pound ground beef
¾ cup old fashioned oats
2 eggs, beaten
½ cup chopped onion
1½ teaspoons salt
¼ teaspoon pepper

¼ teaspoon garlic salt
3 8-ounce cans tomato sauce
1 tablespoon Worcestershire sauce
2 cups grated Mozzarella cheese
¼ teaspoon oregano
¼ teaspoon paprika

Preheat oven to 350 degrees. Cut tops off bell peppers, remove seeds, and cook in boiling salted water for 5 minutes. Set upside down and drain well. Combine beef, oats, eggs, onion, salt, pepper, garlic salt, 1 can tomato sauce, and Worcestershire. Fill peppers ¾ full with meat. Fill remainder of each pepper with ¼ cup of cheese. Arrange peppers upright in casserole. In a small bowl, mix remaining 2 cans tomato sauce, oregano, and paprika. Pour over peppers. Cover and bake for 45 minutes. Remove cover and bake for 15 minutes more. Will freeze. Serves 8.

Mrs. Edwin Prichard (Marjorie Reynolds)

Hamburger-Hominy Pie*

1 pound ground beef
1 onion, chopped
Salt
Pepper
2 tablespoons flour

1 teaspoon chili powder
1 16-ounce can tomatoes
1 16-ounce can hominy
Grated Cheddar cheese

Brown ground beef with onion, salt, and pepper. Add remaining ingredients, except cheese. Pour into greased casserole; sprinkle with cheese. Bake at 350 degrees for 30 minutes. Serves 4 to 6.

Mrs. Gerald A. Reeves (Lois Arnett)

Pork

Marty's Pork Roast

Pork roast
Salt
Pepper

Garlic salt
Flour
Soy Sauce

Cover pork roast well with salt, pepper, and garlic salt. Flour and brown quickly. Remove grease and shake soy sauce heavily over the roast. Cover the bottom of pan (about ½ inch) with water. Cook roast uncovered in a 325-degree oven about 35 to 40 minutes per pound. Shake more soy sauce over meat and add more water, if needed, every 45 minutes.

Mrs. A. Jackson Ashmore (Gay Griffith)

Pork Roast in Mustard

Pork roast
Prepared mustard
Salt

Pepper
Flour

Coat roast with mustard until well covered. Sprinkle with salt and pepper to taste. Sift a thin layer of flour over entire roast. Place in open pan in preheated 450-degree oven for 30 minutes. Turn down to 300 degrees until done, about 30 minutes per pound. This is also a good way to prepare lamb roast.

Mrs. Jeff E. Bell, Jr. (Mary Daimwood)

Crown Pork Roast

5-pound crown roast of pork
1½ to 2 teaspoons salt
1 teaspoon pepper

1 teaspoon poultry seasoning
½ teaspoon paprika
1 teaspoon ground cloves

Preheat oven to 325 degrees. Mix spices and rub pork with mixture. Protect each rib with piece of foil during roasting to prevent too much browning. Fill center with crushed foil to keep crown shape during roasting. Roast uncovered for about 45 minutes per pound. Prepare your favorite stuffing and stuff for last 45 minutes.

Mrs. A. Jackson Ashmore (Gay Griffith)

Sweet and Sour Pork

1 pound lean pork, cut into
½-inch thick, bite-sized pieces
1 tablespoon dry Sherry
1 tablespoon soy sauce
1 egg, lightly beaten

1 tablespoon corn starch
3 tablespoons flour
Cooking oil
3 slices pineapple, quartered

Mix pork with wine, soy sauce, egg, corn starch, and flour. Heat oil to 375 to 400 degrees. Deep fry pork until well done and crisp on edges. Remove to oven-proof platter and keep warm.

SAUCE:

3 tablespoons oil
2 onions, quartered
3 bell peppers, quartered
1 clove garlic, minced
1/3 cup sugar
¼ cup catsup

1 tablespoon dry Sherry
2 tablespoons vinegar
¼ cup soy sauce
1 tablespoon corn starch mixed
  with 1/3 cup water

Heat 3 tablespoons oil and sauté onion, bell pepper, and garlic over high heat for 2 minutes or longer. Mix sugar, catsup, Sherry, vinegar, and soy sauce and add to vegetables; bring to boiling point. Thicken with corn starch mixture, stirring constantly. Add fried pork and pineapple, mix well, and serve hot. May be served over rice. Serves 4.

Mrs. W. Richard McCracken (Lucy McFadyen)

Pork Chops

8 lean pork chops
Flour
Drippings
½ cup soy sauce
½ cup catsup

¼ teaspoon celery seed
½ teaspoon nutmeg
1 bay leaf
½ cup water

Flour chops and brown in drippings. Combine other ingredients and pour over chops in casserole. Cover. Bake at 325 degrees for 1 hour 30 minutes, turning once during cooking. Serves 8.

Mrs. John Pitcairn (Sue Kowalski)

Pork Chops à l'Orange

4 1-inch thick loin pork chops
Seasoned salt
2 tablespoons water
5 tablespoons sugar
1½ teaspoons corn starch
Dash salt

¼ teaspoon cinnamon
10 whole cloves
2 teaspoons orange rind
½ cup orange juice
4 slices orange

Brown pork chops. Sprinkle with seasoned salt. Add water, cover, and simmer 1 hour or until tender. Make syrup of remaining ingredients, boiling until clear and slightly thickened. Pour over chops. Serves 4.

Mrs. Jack Best (Betty Reno)

Pork Chop Casserole

6 thick pork chops
Salt
Pepper
Flour
Cooking oil
1 cup rice
6 slices onion
6 thick slices bell pepper

6 thick slices tomato
2½ cups beef bouillon
¼ teaspoon thyme
½ teaspoon marjoram
½ teaspoon basil
Salt
Pepper

Flour seasoned pork chops. Brown on both sides in small amount of cooking oil. Place rice in large, shallow casserole. Place chops on top of rice, putting sliced onion, bell pepper, and tomato on each chop. Pour bouillon over all. Sprinkle with herbs, salt, and pepper. Cover and bake at 350 degrees for about 50 minutes. Serves 6. Can be prepared ahead of time or day before. An excellent 1-dish meal.

Mrs. John Pitcairn (Sue Kowalski)

Pork Chops with Rosemary

½ teaspoon salt
Dash pepper
6 lean pork chops
1 egg, lightly beaten
½ cup bread crumbs

¾ teaspoon rosemary, crumbled
2 tablespoons cooking oil
1 cup chopped celery
½ cup water

Salt and pepper the pork chops. Dip in beaten egg, then in bread crumbs mixed with rosemary. Brown the breaded chops in oil. Add celery and water. Cover and simmer 30 minutes. Uncover the last 5 minutes to crisp the coated chops. Serves 6.

Mrs. Robert C. Wolter (Frances Overton)

Ham

Baked Ham

8- to 10-pound fully cooked
    ham
Cloves

Cherries
1 18-ounce jar apricot
    preserves

Order ham from butcher and have him cut the rind off. Place in paper bag or wrap in butcher paper and bake at 325 degrees for 20 minutes per pound. Let cool slightly and score deeply. Where scores cross, alternate clove studs and cherries on toothpicks. Spread apricot preserves and bake uncovered at 350 degrees to glaze. Watch closely, as the ham only needs to brown slightly. Serves 12.

Mrs. Earl Sams Lightner (Robin Holmes)

Orse Lee's Coke and Honey Ham

5-pound ham   1 teaspoon dry mustard
½ cup brown sugar   Pineapple slices
3 tablespoons honey   1 6-ounce bottle Coca Cola

Trim fat from ham. Place pineapple slices on top of ham. Mix brown sugar, dry mustard, and honey together and spread over ham. Bake at 325 degrees for 30 minutes or until it begins to brown. Pour Coke over it and continue cooking for 30 minutes longer, basting once the last 15 minutes.

Mrs. James Cliff Avant (Sally Dixon)

Ham Hash

3 cups potatoes   1 bell pepper, chopped
3 cups cubed ham   2 cups milk

Boil potatoes in jackets. Cool, peel, and cube. Place all ingredients in skillet. Cook uncovered over low heat for 1 to 1½ hours. Stir occasionally so hash does not scorch. Serves 4 to 5.

Mrs. John Pitcairn (Sue Kowalski)

Ham Loaf

1½ pounds ground ham   ½ cup vinegar
1½ pounds ground pork   ½ cup water
  shoulder   1½ cups brown sugar
1 cup milk   1 tablespoon prepared mustard
1 cup crushed cracker crumbs   ½ to 1 teaspoon ground cloves
2 eggs, beaten

Mix ground meats, milk, cracker crumbs, and eggs. Shape into 3 loaves. Mix remaining ingredients for sauce and pour over ham loaves. Bake uncovered at 400 degrees for 15 minutes. Baste often. Reduce heat to 275 degrees for 1 hour longer. Serves 6 to 8.

Mrs. A. Jackson Ashmore (Gay Griffith)

Ham Loaf with Sauce

8 ounces ground smoked ham	1 egg, beaten
8 ounces ground pork	¾ cup milk
½ cup cracker crumbs	¼ teaspoon salt
1 small onion, chopped	Dash pepper

Mix all ingredients and shape into a loaf in a flat pan. Bake with either of the following sauces according to sauce directions. Serves 4.

SAUCE 1:

1 cup brown sugar	1 teaspoon dry mustard
3 tablespoons vinegar	

Bake ham loaf at 350 degrees for 30 minutes. Mix above ingredients, boil for 1 minute, and pour over ham loaf. Bake 25 minutes longer.

SAUCE 2:

1 16-ounce can tomatoes	1 teaspoon flour
2 teaspoons granulated sugar	2 eggs
1 teaspoon salt	½ teaspoon vinegar
1 cup brown sugar	1 can condensed beef consommé
1 teaspoon dry mustard	

Mix tomatoes, granulated sugar, and salt. Pour over ham loaf. Bake at 350 degrees for 1 hour 30 minutes. Mix remaining ingredients in an electric blender. Cook in the top of a double boiler until thick. Serve in a sauce boat with ham loaf.

Mrs. Gerald Heinzelmann (Carolyn Jones)

When making ham loaf, sprinkle brown sugar in the bottom of a loaf pan. Top with a row of pineapple rings. Place half a maraschino cherry in the center of each ring. Pack ham loaf into pan. Bake as directed. Invert on a platter to serve.

Mushroom and Ham Stuffed Tomatoes

4 large tomatoes
Salt
Pepper
¼ cup minced onion
2 tablespoons olive oil

1/3 cup soft bread crumbs
2/3 cup ground, cooked ham
1 cup minced fresh mushrooms
1¼ tablespoons minced parsley

Cut top 1/3 off tomatoes, scoop out centers, and season insides with salt and pepper. Sauté onion in oil, add bread crumbs, and cook 1 minute. Add remaining ingredients and season to taste. Stuff mixture into tomato shells. Bake at 350 degrees for 30 minutes. Serves 4.

Mrs. Lev H. Prichard, III (Ella Wall)

Ham and Asparagus

1 15½-ounce can asparagus
1 cup cubed cooked ham
¼ cup grated American cheese
1 tablespoon lemon juice
2 tablespoons tapioca
2 tablespoons chopped bell
   pepper
2 tablespoons chopped onion

2 tablespoons minced parsley
4 hard-cooked eggs, chopped
½ cup milk
1 can condensed cream of
   mushroom soup
½ cup bread crumbs
2 tablespoons melted butter

Mix everything, except bread crumbs and butter, and put in flat 2-quart baking dish. Top with the bread crumbs mixed with butter. Bake at 375 degrees for 25 to 30 minutes. Serves 6.

Mrs. R. Michael Dulaney (Florence "Sue" Williams)

Zesty Ham and Rice Casserole

1 cup rice
1 can condensed cream of
celery soup
1 soup can water
2 cups diced ham
½ cup mayonnaise
1 5-ounce can water chestnuts,
drained and sliced

¼ cup chopped pimiento
2 tablespoons grated Parmesan
cheese
1 tablespoon minced parsley
2 teaspoons Worcestershire sauce
1 teaspoon salt
⅛ teaspoon cayenne pepper

Mix above ingredients and pour into a tightly covered casserole. Bake at 350 degrees for 45 minutes to 1 hour, or until rice is done. Toss once with a fork while baking. Serves 6.

Mrs. A. Jackson Ashmore (Gay Griffith)

Sausage

Sausage and Wild Rice Casserole

1 pound hot bulk sausage
2 medium onions, chopped
2 3-ounce cans button
mushrooms
¼ cup flour
½ cup half and half
2½ cups condensed chicken
broth

1 teaspoon monosodium glutamate
½ teaspoon poultry seasoning
1 tablespoon salt
2 6-ounce packages long grain
and wild rice, cooked
½ cup toasted almonds, slivered

Sauté sausage. Drain on paper towel. Break in small pieces. Sauté onion in sausage drippings. Add mushrooms and cooked sausage. Mix flour with cream, add chicken broth, and cook until thickened. Add seasonings. Combine all ingredients except almonds and pour into casserole. Bake 25 to 30 minutes at 350 degrees. Sprinkle with almonds when ready to serve. Serves 12.

Mrs. Curtis B. Dyer, Jr. (Jerry Bramlet)

Lamb

Marinated Leg of Lamb

¾ cup olive oil
2/3 cup chopped onion
1/3 cup vinegar
1 teaspoon peppercorns
1 teaspoon salt

¼ teaspoon oregano
1 bay leaf (optional)
1 clove garlic
6-pound leg of lamb, boned

Mix oil, onion, vinegar, and seasonings. Shape lamb on a large piece of foil that has been placed on a pan so it lies flat. Pour marinade over meat and pull foil so marinade covers it. Allow to marinate 6 hours or overnight. Drain and broil the lamb 10 minutes on each side. Remove to a roasting pan. Baste and cook at 350 degrees for 20 minutes per pound. Slice in ¾-inch strips. Serves 8 to 10. Peas cooked with lettuce and pears with currant jelly are good accompaniments.

Mrs. J. Franklin Critz (Isabelle Pattee)

Roast Leg of Lamb

6- to 7-pound leg of lamb
2 cloves garlic, cut in
    5 or 6 slivers
2½ teaspoons oregano
1 teaspoon salt

½ teaspoon coarsely ground
    pepper
½ cup olive oil
1½ tablespoons lemon juice

Make 5 or 6 slits ½-inch wide and 2 inches deep at even intervals over top of leg of lamb. Place sliver of garlic in each slit. Mix ½ teaspoon oregano, 1 teaspoon salt, and ½ teaspoon pepper and rub into lamb.

Combine remaining 2 teaspoons oregano, olive oil, and lemon juice in sauce pan. Cook for 5 minutes and rub into the lamb. Place lamb on rack in uncovered roasting pan. Roast at 325 degrees for 3 hours 30 minutes, basting several times. Thicken pan juices for a gravy. Serves 10.

Mrs. John Pitcairn (Sue Kowalski)

Leg of Lamb Supreme

Leg of lamb
1/3 cup fat or cooking oil
1 clove garlic, minced
2 teaspoons marjoram

3/4 teaspoon dry mustard
1 teaspoon salt
1/2 teaspoon paprika

Wipe lamb with damp cloth. Mix remaining ingredients together. Rub over lamb. Put lamb on rack in uncovered roasting pan. Roast at 300 degrees for 30 to 35 minutes per pound. This coating makes marvelous drippings for gravy.

Mrs. James C. Freeman (Cornelia Herz)

Leg of Lamb with Plum Sauce

1 leg of lamb
Salt
Pepper
2 10-ounce jars plum jelly
1/4 cup lemon juice

2 tablespoons soy sauce
2 teaspoons Worcestershire sauce
1 teaspoon basil, crushed
1 clove garlic, pressed

Season lamb with salt and pepper and place fat side up on rack in roasting pan. Roast in 325-degree oven for 2½ to 3 hours or until meat thermometer reads 175 to 180 degrees. Mix remaining ingredients and baste lamb several times during last hour of cooking. Simmer remaining sauce and serve with meat.

Mrs. Earl Sams Lightner (Robin Holmes)

Navarin of Lamb

2 tablespoons olive oil
1 large onion, diced
3 cloves garlic, minced
2 cups lamb gravy or stock
1 7½-ounce can tomatoes
½ cup tomato sauce
2 cups cubed, cooked lamb
¼ teaspoon oregano
½ teaspoon basil

2 teaspoons salt
½ teaspoon pepper
½ bay leaf
1 tablespoon minced parsley
2 cups sliced carrots
2 cups cubed potatoes
1 8-ounce can green beans
1 8½-ounce can green peas
Grated Parmesan cheese

Heat oil over moderate flame in large dutch oven. Add onion and garlic and sauté until they begin to brown. Add gravy, tomatoes, and tomato sauce. Bring to a boil and reduce to a simmer. Add lamb, seasonings, and carrots. Cover and simmer 30 minutes. Add potatoes and simmer about 30 minutes longer, until carrots and potatoes are tender. Add peas and beans and heat through. Serve Parmesan cheese to sprinkle on top the stew. Crusty French bread and butter and a robust red wine will complete the meal. Serves 8.

Mrs. Lev H. Prichard, III (Ella Wall)

This is a traditional stew from Provence, France. Turnips are frequently added with the carrots. This is a perfect meal for the day you clean the refrigerator, since ingredients can vary so widely, and both cooked and uncooked vegetables can be used simply by varying the cooking time. Beans or peas can be added in any quantity, depending on taste and what you have on hand. Leftover lamb pot roast (such as a shoulder roast) is the best source of both meat and gravy.

Meat recipes found in Chapter 1. MEXICAN FOOD:

Mamie's Tamales
Ester's Enchiladas
Peggy's Enchiladas
Tacos
Quick Tortilla Stuffer
Flautas
Chili Casserole

Mexican Beef Casserole
Chili-Bean Casserole
Mexican Meat Loaf
South of the Border Spaghetti
Mamie's Calabaza
Mexican Pork Chop Supper

Game

11. GAME

The underbrush and scrubby trees that grow on South Texas ranch lands provide homes for a great variety of game including deer, dove, quail. The marshlands along the coast attract migratory water fowl during the winter. It is not uncommon to see ducks a hundred feet from shore in downtown Corpus Christi. From the opening of white-wing dove season in early September until quail season ends in January, the crack of gun fire is a familiar sound in rural areas.

Venison

Venison Ham

Venison ham
Flour
Salt
Pepper
Bacon drippings

1 large onion, sliced
1 cup water
1 4-ounce can mushrooms
½ cup dry white wine

Dust roast with flour, salt, and pepper. Brown well in bacon drippings in a heavy dutch oven over high heat. Add onion slices and water. Cover, reduce heat, and simmer about 40 minutes per pound. One hour before roast is done, add mushrooms and white wine.

Mrs. George Taggart (Ethleen Reimers)

Venison Diane

Venison backstrap (tenderloin)
½ cup lemon juice
Salt
Pepper
½ cup butter

1 teaspoon dry mustard
1 3-ounce can sliced mushrooms
1 tablespoon Worcestershire sauce
Parsley

Soak venison in lemon juice for 1 hour. Slice into cutlets and pound until ¼- to ½-inch thick. Salt and pepper. Place butter and mustard in a skillet and stir until blended; add meat and cook until brown. Place on platter. Add chopped mushrooms and Worcestershire sauce to pan drippings in skillet. Pour over meat. Sprinkle with chopped parsley.

Mrs. Earl Sams Lightner (Robin Holmes)

Have a very slow fire started in a covered grill. Make a tray of double heavy duty foil; cup up the sides. Do absolutely nothing to the venison ham; just put it on the grill, cover, and cook about 12 hours. When the juices that run out are clear, it's done. Let stand 30 minutes and slice thin for hors d'oeuvres *or use as meat course.*

Stuffed Venison Round Steak

8-ounce venison round steak	*½ cup chopped parsley*
Salt	*4 slices bacon, diced*
Pepper	*2 carrots, grated (optional)*
1 onion, chopped	*Sliced bacon*
2 ribs celery, chopped	

Pound steak until tender; season with salt and pepper. Mix onion, celery, parsley, diced bacon, and carrots. Spread a generous layer of chopped vegetable stuffing on top of the steak. Roll up and secure with skewers or toothpicks. Place in flat pan. Spread remaining vegetables on top. Cover with slices of bacon. Bake at 325 degrees for 1 hour or until done. Serves 2.

Mrs. Max J. Luther, III (Maxine Jenkins)

Pauline's Venison Stroganoff

3-pound venison steak	*1 3-ounce can mushrooms*
Shortening	*1 tablespoon paprika*
1 large onion, chopped	*1 teaspoon salt*
½ cup water	*Pepper*
1 to 2 cans condensed cream of	*1 cup sour cream*
mushroom soup	*½ cup dry red wine (optional)*

Cut meat into bite-sized pieces or into strips. Brown meat and onion in shortening; add water; cover and simmer 30 minutes. Add additional water during cooking, if needed. Add soup, mushrooms, paprika, salt, and pepper. Simmer 1 hour. Add sour cream and cook until heated. If venison still tastes gamey, add wine. Serve over noodles or rice. Serves 8. This recipe can be doubled. Freeze before adding sour cream.

Mrs. James W. Cottingham (Linda Yancy)

Venison Backstrap

Venison backstrap (tenderloin)   Pepper
Fresh lemon juice   3 tablespoons butter
Salt

Slice backstrap into filets and tenderize with a meat mallet. Squeeze lemon juice on both sides of filets and season with salt and pepper to taste. Melt 2 tablespoons butter in a heavy skillet and sauté the filets over high heat. Remove filets from skillet, melt remaining butter in the skillet, and pour the pan juices over the filets before serving.

Mrs. Richard W. Sallee (Alice Heldenfels)

Sweet and Sour Venison

4-pound venison roast   1 large onion, sliced
4 ounces salt pork, cut in thin   1 teaspoon salt
  strips   10 peppercorns
1½ cups vinegar   2 bay leaves
½ cup Burgundy wine   2 tablespoons shortening
1 cup water   1 tablespoon brown sugar
½ cup olive oil   6 tablespoons gingersnap crumbs
2 cloves garlic, minced

Lard venison roast with strips of salt pork. Place in a large ceramic bowl. Combine vinegar, wine, water, olive oil, garlic, onion, salt, peppercorns, and bay leaves. Bring to a boil and pour over the venison. Marinate for at least 2 days in refrigerator, turning meat several times. Remove meat from marinade, draining well. Brown on all sides in hot shortening in a dutch oven or kettle with a well-fitting lid. Add marinade to depth of ½ inch. Cover tightly and cook over low heat for 3 hours, adding additional marinade if necessary. When venison is tender, remove to hot platter. To make sweet and sour sauce, skim off excess fat from cooking liquid. Add additional marinade and wine to make 2 cups. Stir in brown sugar and the gingersnap crumbs. Cook over low heat until gravy thickens. Garnish the roast with spiced pears and serve with sauce. Serves 10. Moose, elk, caribou, or antelope may be substituted for the venison.

Mrs. Charles A. Mella (Kathryn Mitchell)

Venison Cutlets Italiano

2 to 3 pounds venison cutlets
Salt
2 eggs, beaten
Herb-seasoned bread crumbs
½ cup cooking oil

½ recipe Sauce for Venison
Grated Parmesan cheese
6 ounces Swiss or Mozzarella
  cheese

Remove fat. Tenderize cutlets with a mallet. Salt, dip in beaten eggs, and roll in seasoned bread crumbs. Fry quickly in hot oil, turning once. Remove cutlets to a platter. Coat a 9-by-13-inch baking dish with sauce. Add the cutlets. Sprinkle Parmesan cheese on the cutlets. Cover with additional sauce. Place a slice of cheese on each cutlet. Cover and bake 30 minutes at 350 degrees. Serves 6.

Mrs. James W. Cottingham (Linda Yancy)

Sauce for Venison

¼ cup olive oil
½ cup chopped onion
2 cloves garlic
1 12-ounce can tomato paste
1 28-ounce can tomatoes
3 cups water
½ teaspoon cayenne pepper
  (optional)

1½ teaspoons salt
1 teaspoon sugar
2 bay leaves
1 teaspoon basil
1 teaspoon thyme
¼ teaspoon oregano

Brown garlic and onion in oil. Add remaining ingredients and simmer 1 hour. Use with Venison Cutlets Italiano and Venison Sausage Supper.

Mrs. James W. Cottingham (Linda Yancy)

Venison Sausage Supper

2 pounds venison link sausage	1/4 cup olive oil
3 to 4 large bell peppers,	Salt
chopped	1 1/2 cups cooked rice
2 cups chopped onion	12 tomato cups
1/2 cup chopped celery	1/2 recipe Sauce for Venison

Place sausages in a flat baking dish, pierce skins with a fork, and bake 45 minutes at 350 degrees, turning once or twice. Place chopped vegetables in a baking pan, pour oil over them, sprinkle with salt, and bake 30 minutes at 350 degrees. Remove sausage from oven, slice, and mix with the vegetables and rice. Fill tomato cups with the sausage mixture, pour sauce over the tops, and bake 30 minutes at 350 degrees. Makes 12.

Mrs. James W. Cottingham (Linda Yancy)

Venison Sausage and Wild Rice

2 6-ounce boxes long grain	2 cans condensed chicken broth
and wild rice	Oregano
2 pounds bulk venison sausage	Thyme
1 pound fresh mushrooms,	Marjoram
sliced	1 teaspoon salt
2 large onions, chopped	1/4 teaspoon pepper
1/4 cup flour	Dash Tabasco brand pepper sauce
1/2 cup heavy cream	

Cook rice according to directions. Make sausage into patties, sauté, drain well, and crumble. Sauté mushrooms and chopped onion in sausage drippings. Pour off grease. Add sausage. Make a smooth sauce of flour and cream and add to sausage. Add chicken broth. Cook until thick; season with generous pinch each of oregano, thyme, and marjoram. Add salt and pepper. Combine rice, sauce, and vegetables. Toss together and add Tabasco. Correct seasonings. Bake in a casserole 25 to 30 minutes at 350 degrees. Serves 8. This can be frozen, but add 1 additional can chicken broth.

Mrs. Jack Best (Betty Reno)

Game Birds

Fried Quail

12 quail
1 6-ounce can frozen orange
juice concentrate, thawed

Pioneer brand pancake mix
Cooking oil

Soak quail in orange juice concentrate for less than 3 hours, adding enough water to cover the birds. Drain and dredge birds in pancake mix and deep-fat fry for 5 minutes. Drain on paper towels and serve immediately. Serves 4.

Mrs. Richard King, III (Jimmie Rose Harrison)

Baked Quail

8 quail
1/4 cup butter
1 teaspoon marjoram
1 teaspoon rosemary
1 teaspoon tarragon

1 can condensed cream of
celery soup
1 13¾-ounce can chicken broth
1 3-ounce can mushrooms
1/4 cup piñon nuts (optional)

Skin quail and brown lightly in butter. Mix remaining ingredients and pour over quail in a casserole. Cover and bake at 300 degrees from 1 to 2 hours, basting frequently. Serves 4.

Mrs. Robert B. Wallace (Beverley Bird)

Berried Quail

8 quail
Salt
Pepper
1/4 cup lemon juice

1/4 cup cooking oil
8 bay leaves
3 cups blueberries

Salt and pepper quail; then rub with a mixture of lemon juice and oil. On each of 8 squares of foil place 1 bay leaf. Stuff cavity of quail with drained blueberries. Place on foil breast down. Seal tightly but leave foil loose. Bake at 350 degrees for 1 hour 30 minutes to 2 hours. Serves 4.

Mrs. Robert E. Sallee, III (Phyllis Jasperson)

Smothered Quail

8 quail	Italian herb seasoning
Flour	Salt
1/4 cup shortening	Pepper
1 can condensed cream of	Pimientos
chicken soup	Chives
1 can water	Parsley

Flour quail and brown in hot shortening. Remove to a shallow casserole. Mix soup and water and pour over quail. Sprinkle quail with herb seasoning, salt, and pepper. Decorate with large pieces of pimiento, chives, and parsley. Cover and bake in a 350-degree oven for 1 hour 30 minutes. Remove cover and broil a few minutes before serving. Serves 4. Serve with rice.

Mrs. Jack Best (Betty Reno)

Quail in Wine Sauce

8 quail	Pepper
2 tablespoons butter	1/4 cup Cognac
2 tablespoons oil	1 cup dry white wine
1 small onion, minced	1 can condensed cream of
Salt	chicken soup

Brown quail in oil. Add onion, salt, and pepper. Add warmed cognac and flame. Add white wine and simmer until very tender, about 1 hour. If pan gets dry, add a small amount of chicken stock or more wine. A few minutes before serving, add soup and stir to blend. Serves 4. Serve sauce over rice.

Mrs. Jack M. Painter (Darlene Downer)

Jack's Sautéed Quail*

12 quail
Salt
Pepper

½ cup butter
2 large limes

Take breasts of quail off bone and cut the legs from backbone so they will be attached but will lie flat. Salt and pepper to taste. Melt butter in a large iron skillet. Sauté birds in butter over medium heat for 12 minutes, squeezing limes over the birds as they are cooking. Serves 4 to 6. Serve on toast with a white wine and green salad.

Mrs. Jack Modesett, Jr. (Marcia Heyne)

Baked Doves

10 to 15 doves
1 can condensed cream of
  mushroom soup
1 envelope dry onion soup mix

¼ cup chopped celery
1 cup dry vermouth
1 cup water
Pinch Italian seasoning

Preheat oven to 350 degrees. Place doves in a casserole. Mix remaining ingredients and add to casserole. Cover and cook for 2 hours 30 minutes to 3 hours, turning and basting the doves frequently. Serves 4 to 6.

Mrs. E. Jackson Giles (Mary Kathryn Garrett)

Carolyn Lasater's Mourning Doves

12 doves
3 tablespoons flour
½ cup butter
1 can condensed beef broth

2 cups water
1 cup dry white wine (or
  vermouth)
2 chili pequins, crushed

Flour doves and brown in butter in a heavy dutch oven. Add remaining ingredients, cover, and cook over an open fire for 2 hours. If preparing doves at home, cook at 350 degrees for 2 hours 30 minutes. Add water if gravy becomes too thick. Serves 4 to 6. Serve with rice or noodles.

Mrs. Richard King, III (Jimmie Rose Harrison)

Drunken Duck

6 wild ducks
Salt
Pepper
6 onions, quartered

6 apples, quartered
2 cans beer
1 envelope dry onion soup mix

Salt and pepper the cavities of the cleaned ducks. Place quartered onions and apples in the cavities. Place onion soup mix and beer in a covered roasting pan. Roast ducks with their breasts down at 350 degrees until almost done. Turn ducks, uncover roasting pan, and cook until breasts are browned and meat is fork-tender. Allow about 1 hour 30 minutes for teals, at least 2 hours 30 minutes for mallards. Serves 6.

Mrs. John Pitcairn (Sue Kowalski)

Stuffed Wild Duck

Ducks
Salt
Pepper
Apple wedges
Onion wedges

Parsley
Orange marmalade
Cinnamon
Orange juice
Dry Sherry

Salt and pepper inside each duck. Stuff each duck with wedges of apple and onion and a sprig of parsley. Rub with orange marmalade and sprinkle with cinnamon. Pierce skins of ducks. Place in a foil-lined pot, add mixture of orange juice and dry Sherry, and cover. Cook at 325 degrees for 2 to 3 hours depending on the size of the ducks, basting occasionally.

Mrs. William A. Clark (Margaret Lasater)

Venison recipes found in Chapter 1. MEXICAN FOOD:

Picadillo
Chili con Carne

Mamie's Tamales

Vegetables

12. VEGETABLES

South Texas is part of the pattern of the western migration, and nowhere else do the cooks show their ancestry as they do in the vegetables. This is largely Southern cooking: greens, peas and beans, squash. Many of these vegetables come from backyard gardens, from the huge farms of the Rio Grande Valley, or from Mexico.

Eggs and Asparagus au Gratin

1 cup buttered bread crumbs
2 tablespoons butter
2 tablespoons flour
½ teaspoon salt
Dash pepper
¼ cup grated onion

1 cup milk
1 cup grated American cheese
4 hard-cooked eggs, sliced
1 15-ounce can asparagus
2 pimientos, cut in strips

Place half of crumbs in greased baking dish. Make white sauce of butter, flour, seasonings, onion, and milk. Add cheese and blend. Place alternate layers of eggs, asparagus, pimiento, and cheese sauce in baking dish. Cover top with remaining crumbs. Bake at 350 degrees for 15 minutes. Serves 4 to 6.

Mrs. Richard Scott Bonner (Karen Olsen)

Crider's Baked Beans

1 large onion, diced
1½ tablespoons Worcestershire sauce
½ teaspoon Louisiana hot sauce
1 teaspoon garlic salt
2 heaping tablespoons brown sugar

1½ teaspoons dry mustard
1 teaspoon vinegar
2 15½-ounce cans pork and beans
Bacon strips
Ham (or bacon) drippings

Cook onion, Worcestershire sauce, hot sauce, garlic salt, dry mustard, brown sugar, and vinegar in a little water until onion is tender. Mix with beans and turn into casserole dish. Strip with bacon; sprinkle with extra brown sugar and ham or bacon drippings. Bake 1 hour at 325 degrees. Serves 6.

Mrs. Joseph P. Mueller (Patty Puig)

Broccoli and Rice Casserole

2 large onions, chopped
2-2/3 tablespoons margarine
1 9-ounce package frozen
   chopped broccoli
2 cups cooked rice
2/3 cup Cheez Whiz brand
   cheese spread

Dry mustard (or Worcestershire
   sauce)
1 can condensed cream of
   mushroom soup
Salt
Pepper

Sauté onion in margarine in skillet. Add broccoli and stir until broccoli is soft. Add rice. Add Cheez Whiz and dry mustard or Worcestershire to taste. Add mushroom soup. Stir. Salt and pepper to taste. Stir again. Pour into baking dish. Refrigerate 12 to 24 hours. Bake at 350 degrees for 30 to 40 minutes. Serves about 8.

Mrs. Robert C. Wood (Helen Heaney)

Broccoli Puff

1 9-ounce package frozen
   chopped broccoli
1 can condensed cream of
   mushroom soup
2 ounces sharp Cheddar cheese,
   grated
1/4 cup milk

1/4 cup mayonnaise
1 egg, beaten
Salt
Pepper
1/4 cup fine dry bread crumbs
1 tablespoon margarine, melted

Cook broccoli. Drain and place in a 1-quart baking dish. Stir together soup and cheese. Gradually add milk, mayonnaise, egg, salt, and pepper. Stir until well blended. Pour over broccoli. Combine bread crumbs and margarine. Sprinkle over the top. Bake at 350 degrees for 45 minutes. Serves 4.

Mrs. Donald P. McClure (Sally Garrett)

Brussels Sprouts and Grapes Casserole

2 10-ounce packages Brussels
   sprouts
¾ cup sour cream
½ cup slivered almonds
2/3 cup drained mushrooms
1 cup seedless white grapes

2 teaspoons salt
1 teaspoon sugar
½ teaspoon pepper
¾ cup grated American cheese
¼ cup chopped pimiento

Cook Brussels sprouts as directed; drain. Add sour cream, almonds, mushrooms, grapes, pimiento, and seasonings. Put in serving dish and sprinkle with cheese and paprika. Heat. Serves 6 to 8.

Mrs. Richard Scott Bonner (Karen Olsen)

Brussels Sprouts Cartier

2 10-ounce packages frozen
   Brussels sprouts
¼ cup butter

1 teaspoon curry powder
¼ teaspoon paprika
Salt

Cook Brussels sprouts until done. Drain well. In a sauce pan, melt butter and add curry powder and paprika. Mix the spices with the butter. Then add the well drained Brussels sprouts and mix until well coated. Salt to taste. Serves 6 to 8.

Mrs. A. Jackson Ashmore (Gay Griffith)

Baked Carrots

6 medium carrots
4 strips bacon
1 small onion, minced
3 tablespoons brown sugar

¼ cup butter, melted
Salt
Pepper

Peel carrots and boil until barely tender; slice diagonally. Fry bacon until crisp and drain well and crumble. Drain off some of the bacon drippings and brown onion in remainder. Add bacon, onion, salt, and pepper to carrots in buttered baking dish. Sprinkle with brown sugar and pour melted butter over all. Bake carrots, covered, for a short while in 400-degree oven, stirring occasionally, until sugar is melted and carrots are glazed. Serves 6.

Mrs. Willard Shuart (Marjorie Parris)

Carrot Casserole

2 cups grated carrots
1 cup margarine
½ cup brown sugar
1 egg
1 tablespoon water
1½ cups flour

½ teaspoon cinnamon
½ teaspoon baking soda
½ teaspoon salt
1 teaspoon baking powder
½ teaspoon nutmeg

Mix together and pour into a greased ring mold or loaf pan. Refrigerate overnight. Take out 30 minutes before baking. Bake at 350 degrees for 1 hour. Serves 8.

Mrs. Ben Donnell (Elinor Drake)

Creamed Celery

4 cups diagonally sliced celery
1 6-ounce can water chestnuts, sliced thin
1 can condensed cream of chicken soup

1 tablespoon pimiento
Toasted bread crumbs
1/3 cup toasted sliced almonds
2 tablespoons butter, melted

Cook celery until tender in lightly salted water. Drain. Add water chestnuts, soup, and pimiento. Top with bread crumbs, almonds, and melted butter. Bake at 350 degrees for 25 to 30 minutes. Serves 6 to 8.

Mrs. Roy Caldwell (Ella Mae McCampbell)

Creamy Corn Scallop*

1 can condensed cream of celery soup
1 tablespoon minced onion
Dash pepper

1 16-ounce can whole kernel corn, drained
1 cup crumbled soda crackers
2 tablespoons margarine

Combine soup, onion, and pepper. In 1-quart casserole, arrange alternate layers of corn, soup mixture, and crackers. Dot with margarine. Bake in 400-degree oven for 25 minutes. Serves 6.

Mrs. Louis Russell (Margaret Keys)

Corn Casserole

2 egg yolks
1 cup cream style corn
½ cup evaporated milk
½ teaspoon seasoned salt
¼ cup butter, melted

3 or 4 crackers, soaked in
  evaporated milk
2 egg whites, beaten stiff
2 tablespoons pimiento or
  chopped bell pepper (optional)

Beat egg yolks in bowl. Add corn, milk, salt, butter, and crackers. Fold in stiffly beaten egg whites. Add pimiento or bell pepper if desired. Pour into greased casserole and bake at 350 degrees for 45 minutes. Serves 6. This light corn dish is not quite a soufflé and therefore does not have to be served immediately.

Mrs. James A. Howry (Joan Priour)

Hauser Corn

3 or 4 green onions, chopped
2 tablespoons margarine
1 12-ounce can niblet corn (or
  fresh corn cut off the cob)

Grated Parmesan cheese
Tomatoes
Evaporated milk

Sauté onion in margarine. In a greased baking dish, put layers of corn, onion, cheese, and tomatoes. Repeat until corn is used. Pour evaporated milk over this layered mixture until half full. Bake 1 hour at 350 degrees. Serves 4.

Mrs. Kenneth McKamey (Hattie Bell Colston)

Elegant Eggplant

2 to 3 eggplants
¼ cup butter
1 egg
5 green onions, chopped
Shortening

4 ounces grated sharp Cheddar
  cheese
½ cup herb-seasoned bread
  crumbs
¼ cup grated Parmesan cheese

Peel eggplants and boil in salted water. Drain and mash, with potato masher, in butter. Blend in egg. Sauté onions. Mix and cover with cheese. Bake in greased casserole, topped with crumbs and Parmesan cheese, at 350 degrees for 30 minutes. Serves 6 to 8.

Mrs. James W. Cottingham (Linda Yancy)

Eggplant Extraordinaire

1 small eggplant	Tomato slices
1 egg	Onion, sliced thin
2 tablespoons milk	Salt
½ cup corn meal	Pepper
½ cup grated Parmesan cheese	1 tablespoon butter, melted

Preheat oven to 325 degrees and grease a cookie sheet. Pare and slice eggplant ½-inch thick. Beat egg and add milk. Dip eggplant slices in egg mixture and then into corn meal and cheese mixture. Place slices of tomato on each slice of eggplant. Season with salt and pepper. Top with thinly sliced onion, sprinkle melted butter over it, and bake until tomato and onion are slightly cooked. Serves 4.

Mrs. James C. Freeman (Cornelia Herz)

Mama's Eggplant

1 medium eggplant	Salt
1 small onion, minced	Pepper
2 ribs celery, minced	Margarine
1/3 bell pepper, minced	Worcestershire sauce
3 to 4 tablespoons cooking oil	1 egg, beaten
1 16-ounce can tomatoes, drained	Corn flakes

Peel and cut eggplant in small pieces. Parboil in salted water until it begins to clear. Lightly sauté onion, celery, and bell pepper in oil. Drain eggplant and add to skillet. Add tomatoes; season with salt, pepper, and Worcestershire sauce; and stir in egg. Pour into casserole, dot with margarine, and cover with crushed corn flakes. Bake uncovered 30 to 40 minutes in 350-degree oven. Serves 6 to 8.

Mrs. Robert H. Montgomery (Anne Attwell)

Bacon Green Beans

6 slices bacon, diced
1/4 cup minced onion
2/3 cup wine vinegar
1 tablespoon dill weed

1 tablespoon salt
1/2 teaspoon pepper
4 8-ounce packages frozen green
  beans (any style)

Fry bacon crisp; add onion and sauté until limp. Stir in vinegar, dill, salt, and pepper. Simmer 20 minutes. Cook beans according to label directions. Toss all together and serve. Serves 12.

Mrs. Earl Sams Lightner (Robin Holmes)

Green Beans en Casserole

2 8-ounce packages French
  style frozen green beans
1 3-ounce can sliced mushrooms
1 can condensed cream of
  chicken soup

1/4 teaspoon salt
1 tablespoon minced onion
1 cup soft bread crumbs
3 tablespoons margarine, melted
1/2 cup grated Cheddar cheese

Preheat oven to 350 degrees. Cook beans according to package directions. Drain mushrooms and reserve 1/4 cup broth. In a bowl, combine soup, broth, salt, minced onion, and mushrooms. Put drained beans in 1 1/2-quart greased casserole and stir in soup mixture. Mix crumbs, margarine, and cheese. Sprinkle over beans. Bake 20 minutes or until top is golden. Serves 8.

Mrs. Joseph W. Holt (Shirley Dawson)

Sweet and Sour Beans

2 16-ounce cans French style
  green beans, drained, juice
  reserved
2 small onions, sliced
1/2 cup sugar
1/2 cup vinegar

1/4 cup bean juice
1/4 cup cooking oil
1 teaspoon monosodium glutamate
Salt
Pepper

Put 1 can of beans on bottom of casserole. Layer onions on top. Add other can of beans. Combine other ingredients and pour over all. Serve hot or cold. Serves 6 to 8.

Mrs. George Taggart (Ethleen Reimers)

Hominy Casserole

1 can condensed cream of
mushroom soup
½ cup half and half (or
hominy juice)
Dash Tabasco brand pepper
sauce
½ to 1 cup grated jalapeño
cheese (optional)

1 4-ounce can green chilies
(split open, rake out seeds,
chop finely), or 1 to 2
chopped jalapeños
3 16-ounce cans yellow hominy,
drained
¼ cup margarine, melted
2 to 4 slices bread, crumbed

Mix all together, except bread crumbs and butter. Top with bread crumbs mixed with melted butter. Bake 45 minutes in 350-degree oven until bubbly and brown. (You may have to run under broiler last few minutes to brown properly.) Use 9-by-13 inch casserole. Serves 8 to 10.

Mrs. Emil Tejml (Sue Rosson)

Ford Hook Lima Bean Dish

2 10-ounce packages frozen
Ford Hook lima beans
2 slices bacon
1 medium onion, chopped
1 cup celery, cut in 1-inch
pieces

½ cup butter
2 tablespoons flour
1 cup milk
Salt
Pepper
Dash nutmeg (optional)

Cook beans with bacon until tender. Sauté onion and celery in butter until tender but not brown. Add flour, milk, salt, pepper, and nutmeg. Add to beans and simmer until ready. Serves 8. Delicious with baked ham.

Mrs. James E. Kirkland (Barbara Kirksey)

Stuffed Mushrooms

2 pounds large fresh
mushrooms
½ cup grated Parmesan cheese
¾ cup dry bread crumbs
½ cup grated onion
2 cloves garlic, pressed

3 tablespoons minced parsley
1 teaspoon salt
½ teaspoon pepper
½ teaspoon oregano
¾ cup olive oil

Wash mushrooms and cut stems from caps. Chop stems and mix with remaining ingredients. Loosely stuff mushroom caps. Grease muffin tins lightly with olive oil. Place a stuffed mushroom cap in each tin. Bake 25 minutes at 350 degrees.

Mrs. Gerald Heinzelmann (Carolyn Jones)

Bill Shuart's Okra and Tomato Dish

6 slices bacon, minced
1 cup chopped onion
2 pounds okra, thinly sliced
¼ cup vinegar
2 16-ounce cans tomatoes
1 8-ounce can tomato sauce

½ rounded teaspoon sugar
3 tablespoons chili powder
Worcestershire sauce
Seasoned salt (to taste)
Salt
Freshly ground pepper

Sauté bacon slightly; do not cook crisp. Add onion. Sauté until onion is clear. Add okra gradually, stirring into onion and bacon. Add vinegar slowly, thoroughly mixing with okra mixture. Add tomatoes and tomato sauce slowly, mixing well. Add sugar. Stir chili powder in, 1 tablespoon at a time. Sprinkle Worcestershire over top. Add salt and pepper. Cook over low heat until okra is tender. It can be frozen. Serves 12.

Mrs. Willard Shuart (Marjorie Parris)

Kalista's Onion Soufflé

6 medium onions
1/2 teaspoon salt
1/4 teaspoon white pepper
Pinch nutmeg
Pinch cayenne pepper

1/4 cup butter
1/4 cup flour
1/3 cup heavy cream
1/3 cup onion water
3 eggs, separated

Peel and cube onions and boil until very soft. Purée and strain the cooked onions, reserving the liquid. Season the onion purée with salt, white and cayenne peppers, and nutmeg and set aside to cool. In a double boiler, cook butter, flour, cream, and onion water as you would cook a white sauce, until it is very thick. Cool slightly. Stir in onion purée and slightly beaten egg yolks.

Preheat oven to 400 degrees. Beat egg whites with a dash of salt until very stiff. Fold egg whites into onion mixture. Pour into buttered soufflé dish, reduce oven temperature to 375 degrees, and bake dish 35 to 40 minutes or until knife inserted in center comes out clean. Serve at once. Serves 6.

Mrs. Lev H. Prichard, III (Ella Wall)

Margaret Walsh's Hopping John

1 cup dried black-eyed peas
4 cups boiling water
1/3 pound salt pork (or fat
    bacon)
1 large onion, sliced
1 sprig celery leaves

1 small bay leaf
2 1/2 teaspoons salt
1/8 teaspoon pepper
1/2 cup rice
2 tablespoons minced parsley

Place peas and 2 cups boiling water in sauce pan. Cover and let stand 2 hours. Do not drain. Cut salt pork or bacon in squares and brown in hot skillet. Sauté onions and celery in this and add to soaked peas, along with bay leaf, salt, and pepper. Add 2 more cups boiling water. Simmer in covered sauce pan until peas are nearly tender. Discard bay leaf. Add the rice and simmer covered until rice is done. More water may be added if necessary. Top with chopped parsley to serve.

Mrs. Sam L. Allen (Phyllis Coffee)

Ranch Style Black-Eyed Peas

4 peeled tomatoes, chopped
1 medium onion, chopped
2 tablespoons water
Salt

Pepper
Picante sauce
Cooked black-eyed peas

Put tomatoes and onion in sauce pan and add water. Add salt, pepper, and *picante* sauce to taste. Cook over medium heat until onion is tender and sauce has cooked down considerably. The sauce may be made as hot or as mild as you like. Add to cooked black-eyed peas and heat together.

Mrs. Lawrence Riley Williams (Ann Reading Parsley)

Potato Puffs*

1 cup cold mashed potatoes
1 cup flour
2 teaspoons baking powder

1/4 cup milk
2 eggs
Salt

Mix together, shape in small balls, and fry in deep fat. Serves 8 to 10.

Mrs. R. Michael Dulaney (Florence "Sue" Williams)

Grated Potato Casserole*

1/2 cup milk
3 eggs
1/2 teaspoon salt
1/8 teaspoon pepper
1 cup cubed sharp Cheddar
  cheese

2 tablespoons butter, softened
1/2 small onion, diced
3 medium potatoes, pared and
  cubed (about 3 cups)

Place ingredients into blender in order listed. Cover and blend on high speed just until all potato is grated. Do not overblend. Pour into greased 10-by-6-inch dish. Bake at 375 degrees for 35 to 40 minutes. This casserole can be prepared ahead of sreving time. Serves 6.

Mrs. A. Jackson Ashmore (Gay Griffith)

Paris Potatoes

5 cups cubed potatoes
2 cups creamed cottage cheese
1 cup sour cream
4 medium green onions and
tops, minced

½ teaspoon garlic salt
Salt (to taste)
Pepper (to taste)
1 cup shredded sharp Cheddar
cheese

Cook potatoes until tender but not soft. Combine all ingredients except cheese. Bake in greased casserole in pre-heated 350-degree oven for 30 minutes. During last 10 minutes, sprinkle cheese on top. Serves 6.

Mrs. Curtis B. Dyer, Jr. (Jerry Bramlet)

Tomato-Scalloped Potatoes

3 cups thinly sliced onion
2 cloves garlic, pressed
2 tablespoons olive oil
¼ cup butter
2 pounds tomatoes
2½ pounds potatoes
1½ teaspoons salt

Freshly ground pepper
2 tablespoons chopped parsley
½ teaspoon basil
¼ teaspoon oregano
1 cup grated Swiss cheese
2 tablespoons grated Parmesan
cheese

Sauté the onion and garlic in olive oil and 2 tablespoons of butter. Peel tomatoes and dice. Peel potatoes and cut them in thin slices. Add tomatoes to onion along with salt, pepper, parsley, basil, and oregano. Mix gently. Butter the bottom and sides of a shallow 3-quart casserole. Preheat oven to 325 degrees. Spoon 1/3 of the tomato-onion mixture on the bottom. Add ½ of the potatoes, ½ cup grated Swiss, and 1 tablespoon Parmesan. Repeat once again. Top with last 1/3 of tomato-onion mixture. Dot surface with 2 tablespoons butter. Bake at 325 degrees for 2 hours or until potatoes are tender. Serves 16.

Mrs. Gerald Heinzelmann (Carolyn Jones)

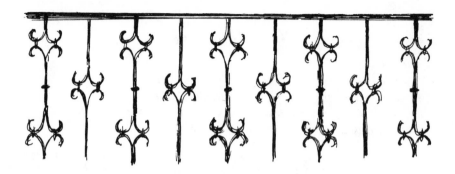

Potatoes Deluxe

1 cup margarine, melted
1 2-pound package frozen hash
  brown potatoes (thawed)
½ cup chopped green onion
1 cup sour cream

2 cups grated sharp Cheddar
  cheese
1 can condensed cream of
  chicken soup
2 cups crushed corn flakes

Melt ½ cup of the margarine in oven-proof baking dish in slow oven. Mix potatoes, onion, cheese, sour cream, and soup and place in casserole. Bake at 350 degrees for 30 minutes. Meanwhile, mix corn flakes with remaining melted butter. Put on top and bake 15 minutes longer. Serves 8 to 10.

Mrs. William Hall Keys (Rose Mary Blackshear)

Sweet Potato Casserole

1 30-ounce can yams
¼ cup butter, melted
½ cup sugar
1 egg

Milk
Nutmeg
½ teaspoon vanilla
Marshmallows

Drain yams and mash thoroughly with butter and sugar. Beat the egg with enough milk to keep it from being stiff. Add nutmeg, to taste, and vanilla. Mix this with yam mixture and put in buttered casserole dish. Top with butter and bake at 350 degrees until bubbly. For the last few minutes, cover the top of casserole with marshmallows and brown. Serves 4.

Mrs. F. William Foran (Sylvia Sarphie)

Louisiana Red Beans and Rice

1 pound red beans
8 ounces ham hock
2 quarts water
3 cups chopped onion
1 bunch green onions, chopped
2 cloves garlic, minced
1 tablespoon salt
1 cup bell pepper, chopped
1 cup parsley, minced

1 teaspoon cayenne pepper
1 teaspoon black pepper
⅛ teaspoon Tabasco brand
* pepper sauce*
1 tablespoon Worcestershire sauce
1 8-ounce can tomato sauce
¼ teaspoon oregano
¼ teaspoon thyme

Soak red beans overnight. (These are not red kidney beans but a smaller distinctive bean.) Put drained beans and ham hock in large soup kettle, add water and salt, bring to boil, and cook slowly for 45 minutes. Add all other ingredients and cook slowly for 2 hours or until beans are tender and liquid thick. Serve over steamed rice. Beans can be frozen. Serves 12.

Mrs. Lev H. Prichard, III (Ella Wall)

Spinach in Pimiento Cream

1 pound spinach
1 tablespoon instant minced
* onion*
1 tablespoon water

2 tablespoons margarine
1 tablespoon chopped pimiento
½ cup half and half
Salt

Wash spinach; discard stems. Cook in small amount of water until done. Drain spinach, pressing out as much liquid as possible. Mince. You should have about 1¼ cups. Measure instant minced onion into water; let stand a few minutes. Sauté onion in margarine. Add pimiento and cream, heating slowly, until mixture is bubbly hot. Add spinach and salt to taste. Double this recipe for 6 hearty servings.

Mrs. James D. Cable (Mary Pearle Garrett)

Spinach Kitty*

2 10-ounce packages chopped spinach	Nutmeg
	1 8-ounce package cream cheese
Salt	Sour cream
Pepper	Paprika

Slightly cook and drain spinach; add salt, pepper, and nutmeg. Mix cream cheese into spinach. Put in buttered casserole. Cover top completely with sour cream and paprika. Bake at 300 degrees for 30 to 45 minutes. Can be prepared ahead and then baked. Serves 6.

Mrs. Tom McArdle (Marion Hall)

Easy Creamed Spinach*

2 10-ounce packages frozen chopped spinach	1 cup onion flavored sour cream
	1 2-ounce can sliced mushrooms

Cook and drain spinach. Mix with other ingredients. Heat and serve. Serves 6.

Mrs. Donald P. McClure (Sally Garrett)

Spinach-Stuffed Mushrooms

12 mushroom caps, about 1½ inches in diameter	Worcestershire sauce
	Pepper
Garlic salt	Lemon juice
1½ cups chopped spinach, cooked slightly	Butter
	Mace
Salt	Grated Parmesan cheese

Arrange mushrooms in buttered baking dish. Sprinkle lightly with garlic salt. Mix drained spinach with Worcestershire sauce, salt, pepper, and lemon juice to taste. Put dab of butter in each mushroom. Heap spinach mixture in each mushroom cap. Sprinkle with mace and Parmesan cheese. Bake at 300 degrees for 30 minutes.

Mrs. Max J. Luther, III (Maxine Jenkins)

Herbed Spinach Bake*

1 10-ounce package frozen
  chopped spinach, thawed
1 cup cooked rice
2 eggs, slightly beaten
1/3 cup milk
1 teaspoon salt

2 tablespoons chopped onion
1 cup grated Cheddar cheese
2 tablespoons melted butter
1/2 teaspoon Worcestershire sauce
1/4 teaspoon rosemary or thyme,
  crushed

Mix ingredients together and pour into buttered baking dish. Bake at 350 degrees for 20 to 25 minutes. Serves 6.

Mrs. W. Richard McCracken (Lucy McFadyen)

Nana's Spinach and Broccoli Casserole

2 10-ounce packages frozen
  chopped spinach
2 10-ounce packages frozen
  chopped broccoli

1 pint sour cream
1 envelope dry onion soup mix
Grated Cheddar cheese

Cook spinach and broccoli together and drain well. Mix the sour cream and onion soup together and stir into the vegetables. Place in 9-by-13-inch greased baking dish and top with grated cheese. Bake at 325 degrees for 40 minutes. Serves 10 to 12.

Mrs. A. Jackson Ashmore (Gay Griffith)

Squash and Things

5 yellow squash
Instant minced onion
6 tablespoons butter
1/3 to 1/2 can Ro-Tel brand
  tomatoes and green chilies

1 cup grated Cheddar cheese
Salt
Pepper
Cracker crumbs

Peel, slice, and cook squash in salted water with instant onion. Drain. Add 4 tablespoons of butter, tomatoes, cheese, salt, and pepper. Stir to blend. Pour into buttered casserole. Melt remaining butter, pour over, and sprinkle with cracker crumbs. Bake at 350 degrees until bubbly, about 30 minutes. Will freeze. Serves 4 to 6.

Mrs. Edwin Prichard, Jr. (Marjorie Reynolds)

Baked Summer Squash

1 pound summer squash
½ cup salted water
5 saltine crackers, broken
1 medium onion, chopped
2 tablespoons margarine, melted
½ cup celery, diced

½ cup grated American cheese
2 tablespoons chopped bell pepper
2 eggs, lightly beaten
1½ cups milk
¼ teaspoon salt
Dash pepper

Cook squash in salted water for 10 minutes or until tender. Drain, mash, and drain again. Add all other ingredients in order listed. Pour into greased 1½-quart baking dish. Bake at 350 degrees for 45 minutes or until knife inserted in center comes out clean. Serve at once. Serves 6.

Mrs. Lev H. Prichard, III (Ella Wall)

Baked Yellow Squash

2 pounds yellow squash
1 tablespoon butter
1 bell pepper, chopped
1 onion, chopped
6 ounces cream cheese (optional)

8 ounces Velveeta brand process cheese, cubed
Salt
Pepper
Cayenne pepper

Cook squash; drain and mash. Sauté bell pepper and onion in butter until clear. Add bell pepper, onion, cheese, and cream cheese, if desired, to squash. Season with salt, pepper, and cayenne pepper. Stir. Bake in buttered casserole 30 minutes at 350 degrees. Serves 6.

Mrs. George Denton (Ann Scott)
Mrs. Terry Hart (Lois Young)

Golden Surprise Acorn Squash

2 acorn squash prepared for
  stuffing*
3 tablespoons chopped bell
  pepper
1 tablespoon minced onion
1 cup fine dry bread crumbs
¼ cup margarine

1 cup grated sharp Cheddar
  cheese
¼ cup heavy cream
½ teaspoon salt
White pepper
½ teaspoon butter

Sauté bell pepper and onion in margarine in skillet until barely tender. Remove squash pulp from shells. Mash and mix in cream, onion and bell pepper mixture, cheese, bread crumbs, salt, and pepper. Pile lightly back into shells and top with butter. Bake at 350 degrees for 15 to 20 minutes. Serves 4.

*Acorn squash may be prepared for stuffing by cutting lengthwise into halves, removing seeds and fibers, and then either parboiling or placing halves upside down in a baking pan with about ¼-inch water and baking at 400 degrees until tender (about 30 to 40 minutes depending on size of squash). Also, if squash are small, turn right side up after about 20 minutes in oven.

Mrs. Max J. Luther, III (Maxine Jenkins)

Stuffed Acorn Squash

2 medium acorn squash,
  prepared as above for stuffing
3 tablespoons melted margarine
2 tablespoons heavy cream
1 tablespoon brown sugar

¼ teaspoon salt
¼ teaspoon pepper
⅛ teaspoon ground ginger
⅛ teaspoon nutmeg
Chopped nuts

Scoop out squash without breaking shells and mash. Blend thoroughly with melted margarine and cream. Add mixture of sugar and seasonings and mix well. Pile lightly into shells. Sprinkle top with chopped nuts. Bake 8 to 10 minutes at 350 degrees, or until squash is reheated and lightly browned. Serves 4.

Mrs. Max J. Luther, III (Maxine Jenkins)

Zucchini Casserole

6 medium zucchini, scrubbed
    and sliced
Garlic salt
Oregano
Coarsely ground pepper

4 ripe tomatoes, peeled and sliced
Chopped onion
Grated Cheddar cheese
Bacon

Cover bottom of baking dish with ½ the sliced zucchini. Sprinkle with garlic salt, pinch of oregano (crushed in palm of hand), and pepper. Place thin tomato slices over squash, then enough chopped onions to cover tomatoes. Repeat these 3 layers, seasoning and all. Top with cheese and several slices of bacon, cut into pieces. Bake at 350 degrees for 30 to 45 minutes. Serves 6.

Mrs. Gerald Heinzelmann (Carolyn Jones)

Stir-Fried Vegetables

3 tablespoons cooking oil
½ teaspoon salt
1½ cups sliced bell pepper

1½ cups onion, sliced
    lengthwise
1½ cups sliced zucchini

Heat oil and salt in skillet over highest heat. Add all vegetables at once. Begin turning vegetables immediately with a pancake turner to avoid burning. Constantly turn and stir vegetables for 3 minutes over highest heat. Serve with soy sauce preferably, or with salt and pepper. Vegetables may be held for 5 minutes over low heat, but don't try to hold them long as they get mushy. They should be crisp. Other vegetable combinations may be used; onion, celery, and fresh bean sprouts are good. Serves 4 to 6.

Mrs. Jack M. Painter (Darlene Downer)

Vegetable recipes found in Chapter 1. MEXICAN FOOD:

Frijoles
Refritos

Kay's Calabaza

Sauces and Condiments

13. SAUCES AND CONDIMENTS

Sauces and condiments are used to add even more taste to the already well-flavored meats and vegetables of South Texas. Preserving is still an honored tradition, and a prized Christmas gift may well be a homemade jelly made from the fruit grown in one's own garden.

Sauces

Beef Marinade Sauce*

1½ cups corn oil
¾ cup soy sauce
½ cup Worcestershire sauce
2 tablespoons dry mustard
1/3 cup wine vinegar

1 tablespoon freshly ground
   pepper
1¼ teaspoons salt
1 teaspoon chopped parsley
1/3 cup lemon juice
1 teaspoon garlic powder

Mix in order given. Stored in a glass jar in refrigerator, sauce will keep indefinitely. For a roast, brisket, or spare ribs, marinate in refrigerator. Turn meat every few hours; marinate for at least 24 hours, or longer. About 5 hours before cooking, remove from refrigerator and let meat warm to room temperature. It is best to cook roast and brisket about an hour on grill and ribs about 20 to 25 minutes on each side. You can save sauce and return to refrigerator to be used again.

Mrs. A. Jackson Ashmore (Gay Griffith)

Barbecue Sauce for a Crowd

6 tablespoons liquid smoke
4 14-ounce bottles catsup
1 pint Worcestershire sauce
1 pint lemon juice
1 tablespoon salt

3 tablespoons chili powder
2 quarts water
3 tablespoons celery seed
4 onions, grated

Mix and bring to a boil. Use on any meat, basting frequently. Makes about 1½ gallons.

Mrs. Richard King, III (Jimmie Rose Harrison)

Barbecue Sauce

2 cups butter
1½ teaspoons salt
1 tablespoon pepper
¼ cup vinegar
¼ cup Worcestershire sauce
½ cup catsup

1 6-ounce can tomato paste
8 drops Tabasco brand pepper
sauce
1 tablespoon garlic salt
1 tablespoon onion salt
1 lemon, sliced

Mix together and heat. Use on any barbecued meat or fowl. Makes about 1 quart.

Mrs. William Hall Keys (Rose Mary Blackshear)

Egan's White Clam Sauce for Spaghetti

½ cup butter
1 large onion, chopped
1 7½-ounce can chopped clams

1 heaping tablespoon Spice
Island brand spaghetti sauce
seasoning

Sauté onion in butter until transparent and barely tender. Add spaghetti sauce seasoning and clams with their juice. Simmer and cook until juice has reduced some. Serve over hot cooked spaghetti and pass grated Parmesan cheese. Serves 2. This may be cooked at the table for company in a chafing dish; however, the onions should be precooked in the kitchen and the sauce finished at the table.

Mrs. Jack M. Painter (Darlene Downer)

Northern Chili Sauce

20 tomatoes
4 bell peppers, minced
6 small onions, minced
1 jalapeño pepper

3 cups light brown sugar
3 cups cider vinegar
3 rounded tablespoons salt
½ teaspoon ground cloves

Combine ingredients. Cook approximately 1 hour 30 minutes, or until thickened. Put in 5 or 6 pint jars and seal. Sauce is especially good with roast beef. Once you've eaten it, there is no substitute.

Mrs. James A. Howry (Joan Priour)

Tomato Sauce

1 28-ounce can tomatoes
1 small onion, chopped
1 tablespoon vinegar

2 tablespoons butter or olive oil
Salt
1 tablespoon sugar

Mix all ingredients and cook until thick, 3 to 4 hours, over low heat. Serve with veal cutlets or chopped steak.

Mrs. William N. Woolsey (Sandra Callaway)

Horseradish Sauce

¼ cup prepared horseradish
1½ tablespoons vinegar
1 tablespoon prepared mustard
½ teaspoon salt

4 drops Worcestershire sauce
Dash cayenne pepper
Dash paprika
½ cup heavy cream, whipped

Combine all ingredients except whipped cream. Fold this mixture into whipped cream. Excellent with hams and ham loaf.

Mrs. Ben Donnell (Elinor Drake)

Blender Hollandaise Sauce*

½ cup butter
3 egg yolks
2 teaspoons lemon juice

¼ teaspoon salt
Few grains cayenne pepper

Heat butter until it bubbles. In blender, put egg yolks, lemon juice, salt, and cayenne. Cover and turn blender on and off immediately. Put blender on low and pour hot butter gradually into mixture. To keep warm, set in pan of warm water. If you pour the butter too fast, hollandaise will be thin.

Mrs. Earl Sams Lightner (Robin Holmes)

Add about 1 tablespoon curry powder to 1 cup mayonnaise, blend well, and refrigerate overnight. This is an excellent dip for raw vegetables or artichoke leaves at a cocktail party and is equally good with congealed seafood and vegetable salads.

Blender Mayonnaise*

2 eggs
1 teaspoon dry mustard
½ teaspoon salt

Pinch cayenne pepper
¼ cup vinegar and/or lemon juice
1½ to 2 cups salad oil

Break eggs into blender; add spices and vinegar. Add ¼ cup oil, cover, and turn on low speed. Immediately uncover blender and very slowly pour the remaining oil in a steady stream. Some days the weather will not permit all of the oil to be absorbed. Makes 1 pint. For a different flavor, add mashed garlic or jalapeño pepper juice.

Mrs. George S. Hawn (Gippie Walling)

Garlic Mayonnaise

2 egg yolks
1 to 2 large cloves garlic,
    pressed
1 teaspoon salt
¼ teaspoon dry mustard

Dash Tabasco brand pepper sauce
2 tablespoons vinegar
¼ cup salad oil
1 tablespoon lemon juice

Beat egg yolks, garlic, salt, mustard, and pepper sauce with mixer on medium speed until lemon-colored. Beat in 1 tablespoon vinegar and add oil drop by drop, beating continuously. Beat in remaining vinegar and lemon juice. Cover and refrigerate. Makes about 1 cup. This can be doubled, but not tripled, successfully. It makes an excellent dip for artichokes.

Mrs. Leslie Giddens (Frances Quinn)

Hot Mustard

1 cup cider vinegar
1 cup dry mustard

2 or 3 egg yolks, beaten
1 cup sugar

Mix vinegar with mustard and refrigerate overnight. The next day, mix egg yolks and sugar in top of double boiler. Add mustard mixture to sugar mixture. Cook over boiling water until thick. Cool. Cover and refrigerate. Excellent with ham or on any meat sandwich. Makes about 1 pint.

Mrs. Gerald Heinzelmann (Carolyn Jones)

Tartar Sauce

1 cup mayonnaise
1½ tablespoons minced onion
1½ tablespoons capers
  (optional)

1½ tablespoons chopped dill
  pickle (or sweet pickle relish)
Salt
Pepper

Mix all ingredients. Chill. Serve with fried, baked, or broiled fish and seafood. Makes 1¼ cups.

Mrs. W. B. Mahan (Martha Painter)

Tartar sauce enhances the flavor of seafood when very little seasoning is used in cooking. The best tartar sauce is made with a good homemade mayonnaise.

Red Sauce*

¾ cup catsup
2 teaspoons Worcestershire
  sauce

2 teaspoons lemon juice
½ teaspoon prepared horseradish
Dash Tabasco brand pepper sauce

Mix all ingredients thoroughly and serve cold with favorite seafood. Makes 1 cup.

Mrs. Lev H. Prichard, III (Ella Wall)

Remoulade Sauce

Yolks of 6 hard-cooked eggs,
  sieved
4 cloves garlic, minced
3 tablespoons dark or creole
  mustard
¼ cup prepared mustard
1 quart mayonnaise
3 tablespoons prepared
  horseradish

2 tablespoons paprika
2 tablespoons Worcestershire
  sauce
¼ cup vinegar
1/3 cup chopped parsley
Dash Tabasco brand pepper sauce
Salt
Pepper

Mix all ingredients well. Refrigerate several hours. If desired, add a little vinegar for a thinner sauce. This makes more than a quart of sauce and will keep well. Serve on shrimp.

Mrs. Gerald Heinzelmann (Carolyn Jones)

Garlic Butter

1 pound butter	Large pinch thyme
8 cloves garlic, pressed	Large pinch summer savory
(or less)	Large pinch marjoram
2 tablespoons grated Parmesan	1 teaspoon chopped parsley
cheese	1 teaspoon chili powder
1 tablespoon paprika	Salt
1 teaspoon onion powder	Pepper

Soften butter and cream in remaining ingredients. Excellent on French or Italian bread.

Mrs. Jack Best (Betty Reno)

Relishes

Apple-Vegetable Relish*

2 cups canned applesauce	½ cup chopped celery
½ cup drained pickle relish	¼ cup chopped onion
½ cup chopped pimiento	

Combine all ingredients and chill well. Makes 3 cups. This is very easy to make and requires no cooking. The ingredients will blend better if refrigerated for a longer time.

Mrs. Lowell Kepp (Betty Ellis)

Pickled Bell Peppers

3 cups water	8 cloves garlic
1½ cups red wine vinegar	8 teaspoons Beau Monde brand
6 tablespoons salt	seasoning
40 chili pequins (or 8 jalapeño	8 to 12 bell peppers
peppers)	

Mix water, vinegar, and salt and bring to a boil. Put 5 *chili pequins* (or 1 jalapeño pepper), 1 clove garlic, and 1 teaspoon Beau Monde seasoning in the bottom of each of 8 half-pint Mason jars. Seed peppers, cut into strips, and stuff into jars. Add the vinegar mix. Seal.

Mr. Forrest C. Allen

Carrot Relish

8 large carrots	2 tablespoons celery seed
8 bell peppers	4 cups sugar
5 large onions	5 cups vinegar
½ cup salt	¼ cup white mustard seed

Grind carrots, bell peppers, and onions. Add salt, tie in cheese cloth, and drain thoroughly. Mix drained vegetables with all other ingredients and pack in sterile jars. Keeps indefinitely.

Mrs. Lev H. Prichard, III (Ella Wall)

Stuffed Pepper Relish

1 8-ounce package cream cheese	½ cup pecans
Vinegar	1 onion, minced
1 large sour (or dill) pickle, chopped	Salt
	1 large or 2 small bell peppers

Cream cheese with just enough vinegar to make it workable. Add pickle, pecans, and onion. Salt to taste. Hollow out pepper and stuff with mixture. Chill overnight. Slice in thin slices and serve as relish. Serves 8.

Mrs. Max J. Luther, III (Maxine Jenkins)

Shawnee Relish

1 16-ounce can sauerkraut, drained well	1 2-ounce jar pimiento, chopped and drained
1 cup coarsely chopped onion	1 cup sugar
½ cup coarsely chopped bell pepper	1 cup cider vinegar

Combine all ingredients in a bowl. Toss until well blended. Store in jar, tightly covered, for at least 24 hours. Delicious when served with ham. You may also add celery and/or carrots, if desired. Makes about 6 cups.

Mrs. Gerald Heinzelmann (Carolyn Jones)

Grace's Pickled Vegetables

5 cups cider vinegar
1 cup water
1 8-ounce bottle olive oil
3 tablespoons salt
5 tablespoons sugar
2 cloves garlic, pressed
1 bay leaf
1 scant teaspoon chili pequins
1 tablespoon mustard seed
2 cups canned whole
   mushrooms, drained
2 4-ounce jars sliced pimientos

5 ribs celery, cut diagonally
2 5¾-ounce cans pitted jumbo
   ripe olives
1 9½-ounce jar pimiento-stuffed
   green olives
1 small cauliflower, broken into
   small flowerettes
12 small white onions
2 bell peppers, cut in ½-inch
   strips
2 cups carrot sticks

Mix vinegar, water, oil, and seasonings in a large sauce pan and bring to a boil. Boil 2 minutes. Set aside to cool. Mix vegetables together in a very large bowl. Pour the vinegar mixture over the vegetables, cover tightly, and refrigerate at least 24 hours. At this time any portion of the mixture not being used immediately may be transferred to 1-quart jars for easier storage. Makes 1 gallon.

Mrs. Robert Dunn (Anne Furman)

Jellies

Grapefruit Jelly

3 cups fresh grapefruit juice
   (white grapefruit if
   available)

1 package dry pectin
4 cups sugar
Red food coloring

Strain grapefruit juice through cheesecloth. Dissolve pectin in juice. Bring to a boil. Add sugar gradually, stirring constantly, and bring to a boil again. Boil hard for 2 minutes. Add color to get right shade of pink. Pour into 6 sterilized half-pint jars and seal. If using pink grapefruit, use less sugar and boil a little longer.

Mrs. Max J. Luther, III (Maxine Jenkins)

Lime Jelly

1 cup fresh lime juice, strained
   (Mexican limes if available)
5 cups water
9 cups suger

2 6-ounce bottles Certo brand
   pectin
Green food coloring

Mix lime juice, water, and sugar thoroughly in large pot or kettle. Bring to a boil and boil hard for 1½ minutes, stirring constantly. Remove from heat and immediately add Certo; stir in thoroughly. Add food coloring. Let cool 5 minutes. Skim with a metal slotted spoon. Pour into 14 sterilized half-pint jars and seal.

To make the jelly pretty, cut slivers of rind from limes with a potato peeler. Place in a small pan, cover with water, add a pinch of baking soda, and boil for about 8 minutes. Drain, rinse, and set aside. Put several strips of the peel into each jar before pouring in jelly.

Mrs. Max J. Luther, III (Maxine Jenkins)

Curried Fruit

1 29-ounce can mixed fruit
1 15¼-ounce can chunk
   pineapple
1 4-ounce jar Maraschino
   cherries

1 large banana, cut in chunks
2 tablespoons corn starch
½ cup brown sugar
1 teaspoon curry powder
2 tablespoons margarine, melted

Drain fruits well. Mix fruits together. Mix remaining ingredients together. Combine the 2 and bake in a 1½-quart casserole at 350 degrees for 40 minutes. Excellent with ham. Serves 6 to 8.

Mrs. Joseph P. Mueller (Patty Puig)

Sauce and condiment recipes found in Chapter 1. MEXICAN FOOD:

Ranchero Sauce
Ann Lively's Ranchero Sauce
Chili Pequin Sauce

Alice Eleanora Nesby's Picante
   Sauce
Jalapeño Jelly

Breads

14. BREADS

A variety of delicious home-baked breads come out of area ovens. Yeast breads and quick breads for dinner, sweet breads and muffins for morning coffees and brunches, pancakes and waffles for extra special breakfasts — all add up to a justly earned reputation these women have for taking pride in what happens in their kitchens.

Yeast Breads

Janet Harte's Whole Wheat Bread

2 packages dry yeast
5 cups warm water
¼ cup granulated sugar
4 teaspoons salt
8 cups hard white flour, sifted

1 cup brown sugar
6 tablespoons shortening
7 to 8 cups stone ground whole
   wheat flour

Soften 2 packages of yeast in 4 cups of warm water with granulated sugar. Add salt and white flour. Beat with a mixer until smooth. Cover and put in warm place until light and bubbly. Stir brown sugar and shortening into 1 cup hot water until dissolved. Cool. Add to yeast mixture. Add 7 to 8 cups whole wheat flour. It is hard to be exact as moisture content of flours varies. Mix and beat until smooth and elastic or turn dough onto a lightly floured board and knead smooth, about 10 minutes.

Place in a greased bowl and turn dough to grease surface. Cover and let rise in warm place until double. Knead down dough. Cut into 4 parts with a knife and shape each portion into a ball.

Cover and let rest for 10 minutes. Roll the dough with a rolling pin into a 10-by-14-inch rectangle, breaking the air bubbles in the surface. Roll the dough toward you and turn the ends to form a loaf. This leaves thin sealed strips to make a smooth uniform crust. Place in greased and floured loaf pans. Lightly grease top of bread, cover, and let rise again until double. Preheat oven to 350 degrees. Bake 50 to 60 minutes. Turn out on a rack to cool. Makes 4 loaves.

Mrs. Edwin A. Durham, II (Kaye Tarrant)

Coffee Can Yeast Bread

1 package dry yeast
½ cup warm water
⅛ teaspoon ground ginger
3 tablespoons sugar
1 cup evaporated milk

1 teaspoon salt
2· tablespoons cooking oil
4 to 4½ cups unsifted flour
Melted butter

Dissolve yeast in water. Add ginger and 1 tablespoon of the sugar. Let stand until bubbly. Stir in remaining sugar, milk, salt, and oil. With mixer on low speed, add flour, 1 cup at a time, beating well. Beat in last cup by hand. Add flour until dough is heavy and stiff but too sticky to knead. Place in well greased 2-pound coffee can. Grease inside of plastic lid and place on can. Let stand in warm place until lid pops off, about 1 to 1½ hours. Preheat oven to 350 degrees. Bake 1 hour in coffee can without lid. Brush rounded top with melted butter after removing from oven. Let cool in can 20 to 30 minutes and remove from can.

Mrs. John Pitcairn (Sue Kowalski)

Dilly Casserole Bread

1 package dry yeast
¼ cup warm water
1 cup cream style cottage
  cheese, heated to lukewarm
1 tablespoon butter
2 tablespoons sugar

1 teaspoon salt
¼ teaspoon baking soda
1 tablespoon instant minced onion
2 teaspoons dill seed
1 egg
2¼ to 2½ cups flour

Soften yeast in water and let stand 10 minutes. Combine in large bowl: cottage cheese; butter; a mixture of sugar, salt, and soda; onion; dill seed; egg; and softened yeast. Beat well to blend. Add flour gradually, beating well after each addition. Cover and let rise in warm place until doubled in size, about 1 hour. Stir dough down and turn into well greased 1½- or 2-quart casserole. Let rise until light, 30 to 40 minutes. Preheat oven to 350 degrees. Bake 35 to 45 minutes. Brush top with butter.

Mrs. A. Jackson Ashmore (Gay Griffith)
Mrs. Albert Slavik (Mary Pat Kelly)
Mrs. R. E. Swetman (Helen Scibienski)

Onion Cake

1 14-ounce box hot roll mix
8 cups thin sliced onion
1/4 cup margarine

3 eggs
2 cups sour cream
1/2 teaspoon salt

Preheat oven to 350 degrees. Prepare roll mix according to package directions. While dough rises, slice onion. Sauté onion in margarine until limp and golden, about 20 minutes. Cool slightly. Beat eggs and sour cream until blended. Add salt and stir sour cream mixture into onions. When dough has doubled, punch down and let it rest 10 minutes. Then roll out to an 11-by-15-inch rectangle. Line a greased 9-by-13-inch pan with dough, turning up 1-inch edge on all sides. Pour onion mixture into the dough-lined pan. Bake 55 minutes or until custard is set. Serves 12.

Mrs. Jack M. Painter (Darlene Downer)

Claudine's Yeast Rolls

2 packages dry yeast
1/2 cup lukewarm water
2 eggs, well beaten
1/3 cup sugar
2 teaspoons salt

1/2 cup cooking oil
1 1/4 cups milk, scalded and cooled
6 1/2 cups flour
Melted butter

Put yeast in water to dissolve. Add yeast, eggs, sugar, salt, and oil to milk. Gradually add 3 cups flour, beating well after each addition. Stir in the rest of the flour, a little at a time, until a good dough stage is reached. The dough should be hard to mix and sticky. Place in a greased bowl. Cover with plastic wrap. Refrigerate until ready to use. Take out of refrigerator and punch the dough down to release the air. Pinch off small bits of dough and roll into a ball. Roll in melted butter. Do this to form 2 more small balls and drop the 3 balls into 1 cup in the muffin pan. Repeat until all the muffin cups are filled. It is not necessary to grease the muffin pan. Let the rolls rise for 1 hour 30 minutes at room temperature. Preheat oven to 350 degrees. Bake for 10 to 15 minutes. You can refrigerate any remaining dough for 2 to 3 days and use.

Mrs. Lawrence Riley Williams (Ann Reading Parsley)

... El pan nuestro de cada dia danosle hoy

Raisin-Nut Bread

¾ cup raisins
Water
1½ cups milk, scalded and
    cooled
2 tablespoons honey
1 tablespoon sugar

2½ teaspoons salt
2 tablespoons cooking oil
1 package dry yeast
4 to 5 cups sifted flour
¾ cup chopped pecans

Add water to raisins to fill 1 cup. Allow to stand overnight to "plump" up the raisins. Mix tepid, scalded milk, honey, sugar, salt, and oil together and stir in the dry yeast. Allow it to "work" for 30 minutes. It should become foamy by that time. Then add 3 cups flour, a cup at a time, until batter is smooth. Continue to add flour until dough thickens, begins to leave the sides of the bowl, and is too stiff to mix with a spoon. Remove dough from bowl, place on a flat surface, and continue to knead in the balance of the flour. Dough should be somewhat elastic and flexible but not very sticky. Add the raisins and work them into the dough. Add the nuts, continuing to knead the dough about 50 times. If dough is too stiff, it won't rise; if too soft, it is full of holes or falls while baking.

Place the dough in a greased bowl and brush the top with oil or margarine. Let it stand, preferably in a warm place, until it doubles in size, then punch it down and knead for another 2 or 3 minutes. Shape it to fit a greased loaf pan. Brush top of loaf with oil or margarine. Let it rise until it comes over the top of the pan. Preheat oven to 375 degrees. Bake bread for 30 minutes; then reduce heat to 325 degrees and bake for another 20 to 30 minutes, or until bread is brown.

Dr. Charles Lewis Concklin

Kolaches

PASTRY:

1 cake yeast	1 egg yolk
¼ cup lukewarm water	½ teaspoon grated lemon rind
1 teaspoon sugar	3 cups sifted flour
¾ cup milk, scalded	3 tablespoons sugar
¼ cup butter	3 tablespoons flour
¼ cup sugar	Butter
½ teaspoon salt	

Soften yeast and sugar in water and let stand 10 minutes. Scald milk and cool to lukewarm. Cream butter; add sugar, salt, egg yolk, and rind; beat until smooth. Stir in softened yeast mixture. Add flour and cooled milk alternately, beating between each mixture to form a smooth, soft dough. Round up dough and put in greased bowl; turn once to bring greased side up. Cover tightly and let rise in warm place 2 hours or until doubled in bulk. Without punching down, turn out on waxed paper and roll ½ inch thick; cut out with 2½- to 3½-inch round biscuit cutter and place on greased cookie sheet. Make wide, deep indentations in each center and fill with desired filling. Let rise 15 minutes. Mix 3 tablespoons sugar and 3 tablespoons flour. Add enough butter to make coarse pellets. Sprinkle this over the top of each kolache before baking. Bake in preheated 400-degree oven for 15 to 20 minutes. Makes 2 dozen.

COTTAGE CHEESE FILLING:

8 ounces dry cottage cheese	1 tablespoon melted butter
2 egg yolks	¼ cup white raisins
2 tablespoons sugar	Dash salt
⅛ teaspoon mace	

Combine all ingredients and mix just enough to blend well.

PRUNE FILLING:

8 ounces pitted prunes	½ teaspoon grated lemon rind
¼ cup sugar	1/16 teaspoon ground cloves
¾ cup water	⅛ teaspoon allspice

Stew prunes with sugar and water. Purée. Add rind, cloves, and allspice to puréed prunes and mix.

APRICOT FILLING:

8 ounces dried apricots	*1 cup water*
1/3 cup sugar	

Wash apricots quickly in cold water. Place in sauce pan with sugar and water. Heat to boiling, reduce heat, cover, and simmer for 45 minutes. When cool, drain off the juice and reserve. Press the fruit through a coarse sieve. If filling is too thick to spread, thin down with reserved juice.

Mrs. Emil Tejml (Sue Rosson)

In recipes that call for sifted flour, always sift the flour before measuring.

Hungarian Coffee Cake

½ cup shortening	*4½ cups flour (or more)*
1 cup milk, scalded	*½ cup margarine (or more)*
½ cup sugar	*¾ cup brown sugar*
2 cakes yeast	*1 teaspoon cinnamon*
2 eggs	*Chopped pecans*
1 teaspoon salt	

Melt shortening in hot milk. Add sugar. Cool to lukewarm, crumble in yeast, and dissolve by stirring. Add eggs, salt, and flour to make workable dough. Let rise until doubled. Punch down and break off bits of dough to form small balls about the size of quarters. Dip balls in melted margarine; then dip balls in a mixture of brown sugar and cinnamon. Be sure balls are well coated with margarine and sugar. Use more margarine or sugar if needed.

Sprinkle an angel food cake pan with chopped pecans. Place a layer of dough balls over pecans. Sprinkle balls with more pecans and add another layer of dough balls. Sprinkle again with chopped pecans. Do not make more than 2 layers of dough balls. Let rise. Preheat oven to 350 degrees. Bake 40 minutes. Cool 10 minutes and turn upside down on serving plate or foil. This makes 2 coffee cakes. Will freeze. Reheat a few minutes in foil to warm.

Mrs. Jack M. Painter (Darlene Downer)

Quick Breads

Hush Puppies

1 large egg, beaten
1 tablespoon Worcestershire
   sauce
1 teaspoon Tabasco brand
   pepper sauce
½ teaspoon soy sauce
1 cup milk
1 tablespoon corn oil
1 cup yellow corn meal

1 cup Masa Harina brand
   instant masa
½ cup flour
2 teaspoons baking powder
1 teaspoon salt
½ teaspoon pepper
1¼ cups minced onion
2 to 3 pickled mild seeded
   jalapeño peppers, minced

Mix egg with all liquid ingredients with an electric mixer until thoroughly blended. Mix dry ingredients and stir into the liquid ingredients. Add chopped onion and jalapeño last. Mix thoroughly. Mixture should be of consistency to pile up on a teaspoon to be pushed into deep oil. Mixture may be adjusted by adding meal or water. Deep fat fry at 350 to 375 degrees until dark brown. Makes about 24. Dough may be frozen. Thaw and add small amount of baking powder 1 hour before frying.

Mrs. Gerald A. Reeves (Lois Arnett)

Corn Bread

1 scant cup corn meal
1½ tablespoons flour
1 heaping tablespoon sugar
2 teaspoons baking powder

1 cup milk (approximately)
1 egg
2½ tablespoons bacon drippings

Preheat oven to 400 degrees. Mix all dry ingredients together. Add milk until mixture is fairly thin; then beat in 1 egg. In a pie pan, small cast iron skillet, or muffin tins, put about 1½ tablespoons bacon drippings and sprinkle corn meal over lightly. Put in oven until drippings are hot and smoking. Remove from oven and put 1 teaspoon hot bacon drippings in the batter; then pour batter into pan. Bake for 12 to 15 minutes. When done, run under broiler to brown top. Serves 6.

Mrs. Gerald Heinzelmann (Carolyn Jones)

Southern Spoon Bread

2 cups corn meal
2½ cups boiling water
1 teaspoon salt
2½ tablespoons cooking oil

1½ cups milk
2 eggs, separated
2 teaspoons baking powder

Preheat oven to 400 degrees. Make a mush of corn meal, water, and salt and allow to cool. Add oil, milk, beaten egg yolks, and baking powder. Fold in stiffly beaten egg whites. Pour into a buttered 8-by-8-inch baking dish and bake 40 minutes. Serves 8 to 10.

Mrs. A. C. Skinner (Marshall Elmore)

Corn Dodgers

1 cup corn meal
¼ cup flour
1 teaspoon salt

1 cup boiling water
Cooking oil

Mix dry ingredients. Add enough boiling water to make a stiff dough. Dip hands in cold water and form into cakes about 3 inches long and ½-inch thick, about the size of the palm of your hand. Fry in hot cooking oil about 1 inch deep until crisp and browned. Serve hot with butter. Serves 6.

Mrs. Jack M. Painter (Darlene Downer)

Corn Fritters

1 8½-ounce can cream style
   corn
1 egg

1 cup flour
1 teaspoon baking powder
1 teaspoon salt

Stir all together; then drop by spoonfuls into deep hot fat. Fry until light brown. Drain and serve. Chopped chives, onions, or parsley may be added. Serves 6.

Mrs. Gerald Heinzelmann (Carolyn Jones)

Mother's Biscuits

1 cup flour	*1 tablespoon sugar*
2 teaspoons baking powder	*1 tablespoon vegetable shortening*
½ teaspoon salt	*Milk*

Mix the dry ingredients together; then cut in the shortening with a pastry blender or 2 knives until well blended. Add milk until the dough is of a sticky consistency. Roll out on a floured board to about a ½- to ¾-inch thickness. Cut with either a biscuit cutter or small glass. Place in a lightly greased pan (touching for soft biscuits, apart for crispy biscuits), dab the top of each biscuit with shortening or butter, and bake 15 minutes in a preheated 400-degree oven.

Recipe can be doubled or tripled successfully. After cutting, place on a cookie sheet and freeze. When frozen solid, remove from the cookie sheet and store in a plastic bag in freezer. When needed, remove desired number and proceed as outlined above.

Mrs. Gerald Heinzelmann (Carolyn Jones)

For easy and delicious bread sticks, quarter sliced hot dog buns, spread cut surfaces with butter, and sprinkle with grated Parmesan cheese. Then heat in a 325-degree oven until browned and crisp.

Poppy Seed Bread

4 eggs	*3 cups flour*
2 cups sugar	*1 5-1/3-ounce can evaporated*
1½ cups oil	*milk*
1 teaspoon salt	*1 box poppy seeds*
1½ teaspoons baking soda	*1 cup chopped nuts (optional)*

Preheat oven to 350 degrees. Beat eggs; then add sugar, oil, salt, baking soda, and flour. Beat well. Add evaporated milk slowly. Add poppy seeds. Add nuts, if desired. Pour into ungreased angel food cake pan or 2 loaf pans and bake for 1 hour 30 minutes. Bread will be brown and crackly on top. Let cool in pan. It is good sliced and spread with cream cheese.

Mrs. Mercer T. Ivey (Jean Nunn)
Mrs. Kenneth McKamey (Hattie Bell Colston)

Ray's Bread

3 cups biscuit mix
3 tablespoons sugar

1 can warm beer

Preheat oven to 375 degrees. Mix together, put in greased loaf pan, and bake 1 hour. Or roll out dough, form into biscuits, and bake 12 to 15 minutes at 400 degrees.

Mrs. George Taggart (Ethleen Reimers)

Popovers

2 eggs
2 cups milk
½ teaspoon salt

1 tablespoon melted butter
2 cups sifted flour

Preheat oven to 425 degrees. Beat eggs slightly. Add milk and salt. Add melted butter and flour. Beat 2 minutes with electric mixer. Pour into 12 sizzling hot, well greased, oven-proof cups or muffin pans. Bake 20 minutes. Serve hot with jam or preserves.

Mrs. F. William Foran (Sylvia Sarphie)

Sweet Breads

Banana Butterscotch Sticky Buns

¾ cup mashed bananas
2 cups biscuit mix
2 tablespoons butter, softened

¾ cup brown sugar
½ cup butter, melted
Chopped pecans

Preheat oven to 450 degrees. Add bananas to biscuit mix. Roll dough on floured board. Knead 10 times and roll into a 16-by-7-inch oblong shape. Spread with 2 tablepsoons butter and sprinkle with ¼ cup brown sugar. Roll at wide side. Cut in 12 slices. In each greased muffin cup, drop 2 teaspoons brown sugar, 2 teaspoons melted butter, and a few pecans. Place rolls, cut side down, in cups. Bake about 10 minutes. Invert pan on tray; remove after 1 minute.

Mrs. Gerald A. Reeves (Lois Arnett)

Danish Coffee Cake

2 cups flour
1 cup butter
2 tablespoons water

1 cup boiling water
1 teaspoon almond flavoring
3 eggs

Mix 1 cup flour, ½ of the butter, and 2 tablespoons water as if making pie crust. Roll or pat on greased cookie sheet. Bring 1 cup water to boil, add remaining butter, and mix until melted. Add almond flavoring and beat in 1 cup flour all at once. Remove from heat and beat the eggs in, 1 at a time. Spread this mixture over the crust. Bake in preheated 350-degree oven for 55 to 60 minutes. Spread with confectioners sugar frosting and chopped nuts after cool. Serves 10 to 12.

Mrs. R. Michael Dulaney (Florence "Sue" Williams)

Banana Bread

½ cup margarine
1 cup sugar
2 eggs, well beaten
4 large bananas
1 teaspoon lemon juice

2 cups sifted flour
3 teaspoons baking powder
½ teaspoon salt
1 cup chopped nuts (optional)

Preheat oven to 350 degrees. Cream margarine and sugar; add beaten eggs. Mash together bananas and lemon juice and add. Sift together flour, salt, and baking powder. Add quickly to banana mixture. Add nuts. Bake in greased loaf pan for 1 hour.

Mrs. Emil Tejml (Sue Rosson)

Cranberry Banana Bread

1 cup margarine
2 cups sugar
6 eggs
5¼ cups flour
2 tablespoons baking powder
1½ teaspoons salt

¾ teaspoon baking soda
3 cups mashed bananas
3 cups cooked cranberries
(cook as for cranberry sauce)
1½ cups nuts (optional)

Preheat oven to 350 degrees. Cream margarine with sugar; add eggs, 1 at a time, beating well after each addition. Sift dry ingredients together. Add flour mixture and then bananas, cranberries, and nuts. Bake 60 to 65 minutes or until done. Cool before slicing. Bakes best in rectangular, deep bread pan. Makes 3 loaves.

Mrs. Joseph P. Mueller (Patty Puig)

 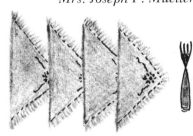

Date Bread

1 cup dates, cut
1½ cups boiling water
1 tablespoon soft butter
1 cup brown sugar
2 egg yolks, beaten
1 teaspoon vanilla

3 cups flour
1 tablespoon baking powder
½ teaspoon baking soda
1 teaspoon salt
1 cup nuts

Preheat oven to 325 degrees. Add water to dates; cool. Cream butter and sugar; add egg yolks and vanilla. Sift flour with baking soda, baking powder, and salt; add to sugar mixtures; add nuts. Pour into well greased loaf pan and bake until done, about 1 hour 30 minutes.

Mrs. Robert L. Browning (Marylee Douglass)

Hattie's Refrigerator Gingerbread Muffins

1 cup sugar	½ teaspoon salt
1 cup shortening	1 cup buttermilk
1 cup dark molasses	1 teaspoon baking soda
4 eggs	1 teaspoon hot water
3½ cups flour	1 teaspoon vanilla
1 teaspoon cinnamon	1 cup raisins
·1 teaspoon ginger	1 cup pecans
1 teaspoon nutmeg	

Cream sugar and shortening. Add molasses and stir. Add beaten eggs. Sift flour with cinnamon, ginger, nutmeg, and salt. Add dry ingredients and buttermilk alternately to the molasses and sugar mixture. Add baking soda that has been dissolved in water and beat. Add vanilla. Stir in raisins and pecans. Put gingerbread dough in greased muffin tins. Bake in preheated 375-degree oven for about 30 minutes. Dough can be kept in refrigerator for several days and used as desired.

Mrs. A. C. Skinner (Marshall Elmore)

An unusual and easy muffin can be made by making your favorite packaged buttermilk pancake mix and pouring it into well greased muffin cups until half full. Then bake at 350 degrees until golden brown, about 20 minutes. Serve with your favorite pancake topping.

Blueberry Muffins

2 cups flour	½ cup butter
1 cup sugar	1 cup milk
2 teaspoons baking powder	1 egg
½ teaspoon salt	1½ cups unsugared blueberries

Have all ingredients at room temperature. Preheat oven to 350 degrees. Sift together flour, sugar, baking powder, and salt. Cream butter until light. Add flour and ½ cup milk. Beat 2 minutes. Add egg and ½ cup milk; beat 2 more minutes. Gently stir in blueberries or use frozen berries that are still frozen and firm. Stir lightly so as not to turn batter blue. Bake in an 8-by-8-by-2-inch pan or in greased and floured muffin tins 30 to 40 minutes.

Mrs. Edwin A. Durham, II (Kaye Tarrant)

Breakfast Foods

Sunday Night Pancakes

2 eggs	1 cup flour
½ cup sugar	1 teaspoon nutmeg
½ cup evaporated milk	½ teaspoon cinnamon
½ cup water	1 teaspoon vanilla
½ teaspoon salt	2½ teaspoons baking powder

Beat eggs; add sugar, milk, and water and beat well. Add remaining ingredients and beat until fluffy. Drop by spoonfuls on lightly greased griddle. Batter will be thin. Turn pancakes when they begin to bubble. They are delicious served with apricot syrup. Serves 4.

Mrs. Robert Dunn (Ann Furman)

Corinne's Hot Cakes

1 egg	1 cup flour
Scant ¼ cup sugar	1 tablespoon baking powder
1/3 cup cooking oil	½ teaspoon salt
¾ cup milk	

Beat egg 5 minutes. Add sugar, oil, and milk. Sift together flour, baking powder, and salt. Add to liquid mixture. Beat well. This may be mixed the night before and will keep in refrigerator for several days. Serves 3 to 4.

Mrs. Kenneth McKamey (Hattie Bell Colston)

Buttermilk Pancakes

1 cup flour	1 cup buttermilk
2 teaspoons baking powder	½ cup water
½ teaspoon baking soda	1 egg
1 tablespoon sugar	2 tablespoons cooking oil

Mix flour, baking powder, baking soda, and sugar. Then add buttermilk, water, egg, and oil. If you have yogurt, you may add a bit. Serves 3 to 4.

Mrs. Jack Best (Betty Reno)

Mother's Waffles

2 cups flour
1 tablespoon baking powder
½ teaspoon salt
2 tablespoons sugar

2 eggs, separated
1½ cups milk
1/3 cup melted shortening

Mix and sift dry ingredients into mixing bowl. Drop in egg yolks and gradually add milk, beating until batter is smooth. Beat in melted shortening. Fold in stiffly beaten egg whites. Bake 3 minutes in waffle iron, which has been preheated 10 minutes. Will make 4 waffles. For variety add to regular waffle mix ¼ teaspoon ginger, ¼ teaspoon cinnamon, and 2 tablespoons molasses.

Mrs. A. Jackson Ashmore (Gay Griffith)

High Protein Cereal

5 cups old fashioned oats
1 cup chopped almonds
1 cup sesame seeds
1 cup sunflower seeds
1 cup shredded coconut

1 cup soy flour
1 cup powdered milk
1 cup wheat germ
1 cup honey
1 cup corn or soy oil

Mix dry ingredients. Beat honey and oil until blended and stir into dry ingredients until thoroughly blended. Spread onto 2 jelly roll trays. Bake at 300 degrees about 30 minutes. Stir once while roasting to keep edges from burning. Cool completely. Store in jars or plastic bags. Serve with milk. Yogurt is an excellent addition. Serves 15 to 20.

Mrs. Edwin A. Durham, II (Kaye Tarrant)

Bread recipes found in Chapter 1. MEXICAN FOOD:

Tortillas de Harina
Jalapeño Corn Bread

Josefinas

Desserts

15. DESSERTS

The sweet conclusion is as important a part of a South Texas gathering as a happy beginning. The desserts often are so good and so varied that they make a party in themselves: informal coffees, formal teas and receptions, or "Drop by for coffee and cake to-morrow."

The freezer of homemade ice cream on the patio in the sum-mer, the school and sorority bake sales, the pie suppers at church all provide excuses for Corpus Christi women to shine.

Pie Crusts

Zwieback or Graham Cracker Crust

2 cups zwieback or graham
   cracker crumbs
½ cup melted butter

1 teaspoon cinnamon
¼ cup sugar

Preheat oven to 375 degrees. Mix together all ingredients. Press into a 9-inch pie pan. Bake for 5 to 7 minutes.

Mrs. William N. Woolsey (Sandra Callaway)

Vanilla Wafer Crust

2 cups vanilla wafer crumbs   5 tablespoons melted butter

Preheat oven to 375 degrees. Mix together all ingredients. Press into a 9-inch pie pan. Bake 5 to 7 minutes.

Mrs. H. William Volk, Jr. (LaVerne Ryan)

Oil Pastry

2/3 cup cooking oil
1/3 cup water

1 teaspoon salt
2 cups flour

Mix all ingredients together with a fork. Divide dough in half and roll each half on waxed paper to size of a pie pan. Invert into pie pan and trim edges. For a baked crust, prick bottom and bake 8 minutes in preheated 475-degree oven. Makes 2 8-inch crusts.

Mrs. Henry Gillespie (Cornelia Martin)

Flaky Pie Crust

3 cups flour
1¼ cups shortening
Dash salt

1 egg
1 tablespoon vinegar
6 tablespoons water

Mix together flour, shortening, and salt. In a separate bowl, beat together remaining ingredients. Combine the 2 mixtures and chill 15 minutes before rolling out. The dough will keep 3 days in the refrigerator or may be frozen. For a baked crust, prick bottom and bake about 10 minutes in a preheated 475-degree oven. Makes 4 to 5 pie crusts.

Mrs. Lev H. Prichard, III (Ella Wall)

Pies

Pineapple Chess Pie

½ cup butter
1½ cups sugar
2 tablespoons flour
3 eggs, beaten

1 cup undrained crushed
pineapple
1 9-inch unbaked pie shell

Preheat oven to 400 degrees. Cream together butter and sugar. Add flour. Slowly fold in beaten eggs and pineapple. Pour into pie shell and bake at 400 degrees for 15 minutes. Reduce temperature to 350 degrees and bake about 35 minutes longer or until center of pie is firm.

Mrs. John F. Cram (Janet Tyson)

Evelyn's Buttermilk Pie

1½ cups sugar
1 tablespoon flour
¼ cup margarine
3 eggs

½ to 1 cup buttermilk
1 teaspoon vanilla
1 pie shell

Preheat oven to 425 degrees. Mix sugar and flour. Mix margarine well with sugar and flour mixture. Add remaining ingredients and pour into an unbaked pie shell. Bake at 425 degrees for 10 minutes. Reduce temperature to 350 degrees and continue to bake for 35 minutes longer.

Mrs. Robert C. Wood (Helen Heaney)

Buttermilk Pecan Pie

½ cup butter
2 cups sugar
2 teaspoons vanilla
3 eggs
3 tablespoons flour

¼ teaspoon salt
1 cup buttermilk
1 9-inch unbaked pie shell
½ cup chopped pecans

Preheat oven to 300 degrees. Cream butter and sugar, adding ½ cup sugar at a time. Blend in vanilla. Add eggs, 1 at a time. Combine flour and salt; add small amount at a time. Add buttermilk. Sprinkle pecans in bottom of pie crust, pour custard mix over the pecans, and bake 1 hour 30 minutes. Best served at room temperature.

Mrs. Lev H. Prichard, III (Ella Wall)

This Buttermilk Pecan Pie was a family recipe often prepared by a career U. S. Navy chef for such dignitaries as the late President Harry S. Truman. Through the years of his military career, the chef refused to share his recipe. Finally, when he retired, he allowed it to be published in a Navy newspaper.

Miss Ella's Pecan Pie

4 eggs, lightly beaten
1 tablespoon flour
1 cup granulated sugar
1 cup light corn syrup
2 tablespoons melted butter
1 teaspoon vanilla extract

½ teaspoon cinnamon
½ teaspoon nutmeg
1 8-inch pie shell
Pinch salt
½ to 1 cup pecans

Preheat oven to 325 degrees. Beat eggs. Stir flour into eggs. Add sugar, syrup, butter, vanilla, cinnamon, and nutmeg. Sprinkle salt on pie crust. Pour custard into crust, add pecans, and bake 1 hour.

Mrs. Frank N. McMillan (Mabel Hall)

Mama's Chocolate Pie

1 cup sugar
Pinch salt
½ cup flour
1/3 cup cocoa
2 cups milk

3 eggs
1 teaspoon vanilla
2 tablespoons butter (optional)
Baked pie shell
Whipped cream

Sift sugar, salt, flour, and cocoa together into a sauce pan. In a separate bowl, beat eggs and milk together to mix well. Add the milk mixture a little at a time to the dry ingredients, stirring to blend. Cook over medium heat until very thick. Remove from heat and stir in vanilla and butter if desired. Pour into a cooled pie shell. Top with whipped cream.

Mrs. Earl Sams Lightner (Robin Holmes)

Mother's Pumpkin Pie

4 medium eggs
2 cups pumpkin
¾ cup brown sugar
¼ cup granulated sugar
½ teaspoon salt (or more)
1 teaspoon cinnamon
½ teaspoon nutmeg

½ teaspoon ginger
⅛ teaspoon ground cloves
1 cup evaporated milk
½ cup whole milk
¼ cup heavy cream
½ cup ground pecans
1 9-inch pie shell

Preheat oven to 350 degrees. Beat eggs. Add pumpkin, sugar, seasonings, and milk and blend. Stir in pecans. Pour into pie shell and bake 45 to 55 minutes or until custard is set. Serve chilled with whipped cream on top if desired.

Mrs. John Chapman (Louise Green)

To make a pie from fresh pumpkin, cut top off pumpkin, scrape out seeds and stringy material, and discard. Scrape sides of pumpkin until you have about 4 cups of pumpkin. Cover with water and simmer uncovered for 1 hour. Drain well.

Sour Cream Raisin Pie

1 cup brown sugar
2 tablespoons flour
½ teaspoon nutmeg
½ teaspoon cinnamon
¼ teaspoon salt

1 cup sour cream
3 eggs, separated
1 cup raisins
6 tablespoons granulated sugar
1 9-inch baked pie shell

Preheat oven to 350 degrees. Combine brown sugar, flour, spices, salt, and sour cream in top of a double boiler and cook until thick. Beat egg yolks in a separate dish. Blend a little of the hot mixture into the eggs; then add egg mixture to double boiler, stirring constantly. Cook for 5 minutes and add raisins. Cool. Place in baked pie shell and cover with a meringue made by beating egg whites and granulated sugar until stiff. Brown in oven about 12 minutes.

Mrs. J. Rogers Rainey, Jr. (Kathleen Lutner)

Banana Pie

3 cups milk
1 cup sugar
4½ tablespoons corn starch
½ teaspoon salt
3 egg yolks, lightly beaten

1 tablespoon butter
2 teaspoons vanilla
1 9-inch baked pie shell
1 cup sliced bananas

Heat milk over medium heat. Meanwhile, combine sugar, corn starch, and salt. Gradually stir into the milk until mixture is smooth and comes to a boil. Boil 1 minute, stirring constantly. Remove from heat; stir in ½ the egg yolks. Pour mixture into remaining egg yolks; mix well. Return to heat and boil 1 minute, stirring constantly. Remove from heat; stir in butter and vanilla. Pour into 9-inch pie shell filled with sliced bananas. Chill until firm. Spread with topping.

TOPPING:

1 cup heavy cream
2 tablespoons sugar

½ teaspoon vanilla

Beat cream at high speed until it begins to thicken. Gradually add sugar. Add vanilla. Beat until very stiff.

Mrs. Jerry E. Fischer (Alice Ann Peters)

Fresh Strawberry Pie

1 cup water
2 cups strawberries
1 cup sugar

3 tablespoons corn starch
1 baked pie shell
Sweetened whipped cream

Bring 1 cup strawberries and ¾ cup water to a boil. Sift together sugar and corn starch and add to strawberries. Add remaining ¼ cup water. Cook until thick. Add red food coloring if desired. Put 1 cup whole strawberries in bottom of the pie shell. Pour the cooked mixture over the strawberries. Chill. Serve topped with sweetened whipped cream.

Mrs. Terry Hart (Lois Young)

Apple Pie Superb

Dough for double pie crust
6 cups pared, thin sliced
  tart apples
¾ cup granulated sugar
¼ cup brown sugar
2 tablespoons flour

½ teaspoon cinnamon
¼ teaspoon ground nutmeg
⅛ teaspoon salt
¼ cup heavy cream
3 tablespoons butter

Preheat oven to 400 degrees. Line a pie pan with half the pastry. Add 1/3 the apples. Mix sugar, flour, cinnamon, nutmeg, and salt together. Sprinkle 1/3 over apples. Repeat twice. Pour cream into center of pie. Dot with butter. Cover with a top crust, slit for steam, brush with milk, and sprinkle with sugar. Bake 1 hour.

Mrs. Donald Everett Jackson (Patricia Ann Alexander)

Apple Cobbler

6 to 8 apples
2/3 cup granulated sugar
Margarine
Cinnamon
½ cup shortening

¾ cup brown sugar
2 to 3 tablespoons water
1 cup flour
½ teaspoon salt

Preheat oven to 350 degrees. Pare and slice apples. Spread half the apples in a 9-by-13-inch baking pan. Sprinkle with half the granulated sugar. Dot with margarine. Dust with cinnamon. Repeat. Blend the brown sugar and shortening. If apples are dry, add water. Add salt to flour and cut into the shortening to make a crust. Roll out the crust; transfer to top of apples. Bake 40 to 45 minutes. Serve with whipped cream or ice cream if desired.

Mrs. Robert H. Montgomery (Anne Attwell)

Cherry Cobbler

2/3 cup sugar (or less)
1 tablespoon corn starch
Dash salt
1 16-ounce can red sour
   pitted cherries

¼ teaspoon almond extract
Red food coloring
6 tablespoons biscuit mix
Dash cinnamon
2 tablespoons melted butter

Preheat oven to 425 degrees. Mix scant ½ cup sugar, corn starch, and salt in sauce pan. Add liquid from canned cherries and cook, stirring, until boiling and thickened. Add cherries, almond extract, and food coloring. Stir carefully and pour into 8-inch pie pan. Combine biscuit mix, remaining sugar, cinnamon, and butter. Sprinkle topping over cherries. Bake 20 to 25 minutes.

Mrs. Dudley A. Chatham (Melba Welsh)

Pear Mincemeat for Pie

7 pounds firm pears, ground	1 teaspoon cinnamon
2½ pounds sugar	1 teaspoon allspice
2 cups butter	1 teaspoon ground cloves
1 cup vinegar	1 teaspoon nutmeg
1 15-ounce box seeded raisins	1 teaspoon salt
Grated peel of 1 lemon	

Boil all ingredients for 1 hour. Seal in hot jars. Makes 8 pints. To make pie, spread 3 cups mincemeat in an unbaked 8-inch pie shell. Cover with a second crust, vent for steam, and bake in preheated 450-degree oven about 30 minutes.

Mrs. Richard King, III (Jimmie Rose Harrison)

Lilia's Strawberry Cheese Cake

2 cups flour	2 8-ounce packages cream cheese
½ cup brown sugar	1 cup confectioners sugar
1 cup margarine, melted	3 10-ounce boxes frozen
1 cup chopped pecans	strawberries
2 2-ounce envelopes whipped	3 tablespoons corn starch
topping mix	½ cup granulated sugar

Preheat oven to 475 degrees. Mix flour, brown sugar, margarine, and chopped pecans to make pastry dough. Pat into 2 8-inch pie pans. Bake 5 to 10 minutes or until lightly browned. Cool pie shell; prepare whipped topping mix according to package instructions and mix with cream cheese and confectioners sugar. Spread in bottom of pie shells. Mix strawberries, corn starch, and sugar and boil over medium heat until mixture gets glossy and thick. Pour over cream cheese mixture. Refrigerate pies before serving.

Mrs. Lawrence Riley Williams (Ann Reading Parsley)

Cheese Cake

2/3 cup zwieback crumbs
3 8-ounce packages cream
    cheese
4 egg whites

1 cup + 2 tablespoons sugar
1½ teaspoons vanilla
1 pint sour cream
2 tablespoons sugar

Preheat oven to 350 degrees. Butter a 9-inch spring mold pan and sprinkle with zwieback crumbs. Allow cream cheese to soften; then cream well. Beat egg whites until stiff; blend in 1 cup sugar. Combine cream cheese, egg whites, and 1 teaspoon vanilla. Pour into pan and bake 25 minutes. Remove from oven and raise oven temperature to 475 degrees. Mix sour cream with 2 tablespoons sugar and ½ teaspoon vanilla and spread over top of cheese cake. Return to oven for 5 minutes. Allow cheese cake to set for at least 12 hours before serving.

Mrs. Robert L. Browning (Marylee Douglass)

Mincemeat Cheese Pie

4 3-ounce packages cream
    cheese
2 eggs
½ cup + 2 tablespoons sugar
Grated peel of 1 lemon
1 tablespoon lemon juice

2 cups mincemeat
Baked 9-inch pastry shell
1 cup sour cream
½ teaspoon vanilla
Twisted lemon slices

Preheat oven to 375 degrees. Beat together cream cheese, eggs, ½ cup sugar, grated lemon peel, and lemon juice with an electric mixer until very smooth. Spoon mincemeat into the baked pastry shell. Pour the cream cheese mixture over the mincemeat. Bake 20 minutes. Mix together sour cream, 2 tablespoons sugar, and vanilla. When pie has baked 20 minutes, remove from the oven and spread sour cream mixture evenly over top. Return to oven for 10 minutes. Then chill pie before cutting and serving. Garnish with twisted lemon slices.

Mrs. Lowell Kepp (Betty Ellis)

Black Bottom Pie

2 cups scalded milk	1 tablespoon unflavored gelatin
1 cup sugar	2 tablespoons water
4 egg yolks, beaten	1 tablespoon dark rum
4 teaspoons corn starch	3 egg whites
2 squares unsweetened chocolate	1/4 teaspoon cream of tartar
1 teaspoon vanilla	1 cup heavy cream
1 9-inch vanilla wafer pie shell	2 tablespoons confectioners sugar

Heat milk and ½ cup sugar in the top of a double boiler. Pour a small amount of the hot liquid into the egg yolks. Stir the egg yolk mixture and add to the milk mixture. Add corn starch. Cook until custard coats a spoon, or about 20 minutes. Measure out 1½ cups custard. Grate 1½ squares of chocolate. Add chocolate and vanilla to the custard. Cool. Pour the chocolate custard into the pie shell and chill. Dissolve gelatin in water and add to remaining custard, which must be hot. Cool; add rum. Beat egg whites until frothy; add cream of tartar and continue to beat until whites are very stiff. Gradually add remaining ½ cup of sugar. Gently fold together the egg whites and custard. Pour over the chocolate custard in the pie shell and chill. Whip cream with confectioners sugar and spread on top of pie. Grate remaining chocolate and sprinkle on the top.

Mrs. H. William Volk, Jr. (LaVerne Ryan)

Louise's Rum Pie

3 egg yolks	1 cup heavy cream
1/2 cup sugar	1/4 cup dark rum (or less)
1/2 tablespoon gelatin	1 8-inch graham cracker crust*
1/2 cup cold water	Grated unsweetened chocolate

Beat egg yolks until light in color. Add sugar slowly, while continuing to beat. Soak gelatin in cold water; bring to a boil over low heat. Add to sugar and egg mixture, stirring briskly. Whip the cream and fold into egg mixture. Add rum. Pour into pie crust. Cool; sprinkle chocolate over the top.

*Add ⅛ teaspoon nutmeg and a smaller amount of cinnamon to the crust for extra flavor.

Mrs. W. Richard McCracken (Lucy McFadyen)

Millionaire Pie

1¼ cups confectioners sugar
¼ cup margarine
1 egg
Vanilla
1 9-inch baked pie shell

1½ cups heavy cream
¾ teaspoon unflavored gelatin
1½ cups crushed pineapple,
   drained
½ cup chopped pecans

Cream 1 cup sugar, margarine, egg, and vanilla with an electric mixer, using high speed, for 10 minutes. Spread evenly over the baked pie shell. Refrigerate. Whip cream, ¼ cup sugar, and gelatin until firm. Fold pineapple and nuts into whipped cream mixture. Spread pineapple mixture into cooled pie shell. Refrigerate several hours before serving.

Mrs. Charles W. Thomasson (Willa Parker)

Pineapple-Cherry Pie*

1 cup heavy cream
1 14-ounce can condensed milk
¼ cup sugar
Juice of 1 lemon
1 20-ounce can crushed
   pineapple, drained

1 16-ounce can red sour pitted
   cherries, drained
1 cup chopped nuts
2 graham cracker pie crusts

Whip the cream as thick as possible. Add condensed milk, sugar, and lemon juice. Then add pineapple, cherries, and nuts. Place in graham cracker crusts and freeze. Serve chilled. Keeps in freezer indefinitely.

Mrs. A. Jackson Ashmore (Gay Griffith)

Pecan Meringue Pie

3 to 4 egg whites
1 cup sugar
22 crushed Ritz brand crackers
1 cup chopped pecans

1 teaspoon vanilla
1 1/4 teaspoons almond extract
(optional)

Preheat oven to 300 degrees. Grease a glass pie pan. Beat egg whites until peaks begin to form; gradually add sugar and continue to beat until very stiff. Fold in remaining ingredients. Spread in pie pan. Bake 45 minutes. Serve the pie with whipped cream or ice cream if desired.

Mrs. John F. Cram (Janet Tyson)
Mrs. Henry Gillespie (Cornelia Martin)
Miss Coleene McCracken

Butterscotch Brownie Pie

1 cup graham cracker crumbs
1 cup chopped nuts
4 egg whites
1/4 teaspoon salt

1 cup sugar
1 teaspoon vanilla
1 cup heavy cream, whipped

Preheat oven to 350 degrees. Combine graham cracker crumbs and nuts. Beat egg whites until foamy. Add salt; add sugar gradually, beating until stiff peaks form. Fold in flavoring. Then fold egg white mixture into crumb mixture. Pour into greased 9-inch pie pan. Bake 30 minutes. Top with sweetened whipped cream.

Mrs. Gerald Heinzelmann (Carolyn Jones)

Brownie Pie*

1/2 cup butter
1 cup sugar
2 eggs

1/2 cup flour
3 tablespoons cocoa
1 teaspoon vanilla

Preheat oven to 350 degrees. Beat and blend all ingredients at once. Spread in 10-inch greased pie pan and bake for 25 minutes. Serve alone or with ice cream.

Mrs. Robert L. Browning (Marylee Douglass)

Cakes

Italian Cream Cake

½ cup margarine
½ cup vegetable shortening
2 cups sugar
5 eggs, separated
1 teaspoon baking soda
1 cup buttermilk

2 cups sifted flour
1 3½-ounce can angel flake coconut
1 cup chopped pecans
1 teaspoon vanilla

Preheat oven to 350 degrees. Grease and flour 3 9-inch layer pans. Cream margarine and shortening; add sugar gradually. Add egg yolks and beat well. Add soda to buttermilk; then add flour and milk alternately to cake batter. Add pecans and coconut. Fold in well beaten egg whites. Bake for 25 minutes. Ice with Cream Cheese Frosting.

Mrs. George Taggart (Ethleen Reimers)

1, 2, 3, 4 Cake

3 cups sifted cake flour
1 tablespoon baking powder
½ teaspoon salt
1 cup butter

2 cups sugar
4 eggs, separated
1 cup milk
1 teaspoon vanilla

Preheat oven to 350 degrees. Grease and flour 3 9-inch round pans, or line bottoms of greased pans with greased brown paper. Sift together the flour, baking powder, and salt. Cream butter and sugar well. Add egg yolks; beat. Add flour alternately with milk, beginning and ending with flour. Fold in stiffly beaten egg whites and vanilla. Bake for 25 to 30 minutes. Use Pineapple Filling between layers and frost with Boiled White Icing.

Mrs. Kenneth McKamey (Hattie Bell Colston)

Colston Chocolate Cake

½ cup margarine	1 teaspoon baking powder
1½ cups sugar	1 teaspoon cinnamon
2 egg yolks	⅛ teaspoon salt
2 squares bitter chocolate	1 teaspoon baking soda
1 cup boiling water	Dash ground cloves
½ cup buttermilk	1 teaspoon vanilla
2 cups cake flour	2 egg whites

Preheat oven to 350 degrees. Grease and flour an 8-by-12-inch glass cake pan. Cream margarine and sugar. Add egg yolks and beat well. Dissolve chocolate in boiling water; cool and add to batter. Add buttermilk alternately with sifted dry ingredients. Add vanilla. Fold in stiffly beaten egg whites. Bake for 30 minutes.

Mrs. Kenneth McKamey (Hattie Bell Colston)

Chocolate Chip Cake

1 cup boiling water	2 teaspoons cocoa
1 8-ounce package pitted dates	Pinch salt
1 teaspoon baking soda	1 teaspoon vanilla
1 cup butter	½ cup chopped pecans
1 cup sugar	1 6-ounce package chocolate chips
2 eggs	Confectioners sugar
1¾ cups flour	

Preheat oven to 350 degrees. Grease and flour an 8-by-12-inch pan. Pour water over chopped dates; add soda and set aside. Cream butter and sugar. Blend in eggs, 1 at a time. Sift together flour, cocoa, and salt. Add to the sugar, butter, and egg mixture. Add vanilla and the date mixture and pour batter in greased pan. Sprinkle nuts and chocolate chips over batter. Bake 30 minutes. When cake is cool, dust with confectioners sugar. This cake will stay moist in an air-tight container for about a week.

Mrs. Joe P. Nelson (Harriet Hornish)

Fresh Apple Cake

1 cup corn oil
1¾ cups sugar
2 eggs
2 cups peeled and grated apples
1 teaspoon baking soda

½ teaspoon salt
2 cups sifted flour
1 tablespoon vanilla
1 cup chopped pecans

Preheat oven to 350 degrees. Grease and flour a tube pan. Cream oil and sugar in electric mixer. Keep mixer on and add eggs. Dredge apples in mixture of soda, salt, and flour. Add to batter; continue mixing. Add vanilla and nuts. Bake in bottom of oven for 1 hour.

Mrs. Jerry E. Fischer (Alice Ann Peters)

Carrot Cake

2 cups flour
2 cups sugar
2 teaspoons baking soda
1 teaspoon salt

2 teaspoons cinnamon
1 cup cooking oil
4 eggs
3 cups finely grated carrots

Preheat oven to 350 degrees. Grease and flour 3 9-inch layer pans. Sift flour, sugar, soda, salt, and cinnamon together. Add oil; stir. Add eggs, 1 at a time, mixing well after each addition. Add 3 cups carrots. Bake for 30 minutes. Frost with Cream Cheese Frosting, substituting raisins for chopped pecans if desired.

Mrs. Earl Sams Lightner (Robin Holmes)

Prune Cake

2 cups sugar
1 cup corn oil
1 cup buttermilk
3 eggs
2 cups flour

1 teaspoon cinnamon
1 teaspoon soda
1 teaspoon salt
1 cup cooked prunes, cut up
1 cup chopped pecans

Preheat oven to 350 degrees. Generously grease and flour a tube pan. Mix ingredients in order listed, sifting flour, cinnamon, soda, and salt together into the batter. Bake 1 hour. Plum jam may be substituted for the prunes.

Mrs. Mercer T. Ivey (Jean Nunn)

Fig Cake

2 cups flour
1 teaspoon baking soda
1 teaspoon salt
1 cup cooking oil
1½ cups sugar
3 eggs
1 cup buttermilk

1 cup chopped pecans
1 cup fig preserves
1 teaspoon vanilla
1 teaspoon cinnamon
1 teaspoon nutmeg
1 teaspoon ground cloves

Preheat oven to 325 degrees. Grease and flour a 9-by-13-inch pan. Sift together flour, soda, and salt. Add the oil and beat well. Add remaining ingredients; mix well. Bake for 45 minutes. Glaze while cake is still warm.

GLAZE:

1 cup sugar
½ cup margarine
1 teaspoon light corn syrup

1 teaspoon vanilla
½ cup buttermilk
½ teaspoon baking soda

Mix all ingredients well and boil for 3 minutes.

Mrs. James C. Freeman (Cornelia Herz)

Sour Cream Cake

1¼ cups sugar
½ cup butter
2 eggs
1 cup sour cream
2 cups sifted cake flour

1 teaspoon baking powder
1 teaspoon baking soda
1 teaspoon vanilla
½ teaspoon cinnamon
½ cup chopped nuts

Preheat oven to 350 degrees. Grease and flour a tube pan. Cream butter and 1 cup sugar. Add eggs and sour cream; beat until smooth. Sift together dry ingredients and add to egg mixture. Add vanilla; blend thoroughly. Pour half of the batter into the pan. Make a topping with remaining sugar, cinnamon, and nuts. Sprinkle half the topping mixture on the batter. Add the remaining batter and sprinkle with the remainder of the topping mixture. Bake for 35 minutes.

Mrs. Lowell Kepp (Betty Ellis)

Sour Cream Pound Cake

1 cup butter	1½ teaspoons vanila
3 cups sugar	1 cup sour cream
¼ teaspoon baking soda	6 eggs
½ teaspoon lemon extract	3 cups sifted flour

Preheat oven to 325 degrees. Grease and flour a Bundt pan. Cream butter and gradually beat in sugar. Add and beat in soda, lemon extract, and vanilla. Add sour cream and mix well. Beat in eggs, 2 at a time. Blend in flour, 1 cup at a time, beating well after each addition. Bake 1 hour 30 to 45 minutes.

Mrs. Kenneth McKamey (Hattie Bell Colston)

Slice a pound cake in strips 3 inches long and ¾-inch wide. Spread with soft butter, roll in a mixture of 1 cup sugar and 6 tablespoons cinnamon, and bake at 450 degrees for 5 minutes.

Lemon Pound Cake

1 cup vegetable shortening	3 cups sifted flour
3 cups sugar	¼ teaspoon salt
6 large eggs	¼ teaspoon baking soda
1 teaspoon vanilla extract	1 cup buttermilk
1 teaspoon lemon extract	1 cup sifted confectioners sugar
Grated lemon rind (optional)	Juice of 2 lemons

Have all ingredients at room temperature. Preheat oven to 350 degrees. Grease and flour a 10-inch tube or Bundt pan. Cream shortening with an electric mixer; add sugar gradually. Add eggs, 1 at a time, beating thoroughly after each addition. Add vanilla and lemon flavorings. Sift together flour, salt, and soda; and with mixer on low speed, add alternately with buttermilk, beginning and ending with flour. Bake at 350 degrees for 15 minutes; reduce the oven temperature to 325 degrees and bake 1 hour. While cake is baking, mix confectioners sugar and strained lemon juice to make a sauce. Spoon the sauce over the cake as soon as cake is done. Put a plate over the cake and wrap the cake in towels and let steam for 4 hours; then invert on a cake plate. The cake will still be hot.

Mrs. Robert Dunn (Anne Furman)

Old Fashioned Pound Cake*

1-2/3 cups sugar
1 cup shortening
2 scant cups flour

5 eggs
Dash salt
1 teaspoon vanilla

Preheat oven to 325 degrees. Grease and flour a Bundt pan. Cream shortening and sugar. Add eggs, flour, salt, and vanilla. Mix well. Bake 45 minutes to 1 hour. Cool in pan 10 or 15 minutes.

Mrs. Howard Lipstreu (Betty Grett)

Sour Cream Coffee Cake

1 cup butter
1 cup granulated sugar
1 cup brown sugar
2 cups flour
2 eggs, beaten

1 cup sour cream
1 teaspoon baking soda
2 teaspoons cinnamon
3/8 teaspoon salt
2 cups pecans

Preheat oven to 325 degrees. Cut butter into sugar and flour until it resembles cornmeal. Reserve 1 cup of mixture for topping. Add eggs, sour cream, soda, 1 teaspoon cinnamon, and 1/4 teaspoon salt to remaining flour mixture. Beat well. Cover bottom of 2 8-by-8-inch pans with pecans. Pour batter over pecans. Mix reserved flour mixture, 1 teaspoon cinnamon, and 1/8 teaspoon salt to make a topping. Sprinkle over the cake batter. Bake 1 hour.

Mrs. Floyd W. Brown (Janet Gowdey)

The Guaranty Cake

1 cup margarine
2 cups sugar
6 eggs
1 12-ounce box vanilla wafers

1/2 cup milk
1 7-ounce package coconut
1 cup chopped pecans

Preheat oven to 275 degrees. Grease and flour a large tube pan. Cream margarine and sugar. Add eggs, 1 at a time, beating well after each addition. Crush vanilla wafers and add alternately with milk. Add coconut and nuts. Bake about 2 hours.

Miss Nancy Bowen

Oatmeal Cake

1 cup quick oats
1-1/3 cups boiling water
½ cup margarine
½ cup sugar
1 cup brown sugar
2 eggs

1 teaspoon vanilla
1-1/3 cups flour
½ teaspoon salt
½ teaspoon nutmeg
1 teaspoon baking soda
1 teaspoon cinnamon

Preheat oven to 350 degrees. Grease and flour a 9-by-11-inch cake pan. Pour boiling water over oatmeal and stir. Cover and let stand 20 minutes or until cool. Cream margarine, sugars, eggs, and vanilla. Sift flour, salt, nutmeg, soda, and cinnamon together and add alternately with oatmeal to sugar and margarine mixture. Bake for about 30 minutes. Frost in the pan with Coconut Frosting.

Mrs. A. Jackson Ashmore (Gay Griffith)

Frances' Fruit Cake

8 ounces candied cherries
8 ounces candied pineapple
2 14-ounce boxes pitted dates
1 quart chopped pecans
1 cup sugar

1 cup cake flour
2 teaspoons baking powder
1 teaspoon vanilla
6 eggs, beaten

Preheat oven to 250 degrees. Grease and flour a heavy Bundt or loaf pan. Cut all fruit into coarse pieces. Mix fruit and nuts together with your hands in a very large mixing bowl. Sift sugar, flour, and baking powder together into the bowl. Mix well by hand. Add vanilla to the eggs; add to mixing bowl. Again, mix well by hand. Pack mixture lightly into pan. Bake for about 2 hours. Cool thoroughly. Sherry, bourbon, or brandy may be poured over the cake before storing. The cake can be made early and stored wrapped in heavy foil, or it can be frozen. Slice very thin to serve.

Mrs. Charles M. Forney (Joyce Smith)

Uncle John R.'s Norwegian Fruit Cake

2 cups sugar	1 pound candied cherries
2 cups butter	4 ounces candied pineapple
6 eggs, separated	1 pound white raisins
3 cups sifted cake flour	1 pound pecans
2 tablespoons lemon extract	1 pound walnuts (optional)

Preheat oven to 250 degrees. Grease and flour a tube pan. In a very large mixing bowl, cream softened butter and add sugar. Beat well and add beaten egg yolks. Continue creaming and beating. Add 2 cups flour; add lemon extract. Cut fruit and nuts, dredge with 1 cup flour, and add to batter. When mixed well, fold in stiffly beaten egg whites. Bake 2 hours 30 minutes.

Mrs. Frank N. McMillan (Mabel Hall)

Cream Cheese Jelly Roll

1 cup flour	3 eggs
1 teaspoon baking powder	¾ cup sugar
½ teaspoon baking soda	½ cup raisins
½ teaspoon cinnamon	½ cup sweetened applesauce
¼ teaspoon ground cloves	Confectioners sugar
¼ teaspoon salt	

Preheat oven to 375 degrees. Line a jelly roll pan with waxed paper. Sift together dry ingredients. Beat eggs and sugar together until lemon-colored and thick. Add raisins and applesauce to egg and sugar mixture. Fold in dry ingredients. Bake 15 to 20 minutes. Remove from pan and invert onto a dish towel that has been well powdered with confectioners sugar. Peel off wax paper and roll, towel and all, and leave for 10 minutes. Open, spread with filling, and reroll. Place on platter or wax paper, seamside down and keep refrigerated.

FILLING:

2 3-ounce packages cream cheese	3 tablespoons evaporated milk
	¼ cup sugar

Mix all ingredients together.

Mrs. Gerald Heinzelmann (Carolyn Jones)

Chocolate Cup Cakes

1/4 cup shortening
1 cup sugar
2 squares unsweetened
  chocolate, melted
2 eggs, beaten

1 teaspoon vanilla
1 cup sifted flour
1 teaspoon baking powder
Pinch salt
1/2 cup milk

Preheat oven to 375 degrees. Cream shortening and sugar. Add chocolate, eggs, and vanilla. Sift flour with baking powder and salt. Add alternately with the milk to chocolate mixture. Spoon batter into cupcake liners. Bake 15 to 18 minutes. Makes 18.

Mrs. R. Michael Dulaney (Florence "Sue" Williams)

Bridge Club Dessert*

Angel food cake
1/3 cup lemon juice
1 14-ounce can condensed milk
1/2 teaspoon almond extract

1/2 teaspoon vanilla
1 9-ounce carton non-dairy
  whipped topping
Sliced almonds

Cut cake into 3 layers. Whip lemon juice, milk, and extracts until consistency of thick icing. Spread between layers and on top of cake. Ice with topping; sprinkle with almonds.

Mrs. Austin Davies (Kathy Jones)

Mother's Chocolate Ice Box Cake

1 package Baker's brand
  German sweet chocolate
1/2 cup butter
3 eggs, separated
3/4 cup confectioners sugar

1 teaspoon vanilla
1 cup chopped pecans
1 10½-ounce bought pound cake
  or angel food cake
Vanilla flavored whipped cream

Melt chocolate and butter in top of a double boiler. Cool slightly and stir in beaten egg yolks. Add sugar. Fold in stiffly beaten egg whites. Add vanilla and nuts. Line an 8-by-8-inch baking dish with a layer of very thinly sliced cake. Pour a thin layer of the chocolate mix over the cake, and repeat until the mix is gone, topping with chocolate. Refrigerate, covered. Serve with whipped cream.

Mrs. John H. Yochem (Phyllis Nigh)

Frostings and Fillings

Great Chocolate Frosting

2 1-ounce squares bitter
  chocolate
½ cup butter
2 cups sifted confectioners
  sugar
1 egg, well beaten

1 tablespoon vanilla
1 tablespoon lemon juice
  (optional)
1 cup chopped toasted pecans
  (optional)

Melt chocolate in double boiler. Add butter and 1 cup sugar and beat well. Remove from heat and add egg, vanilla, and lemon juice, if desired. Add remaining sugar gradually until icing reaches proper spreading consistency. Add nuts last and spread on 8-inch 2-layer cake.

Mrs. Kenneth McKamey (Hattie Bell Colston)

Boiled White Icing

2 cups sugar
1 cup water
2 tablespoons light corn syrup
2 egg whites

⅛ teaspoon salt
⅛ teaspoon cream of tartar
1 teaspoon vanilla

Mix sugar, water, and syrup and cook, stirring often, until sugar is dissolved. Boil until syrup reaches soft ball stage, 234 degrees on a candy thermometer. Beat eggs with salt until frothy. Add 1/3 of boiling syrup to the egg whites in a thin stream, beating constantly. Then return syrup to heat and cook a little more. Add second third of boiling syrup in the same manner. Place remainder of syrup on heat to reach crack stage, about 290 degrees; add to egg whites. Add cream of tartar and vanilla. Whip until creamy. If icing gets too hard and stiff, add a few drops of water at a time until it is right consistency for smooth spreading. Ice the top and sides of a chocolate cake or 1, 2, 3, 4 Cake.

Mrs. Kenneth McKamey (Hattie Bell Colston)

Coconut Frosting

6 tablespoons margarine
1/4 cup heavy cream
2/3 cup brown sugar
1 teaspoon vanilla

1 cup coconut
1/3 cup chopped nuts
1/2 cup confectioners cugar

Mix margarine, cream, and brown sugar together in a sauce pan over moderate heat until margarine melts. Add vanilla, coconut, and nuts and bring to a rolling boil. Remove from heat and gradually add confectioners sugar until desired consistency is reached. This frosting is excellent on Oatmeal Cake.

Mrs. A. Jackson Ashmore (Gay Griffith)

Cream Cheese Frosting

8 ounces cream cheese
1/4 cup margarine
1 pound confectioners sugar

1 teaspoon vanilla
1 to 2 teaspoons milk
Chopped pecans (optional)

Soften cream cheese and margarine; then cream. Add sugar, vanilla, and milk. This frosting is excellent with Italian Cream Cake. The top of the cake may be sprinkled with chopped pecans if desired.

Mrs. George Taggart (Ethleen Reimers)

Pineapple Filling

1 cup sugar
1 heaping tablespoon flour
1 8 1/4-ounce can crushed
   pineapple

3 beaten egg yolks
1 1/2 tablespoons lemon juice
1 tablespoon butter

Blend sugar and flour; combine with pineapple. Add egg yolks, lemon juice, and butter. Cook over low heat, stirring constantly, until thick and smooth, about 20 minutes. Cool and spread between layers of 1, 2, 3, 4 Cake.

Mrs. Kenneth McKamey (Hattie Bell Colston)

Sauces

Miss Alice O'Grady's Lemon Jelly

1 cup sugar	Juice of 2 lemons
3 to 4 tablespoons flour	Grated rind of 1 lemon
3 eggs	1 cup water

Sift sugar and flour into eggs; mix well. Add remaining ingredients. Cook over low heat, stirring constantly, until jelly thickens. Serve hot over cake or gingerbread. It is also delicious cooled and put between layers of 1, 2, 3, 4, Cake. Frost cake with white icing all over.

Mrs. Kenneth McKamey (Hattie Bell Colston)

Rose's Sour Cream Orange Sauce

3 tablespoons butter	3 tablespoons fresh orange juice
½ cup confectioners sugar	1 teaspoon grated orange rind
½ cup sour cream	

Cream together butter and sugar. Beat in sour cream, orange juice, and orange rind. Makes about 1 cup of sauce. Serve on white, sponge, or pound cake.

Mrs. Kenneth McKamey (Hattie Bell Colston)

Blueberry Sauce

1½ cups blueberries, fresh or frozen	2 tablespoons flour
1 cup water	¼ teaspoon salt
½ cup sugar	Juice of 1 lime

Cook blueberries, ¾ cup water, and sugar until blueberries are soft. Then add flour mixed with ¼ cup water and salt. Cook, stirring, until mixture has thickened. Add lime juice. This sauce may be used over pancakes, over crepes filled with cottage cheese or sour cream, or poured over baked pastry shells filled with fresh blueberries. Makes about 3 cups.

Mrs. Dudley A. Chatham (Melba Welsh)

Chocolate Sauce

2 tablespoons butter
2 squares bitter chocolate
¾ cup sugar

1/3 cup evaporated milk
1 teaspoon vanilla

Melt all ingredients except vanilla together, over low heat. When melted, beat with electric mixer until smooth. Add vanilla. Can be rewarmed over hot water later. Makes about 1 cup.

Mrs. Gerald Heinzelmann (Carolyn Jones)

Custards
Pot de Crème

¼ cup sugar
¼ cup water (or coffee)
8 ounces dark sweet chocolate
5 eggs, separated

1 teaspoon vanilla
Whipped cream
Grated chocolate

Add sugar and water to chocolate and melt in top of a double boiler. Stir until smooth. Cool. Add egg yolks and stir briskly. Fold in stiffly beaten egg whites and vanilla. Pour into small cup. Refrigerate for several hours. Serve with whipped cream and shaved chocolate. Serves 10 to 12.

Mrs. Edwin A. Durham, II (Kaye Tarrant)

Crème Brulée

1 pint heavy cream
3 eggs, beaten
¼ cup sugar

Salt
½ teaspoon vanilla
Brown sugar

Preheat oven to 325 degrees. Scald cream. Add sugar and salt to beaten eggs. Mix well; add cream and vanilla. Pour into glass baking cups. Place cups in pan and pour in enough water to reach halfway up the cups. Bake 45 minutes or until knife inserted into custard comes out clean. Refrigerate at least 4 hours before serving. To serve, sprinkle lightly with brown sugar and run under broiler until sugar is bubbly. Serves 4.

Mrs. Earl Sams Lightner (Robin Holmes)

Fudge Pudding

½ cup butter
1 cup sifted sugar
⅛ teaspoon salt
2 eggs

1½ ounces unsweetened chocolate
Scant ½ cup sifted flour
2 teaspoons vanilla

Preheat oven to 325 degrees. Cream butter, sugar, and salt together until fluffy. Add eggs and beat in thoroughly. Melt the chocolate in the top of a double boiler, cool slightly, and combine with the sugar and egg mixture. Sift in flour. Add vanilla and blend. Bake in buttered 8-inch pie pan 30 to 35 minutes. Serve with whipped cream or ice cream. Serves 6.

Mrs. R. Michael Dulaney (Florence "Sue" Williams)

Lemon Delicious

¼ cup flour
1 cup sugar
⅛ teaspoon salt
2 tablespoons butter

3 eggs, separated
1½ cups milk
5 tablespoons lemon juice
Grated rind of 1 lemon

Preheat oven to 350 degrees. Lightly grease a 1-quart baking dish or 6 custard cups. Mix flour, sugar, and salt; cream with butter. Beat egg yolks until thick; add to mixture. Add milk, lemon juice, and rind. Beat egg whites until stiff and fold into mixture. Pour into baking dish. Place dish in pan with 1 inch hot water. Bake about 45 minutes. A delicate crust will form on the top, and a sauce will be on the bottom. Invert on dessert plate before serving if desired. Serves 6.

Mrs. James R. Harris (Betty Fischer)
Mrs. James A. Howry (Joan Priour)
Mrs. William N. Woolsey (Sandra Callaway)

Mix the juice of 1 lemon or lime, 1 ripe banana, and 1 peeled and seeded avocado in an electric blender until smooth. Add honey or sugar to taste. Top with or fold in whipped cream; sprinkle with nuts or coconut. A nutritious pudding.

Desserts

Mrs. E's Lemon Dessert

Lady fingers
8 eggs, separated
1¼ cups sugar
2/3 cup lemon juice

Grated rind of 2 lemons
1½ tablespoons gelatin
¾ cup water
Whipped cream

Line the bottom and sides of an angel food or spring mold cake pan with lady fingers that have been cut in half, lengthwise. Mix egg yolks, ¾ cup sugar, lemon juice, and rind; cook in top of double boiler until thick. While hot, add gelatin that has been soaked in water. Beat well. Cool. Beat egg whites until stiff; gradually add ½ cup of sugar.. Fold into gelatin mixture. Pour into cake pan. Refrigerate for 24 hours before serving. Invert dessert on a platter and cover with whipped cream to serve. Serves 12.

Mrs. Tom Lake Erwin (Jean Sterrett)

Lemon Posset

Grated rind and juice of
  2 lemons
1 pint heavy cream
½ cup dry white wine

Confectioners sugar
3 egg whites
Freshly grated orange peel

Add the grated lemon rind to cream and beat until stiff. Stir in lemon juice and white wine. Add sugar to taste. Beat whites until they form peaks; fold into whipped cream mixture. Serve in a glass serving dish or in individual glasses, garnished with grated orange peel. Serves 4 to 6.

Mrs. Richard King, III (Jimmie Rose Harrison)

Frozen Lemon Dessert

½ cup crushed vanilla wafers
3 eggs, separated
Pinch cream of tartar
½ cup sugar

1 cup heavy cream
¼ cup fresh lemon juice
1 tablespoon freshly grated
lemon rind

Butter a 9-by-9-inch glass dish and coat sides and bottom with about half the crumbs. Place dish in freezer to cool. Beat egg whites until foamy; add cream of tartar and beat until stiff; add sugar slowly and beat until glossy. In a separate bowl, beat yolks; then fold into the whites. In a cold bowl, combine cream, lemon juice, and rind; beat until stiff; fold into egg mixture. Pour into chilled dish; cover with remaining crumbs; freeze 4 to 6 hours. Cut into squares. Serves about 8.

Mrs. Donald P. McClure (Sally Garrett)
Mrs. Lev H. Prichard, III (Ella Wall)

Frozen Mocha Soufflés

4 eggs, separated
¼ cup sugar
2 tablespoons instant coffee
2 ounces sweet chocolate

2 tablespoons water
2 tablespoons dark rum
1 cup heavy cream
3 tablespoons grated chocolate

Beat egg yolks with sugar and coffee until mixture is thick and creamy. Melt chocolate and water in a small sauce pan; add rum and stir into egg and coffee mixture. Whip cream and fold into soufflé mixture. Whisk egg whites until stiff and fold into mixture. Fold in 2 tablespoons grated chocolate, pour into individual soufflé dishes or custard cups, and freeze for 4 hours. Decorate with a little grated chocolate. Serves 6.

Mrs. Richard King, III (Jimmie Rose Harrison)

Fruits

Hot Fruit Compote

2 15¼-ounce cans pineapple
chunks
1 16¼-ounce can pitted
purple plums
1 16-ounce can sliced peaches
1 4-ounce jar maraschino
cherries
1 16½-ounce can applesauce

1 10-ounce package frozen
raspberries (or strawberries)
2 bananas, sliced (optional)
1 cup brown sugar
1/3 cup butter
½ to 1 teaspoon curry powder
½ cup chopped pecans (optional)

Drain all fruit well except raspberries and applesauce. Mix all the fruits. Mix ¾ cup sugar, curry, and melted butter and add to fruits. Put in a buttered 3-quart casserole and top with remaining brown sugar and chopped pecans if desired. Bake covered for 1 hour at 350 degrees. Serves 16. This may be prepared up to 2 days in advance of baking if bananas are omitted.

Mrs. Jack Best (Betty Reno)

Grecian Pears

6 pears
4½ cups sugar
2 cups water
Food coloring (optional)

1 stick cinnmaon
3 to 4 whole cloves
1 cup sour cream
Mace

Peel barely ripe pears and core from the blossom end, leaving stems on. Combine sugar and water in a large sauce pan and cook over low heat, stirring, until sugar is dissolved. Add green or red food coloring if desired. Place pears in syrup and boil gently about 15 minutes, or until tender. Remove from heat. Add cinnamon stick and cloves to the syrup. Refrigerate several hours.

Place pears upright in 6 shallow dessert bowls. Pour a little syrup over each pear. Pour a little sour cream around each pear. Sprinkle with mace. Serves 6.

Mrs. R. E. Swetman (Helen Scibienski)

Ice Cream and Sherbet

Patt's Vanilla Ice Cream

4 to 6 eggs
2½ cups sugar
6 cups milk

4 cups evaporated milk
1 to 2 tablespoons vanilla
½ teaspoon salt

Beat eggs until light. Add sugar gradually, beating until mixture thickens. Add remaining ingredients. Mix thoroughly. Makes 1 gallon.

Mrs. Robert C. Wood (Helen Heaney)

Caramel Ice Cream

8 egg yolks
3 cups sugar
1 quart milk

1 teaspoon vanilla
Pinch salt
1 quart heavy cream

Beat egg yolks and 1 cup sugar together. Scald milk. Put remaining sugar in skillet to caramelize. Add egg mixture to scalded milk and place in top of a double boiler. Cook 2 minutes. Then add caramelized sugar to custard. Cool. Add vanilla and pinch of salt. Cool thoroughly. Add cream and freeze according to freezer instructions. Makes 2 quarts.

Mrs. Mercer T. Ivey (Jean Nunn)

Fresh Fruit Ice Cream

2 cups fresh fruit
1 teaspoon lemon juice
   (optional)
Chopped pecans (optional)
Sugar

2 14-ounce cans condensed milk
1 pint half and half
1 teaspoon vanilla
Pinch salt
Milk to fill container

Prepare approximately 2 cups strawberries, peaches, or bananas with lemon juice and chopped pecans if desired. Sweeten fruit to taste and put in blender briefly or mash. Put all ingredients into the container of a 4-quart ice cream freezer. Freeze. For a richer ice cream, substitute heavy cream for half and half. If using canned fruit, use half the syrup.

Mrs. Thomas L. Goad (Elizabeth Vickers)

Peppermint Ice Cream

2 10-ounce packages
  peppermint candy
1 quart milk (or more)

2 eggs, well beaten
3 cups heavy cream
4 to 6 drops red food coloring

Melt peppermint candy slowly in 1 quart of milk. Remove from heat and quickly beat in eggs until smooth. Cool in refrigerator. Strain into freezer container. Add cream, food coloring, and enough milk to fill container ¾ full. Freeze according to directions. Makes 3 quarts.

Mrs. Maurice Priday (Joan McCroskey)

Rich Ice Cream

8 eggs
1½ cups sugar
½ cup flour
1 teaspoon vanilla
1 13-ounce can evaporated milk

4 to 5 cups cut-up fruit (or
  2 10-ounce packages
  peppermint candy)
Milk

Beat eggs to buttery consistency, slowly adding sugar and flour. Add all other ingredients and freeze according to freezer directions. Makes 6 quarts.

For a 4-quart freezer use 6 eggs, 1 cup sugar, and 1/3 cup flour with the other ingredients remaining the same.

Mrs. William N. Woolsey (Sandra Callaway)

Buttermilk Ice Cream

5 cups heavy cream
2 quarts buttermilk
2 cups sugar

4 teaspoons vanilla
Pinch salt
Pinch baking soda

Mix ingredients together. Pour into freezing can. Freeze as directed. Makes 1 gallon. Though very rich, this ice cream tastes light, almost like a sherbet.

Mrs. Robert Dunn (Anne Furman)

Bourbon Ice Cream*

2 quarts vanilla ice cream
1½ cups chopped pecans,
   lightly toasted

1 10-ounce jar maraschino
   cherries, cut and drained
1 cup bourbon

Soften ice cream. Quickly stir in other ingredients. Refreeze in ice cream container.

Mrs. Robert Dunn (Anne Furman)

Grape Sherbet*

2 quarts pure grape juice
Juice of 4 lemons

2 cups sugar
3 pints half and half

Mix all ingredients well and pour into freezing can. Freeze as directed on ice cream freezer. Makes 1 gallon.

Mrs. Robert Dunn (Anne Furman)

Cookies

Chocolate Cookies

½ cup vegetable oil
4 ounces unsweetened
   chocolate, melted
2 cups sugar
4 eggs
2 teaspoons vanilla

2 cups sifted flour
2 teaspoons baking powder
½ teaspoon salt
1 cup chopped nuts (optional)
1 cup confectioners sugar

Mix oil, chocolate, and sugar. Blend in 1 egg at a time. Add vanilla. Add flour, baking powder, salt, and nuts if desired and mix well. Chill several hours or overnight. Make balls using about 1 teaspoon dough. Roll in confectioners sugar. Place on ungreased cookie sheet about 2 inches apart. Bake in preheated 350-degree oven for 10 to 12 minutes. Do not overbake. Makes about 7 dozen cookies. Cookies can be frozen after they are rolled in confectioners sugar or after baking.

Mrs. Ned Langdon (Cile James)
Mrs. Joe P. Nelson (Harriet Hornish)

Chinese Almond Cookies

2 cups butter
1½ cups sugar
½ teaspoon salt

1 teaspoon almond extract
4 cups flour
84 whole blanched almonds

Cream butter and sugar; add salt and extract. Work in flour, with hands if necessary. Refrigerate overnight. Next day, roll into balls smaller than a walnut. Place on a cookie sheet; press a whole blanched almond on top of each cookie. Bake about 30 minutes in a preheated 300-degree oven. The cookies do not get very brown. Makes about 7 dozen.

Mrs. Gerald Heinzelmann (Carolyn Jones)

Swedish Cookies

1 cup butter
1 cup sugar
1 egg
3 cups flour
¼ teaspoon mace

⅛ teaspoon salt
1 teaspoon baking powder
2 tablespoons heavy cream
1 teaspoon vanilla
36 pecan halves

Cream butter and sugar. Add egg. Sift in dry ingredients. Add cream and vanilla. Mix lightly. Chill dough overnight. Break off bits of dough and flatten down 2 inches apart on lightly greased cookie sheet. Press a pecan on top of each cookie. Bake 8 minutes in a preheated 350-degree oven. Makes 3 dozen.

Mrs. W. Byrd Harris (Beatrice Merriman)

Sand Tarts

1 cup butter
¾ cup sifted confectioners sugar
2 cups sifted flour

1 teaspoon vanilla
1 cup chopped pecans

Preheat oven to 325 degrees. Cream butter and sugar. Add flour gradually and mix well. Add nuts and vanilla and mix. Roll in balls or crescents. Bake about 25 minutes on ungreased cookie sheet, or until cookies are lightly browned. When done, roll in additional confectioners sugar while hot. Makes about 4 dozen.

Mrs. A. C. Gilmore (Clydell Hollon)

Oatmeal Cookies

1 cup brown sugar	½ teaspoon salt
1 cup granulated sugar	2 cups old fashioned oats
1 cup vegetable shortening	1 cup chopped nuts
2 eggs	1 cup coconut (optional)
2 cups flour	1 cup raisins (optional)
1 teaspoon baking soda	1 teaspoon vanilla
1 teaspoon baking powder	

Preheat oven to 350 degrees. Cream sugar and shortening. Add eggs and mix well. Sift together the flour, soda, baking powder, and salt and add to mixture. Add remaining ingredients. Mix well. Roll in walnut-sized balls. Baked on ungreased cookie sheets for 8 to 10 minutes. Makes 8 dozen cookies.

Mrs. Mercer T. Ivey (Jean Nunn)

Christmas Cookies

½ cup margarine	1 pound dark raisins
1½ cups dark brown sugar	1 pound light raisins
4 eggs	1 teaspoon cinnamon
3½ cups flour	1 teaspoon ground cloves
6 cups chopped pecans	1 tablespoon baking soda
1 pound candied red cherries	1 cup bourbon
1 pound candied green pineapple	3 tablespoons milk

Preheat oven to 275 degrees. Grease cookie sheets. Cream margarine and sugar. Beat in eggs, 1 at a time. Sprinkle ½ cup flour on chopped nuts and fruit. Mix 3 cups flour with soda and spices. Add flour mixture to sugar mixture; add milk and bourbon. Add fruit and nut mixture. Drop by teaspoons on cookie sheet and bake for 15 to 20 minutes. The cookie keeps for several weeks in an airtight container. Makes 16 dozen.

Mrs. Jack Scholl (Catherine Dannelly)

Candied Orange Cookies

1 cup butter
¾ cup granulated sugar
½ cup brown sugar
1 egg, well beaten
2 tablespoons frozen orange
  juice concentrate

2 tablespoons candied orange
  peel, minced
2 cups flour
¼ teaspoon baking soda
¼ teaspoon salt
¾ cup chopped pecans

Preheat oven to 375 degrees. Grease a cookie sheet. Cream together butter and sugar until mixture is very light and smooth. Stir in egg, orange juice, and candied orange peel. Sift flour with baking soda and salt. Mix flour lightly into batter; add chopped nuts. Drop the dough from a teaspoon onto a cookie sheet 2 inches apart. Bake 10 to 12 minutes or until lightly browned. Remove from cookie sheet at once and cool on racks. Makes about 9 dozen cookies. This cookie is best when freshly baked.

Mrs. Edwin A. Durham, II (Kaye Tarrant)

Spread a box of cinnamon graham crackers on the bottom of a jelly roll pan. Melt ½ cup butter with 1 cup brown sugar and spread on the crackers. Sprinkle with chopped pecans and bake at 350 degrees for 10 minutes.

Rolled Cookies

1 cup light brown sugar
1 cup granulated sugar
1 cup butter
2 eggs
½ teaspoon salt
1 teaspoon baking powder

3½ cups flour
1 teaspoon baking soda
Hot water
1 teaspoon vanilla (or almond
  extract)

Cream butter and sugar. Add eggs. Sift together salt, baking powder, and flour and add. Dissolve soda in hot water and add to dough. Add vanilla. Mix well. Chill overnight. Roll out dough on a floured board until about ¼-inch thick. Cut out with cutters and decorate as desired. Bake in preheated 375-degree oven for about 8 to 10 minutes. Makes about 5 dozen cookies.

Mrs. Gerald Heinzelmann (Carolyn Jones)

Ice Box Cookies

1 cup butter
1 cup granulated sugar
1 cup brown sugar
2 eggs
3½ cups flour (or more)

2 teaspoons cinnamon
1 teaspoon baking soda
1 teaspoon vanilla
1 cup chopped pecans

Cream butter and sugar. Add eggs, dry ingredients, vanilla, and pecans. Roll into a roll on waxed paper. Chill. When firm, slice thin and bake on greased cookie sheet in preheated 350-degree oven until brown, about 12 minutes. Makes about 14 dozen 1-inch cookies.

Mrs. William Hall Keys (Rose Mary Blackshear)

Refrigerator Sand Tarts

1 cup butter
½ cup confectioners sugar
2 cups flour

1 teaspoon vanilla
1 cup ground or chopped almonds

Mix all ingredients together, roll in waxed paper, and chill thoroughly. Slice and bake on ungreased cookie sheet in preheated 325-degree oven until lightly browned, about 20 to 30 minutes. Roll in additional confectioners sugar while still warm. Makes about 5 dozen.

Mrs. Gerald Heinzelmann (Carolyn Jones)

Brownie Mounds

2/3 cup margarine
1½ cups sugar
2/3 cup light corn syrup
2 eggs, beaten

5 squares unsweetened chocolate,
  melted
3 1/3 cups sifted flour
1 teaspoon baking powder
1½ cups chopped nuts

Preheat oven to 350 degrees. Grease baking sheet. Cream margarine and sugar; stir in syrup and beaten eggs. Add chocolate. Mix together flour and baking powder and add. Add nuts. Drop by heaping teaspoons onto baking sheet. Bake for 10 to 12 minutes.

Mrs. William N. Woolsey (Sandra Callaway)

Brownies

2 squares unsweetened
  chocolate
½ cup butter
1 cup sugar

½ cup flour
1 teaspoon vanilla
2 eggs, beaten
½ cup pecans

Preheat oven to 350 degrees. Grease and flour a 9-by-9-inch pan. Melt chocolate with butter. Remove from heat and add sugar, flour, vanilla, eggs, and pecans. Mix well. Bake 20 to 25 minutes or until firm and pulled from sides of pan. Cool, sprinkle with confectioners sugar, and cut into squares. Makes 3 dozen.

Mrs. Roy Grassedonio (Claire Searcy)

Date-Filled Oatmeal Bars

1¾ cups flour
1¾ cups old fashioned oats
1 teaspoon baking soda
1 cup brown sugar
½ teaspoon salt

1 cup melted butter
1 8-ounce package pitted dates,
  chopped
½ cup granulated sugar
1 cup water

Preheat oven to 350 degrees. Grease a 9-by-12-inch pan. Mix dry ingredients together. Add butter. Cook dates, sugar, and water until dates are mushy. Pour ¾ of the cake mixture into pan, add date mixture, and sprinkle with remaining cake mixture. Cook until brown, approximately 45 minutes. Makes about 3 dozen.

Mrs. Robert L. Browning (Marylee Douglass)

Brown Sugar Squares

½ cup butter
2 cups brown sugar
2 eggs
1½ cups sifted flour

2 teaspoons baking powder
2 teaspoons vanilla
½ cup broken nuts

Preheat oven to 375 degrees. Grease a 9-by-13-inch pan. Melt butter in a sauce pan. Add sugar. Add eggs, 1 at a time. Sift flour and baking powder; add to batter. Add vanilla and nuts. Bake 20 to 30 minutes. Cut in squares or strips. Makes 4 dozen.

Mrs. Sam L. Allen (Phyllis Coffee)

Date Squares

1 cup butter
4 cups brown sugar
1 cup milk
4 cups sifted flour

1 tablespoon baking powder
2½ cups chopped dates
3 cups chopped pecans
4 eggs

Preheat oven to 350 degrees. Grease a 9-by-13-inch baking pan. Combine butter, brown sugar, and milk and cook over medium heat for 5 minutes. Let cool completely. Add remaining ingredients; mix thoroughly with a spoon. Pour into pan. Bake 35 minutes. Makes about 3 dozen.

Mrs. William Hall Keys (Rose Mary Blackshear)

Vanilla Sticks

6 egg whites
1 pound confectioners sugar
1 tablespoon vanilla
½ teaspoon salt

1 pound unblanched ground
  almonds
Flour

Preheat oven to 300 degrees. Beat egg whites until they stand in peaks. Gradually add sugar, vanilla, and salt, and beat 5 minutes longer with electric mixer. Divide mixture in half. Add almonds to 1 half; add flour gradually until dough is the consistency of rolled cookie dough. Roll out to ⅛-inch thickness and cut in 4-by-1/3-inch strips. Spread with meringue mixture. Place on cookie sheets. Let dry 5 minutes. Bake 15 minutes. Makes 12 dozen.

Mrs. R. Michael Dulaney (Florence "Sue" Williams)

Confections

Apricot Balls*

1½ cups ground apricots
2 cups angel flake coconut

2/3 cup condensed milk
Confectioners sugar

Mix all ingredients well. Roll into walnut-sized balls; then roll in confectioners sugar. Makes about 3 dozen. Especially good for a brunch or tea.

Mrs. James D. Cable (Mary Pearle Garrett)

Chocolate Dreams*

2 cups sugar
1/4 cup cocoa
Dash salt
1/2 cup margarine

1/2 cup milk
3 cups quick oats
1 cup nuts
1 teaspoon vanilla

Mix sugar, cocoa, salt, margarine, and milk in a 3-quart sauce pan; bring to a rolling boil. Add remaining ingredients. Drop by a teaspoon onto waxed paper. Cool. Makes 5 dozen.

Mrs. Gerald A. Reeves (Lois Arnett)

Candy

Christmas Fudge Milly

4 1/2 cups sugar
1 13-ounce can evaporated milk
1 7-ounce jar Kraft brand
   Marshmallow Creme
10 1 3/8-ounce milk chocolate
   candy bars

1 tablespoon butter
2 12-ounce packages chocolate
   chips
1 teaspoon vanilla
Pinch salt
1 pound pecans

Cook sugar and milk together, stirring constantly, until mixture comes to a boil. Boil without stirring for 6 minutes. Mix Marshmallow Creme, chocolates, and butter in a heat-proof bowl; pour in the boiling sugar mixture. Fold in pecans. Drop on waxed paper. Let stand 4 to 6 hours. Makes 7 dozen.

Mrs. James C. Sharp, Jr. (Amber DeForest)

Butterscotch Surprises*

2 6-ounce packages butterscotch
   morsels
1/2 cup peanut butter

1 cup nuts
1 1 1/2-ounce can shoestring
   potatoes

Melt butterscotch chips and peanut butter in top of double boiler. Stir in nuts and shoestring potatoes. Drop on waxed paper. Cool in refrigerator. Makes 2 dozen.

Mrs. Gerald A. Reeves (Lois Arnett)

Mother's Caramels

½ cup butter
¾ cup light corn syrup
2 cups sugar

1 13-ounce can evaporated milk
1 cup chopped nuts
1 teaspoon vanilla

Butter an 8-by-8-inch cake pan. In a large kettle, cook butter, sugar, syrup, and half the milk until mixture comes to a hard boil. Gradually add remainder of milk, stirring constantly with a wooden spoon, cooking about 25 minutes. Cook until mixture forms a hard ball in cold water. Cool slightly; add nuts and vanilla. Pour into cake pan to cool. When candy is almost cool, cut it into squares and wrap in waxed paper. Keeps well; ships well. Makes about 3 dozen.

Mrs. John H. Yochem (Phyllis Nigh)

Nunna's Buttermilk Candy

1 teaspoon baking soda
1 cup buttermilk
2 cups sugar
2 tablespoons light corn syrup

2 tablespoons butter
1 teaspoon vanilla
1 cup chopped pecans

In a large sauce pan, combine soda and buttermilk and stir over medium heat. Add sugar, corn syrup, and butter, stirring constantly. Cook until syrup is brown and forms a soft ball in water. Add vanilla and beat until barely creamy. Add nuts. Quickly drop by tablespoons on waxed paper. Makes 4 dozen.

Mrs. A. Jackson Ashmore (Gay Griffith)

Quick Pralines*

1 3-ounce box butterscotch
  pudding
1 cup granulated sugar
½ cup brown sugar

½ cup evaporated milk
1 teaspoon vanilla
2 cups pecan pieces

Mix all ingredients except vanilla and pecans. Boil for 2 minutes, stirring constantly. Add pecans and vanilla; stir and cook 1 to 2 minutes. Drop by tablespoons on waxed paper. Makes 2 dozen.

Mrs. Lowell Kepp (Betty Ellis)

Melt 1½ bars dark baking chocolate in the top of a double boiler and stir in a 14-ounce can of condensed milk. Chill the mixture until firm, roll in small balls, and then roll in coconut, chopped nuts, etc., for an easy candy.

Nuts

Minted Nuts

1 cup sugar
½ cup water
1 tablespoon light corn syrup
⅛ teaspoon salt

6 marshmallows
1 teaspoon essence of peppermint
3 heaping cups of pecan or
    walnut halves

Slowly cook sugar, water, corn syrup, and salt. Remove from heat just before syrup reaches the soft ball stage. Add marshmallows; stir until melted. Add peppermint and nuts and stir with a circular motion until every nut is coated and mixture begins to look creamy. Empty on waxed paper; cool; then separate. Nuts may be stored in cans for several weeks.

Mrs. James D. Cable (Mary Pearle Garrett)

Mexican Spiced Pecans

1 cup sugar
½ cup water
1 teaspoon cinnamon

¼ teaspoon salt
1 teaspoon vanilla
2½ cups pecan halves

Combine sugar, water, cinnamon, and salt in a sauce pan and cook over medium heat until syrup spins a thread (232 degrees on candy thermometer). Remove from heat; add vanilla and pecans. Stir until nuts are well coated and mixture becomes creamy. Pour onto greased baking sheet. With 2 forks, separate nuts as they cool.

Mrs. Lev H. Prichard, III (Ella Wall)

Dessert recipes found in Chapter 1. MEXICAN FOOD:

Nogada Amador Ayala
Pan de Polvo

Cajeta
Flan with Caramel Topping

Dining under Sail

16. DINING UNDER SAIL

MRS. EARL SAMS LIGHTNER, EDITOR

On Sunday afternoons, the Corpus Christi shoreline is dotted with the bright sails of local boats and yachts, out for family cruising or competitive racing. The warm weather and brisk breezes have helped make sailing an increasingly popular sport that is enjoyed year 'round.

Many a wife chooses the role of galley steward instead of weekend widow. Some of them have shared their methods for serving the best food with the least amount of effort, making sailing as pleasurable for them as for their husbands.

These suggestions for food storage and preparation are as applicable to the weekend camper and the picnicker — any time dining is done on the move.

Supply List

Ice and ice chest
Drinks
Bottle opener

Pots and pans, as needed
Utensils for eating and cooking
Paper plates, cups, bowls,
  napkins, and paper towels
Can opener
Pot holders

Several plastic containers for
  leftovers
Garbage bags
Dish pan and soap
Scouring pad

Menus
Foodstuffs
Spices, as needed
Corn meal
Flour
Sugar
Cooking oil

Matches (in an airtight
  container)
Charcoal lighter for campfire
  or portable stove

Fire extinguisher
First aid kit
Sewing kit

Preparation Tips

1. Make menus for each meal each day.
2. Prepare as much food as possible at home before you go.
3. Keep main dishes simple, and, if possible, prepare 1-dish meals such as casseroles. Remember, the beautiful outdoors makes for good appetites, so have plenty. Even the simplest meals taste great when at sea or snuggled around a campfire.
4. For no mess, no bother, cooking a "Seal-a-Meal" is a delight. Fix your favorite stew, spaghetti, stroganoff, creamed chicken, scrambled eggs, etc., and seal in the plastic cooking pouch.
5. The wide-mouth insulated jar is good for chunky soups, stews, or spaghetti.
6. A tea kettle is a must for heating water; it eliminates the chance of a nasty burn.
7. A reflector fold-up oven is available in most camping stores.

Storage Tips

1. Ice: to make ice last longer —
    a. wrap dry ice in plastic and keep in ice chest and
    b. assign 1 person to be in charge of ice, to cut down the times the ice chest is opened.
2. Fresh vegetables and fruits: to keep them fresh longer —
    a. store in a dark, cool area and
    b. check every few days and throw out anything rotten.
3. Eggs: to keep eggs fresh for weeks (even up to a month!) —
    a. buy them very fresh and
    b. seal the eggs by dipping them in paraffin and boiling for one minute.
4. Dry foods: crackers, cereals, flour, cookies, etc., should be kept in watertight containers.

Food Tips

1. Drinks — besides plenty of beer and soft drinks, fruit juices are always a hit. Another good refreshment is hot or cold instant breakfast drink, hot or cold tea, bouillon, and Gatorade brand drink.
2. Soups — fill a thermal jar with hot soup or use Lipton brand Cup a Soup for a quick "picker-upper."
3. Canned meats — Spam or chopped ham can be dressed up for supper by frying and adding pineapple and brown sugar. Canned chicken can be used in salads or added to noodles in a casserole.
4. Nutritional foods — these include cheese, peanut butter, dried and fresh fruits.
5. Pull-top cans — many items are packaged this way including baked beans, bean salad, potato salad, puddings, fruit, and apples.
6. Sandwiches — varying the type of bread helps to avoid monotony.
7. Spreads — make your own at home or dress up canned versions with spices, onion, or cheese.
8. Quick casserole — brown ground meat, drain, and add a can of Spanish rice. Top with cheese.
9. Canned whole chicken — add to canned chicken and dumpling soup for a good quick meal.
10. Jerky — an excellent snack.

Menus

Menus for a 3-day cruise or camping trip:

FIRST DAY:

Breakfast

Juice
Scrambled eggs with chipped beef*   *Toast* and Jelly*
Coffee or Milk

Lunch

Sailor's Sandwich*
Chips   Deviled eggs
Fruit cocktail (individual cans)

Dinner

Fried chicken (prepared at home)
Potato salad (prepared at home)   Off Shore Salad*
Cake (prepared at home)

SCRAMBLED EGGS WITH CHIPPED BEEF:

Break enough eggs in the bowl for the number of servings needed. Salt and pepper to taste. Cut chipped beef into bite-sized pieces and add to eggs. Scramble in skillet.

TOAST:

If you don't have an oven, butter both sides of bread and fry in skillet.

SAILOR'S SANDWICH:

3 tablespoons butter
1 medium onion, minced
½ pound bulk sausage
½ pound lean ground beef
12 brown-and-serve club rolls
1 egg

2 teaspoons Dijon mustard
¼ teaspoon marjoram
½ teaspoon salt
1/3 cup water
1 clove garlic, pressed (optional)

Melt 1 tablespoon of butter; sauté the onion until golden. Add sausage, breaking it up with a fork, and brown over low heat for several minutes. Add ground beef and cook the mixture until the meats are lightly brown. Cut the ends from the rolls and carefully remove as much of the center as possible, leaving only a thin shell. Mix about ¾ of the crumbs from the rolls with the meat mixture. Add egg, seasonings, and water and mix well. Pack the bread shells with the mixture. Melt remaining butter; add garlic. Brush butter on the rolls. Bake at 350 degrees until crusty and brown, about 25 minutes. Wrap in foil. Rolls will keep warm in transit to boat or picnic. Allow 2 rolls per person.

Mrs. Robert H. Blair (Sarah King)

OFF SHORE SALAD:

Celery
Cherry tomatoes
Radishes

Cauliflower
Carrots
Dressing

Wash and clean raw vegetables. Cut celery and carrots into strips. Break cauliflower into small pieces. Mix all vegetables together and put individual servings into small plastic bags. Sailors can help themselves and dip vegetables into dressing without having to balance a plate.

DRESSING FOR OFF SHORE SALAD:

1 cup mayonnaise
Celery salt

Worcestershire sauce
Paprika

Add 2 or 3 dashes Worcestershire to mayonnaise. Add celery salt to taste. Add paprika to turn the dressing slightly pink. Put into a paper cup, cover with plastic wrap, and seal with a rubber band. Refrigerate.

SECOND DAY:

Breakfast

Juice

Cereal with bananas   Sweet rolls

Coffee or Milk

Lunch

Soup

Pickles and Olives   Grilled cheese sandwiches

Pudding (individual cans)

Dinner

Roast beef (prepared at home)

Mashed potatoes (instant)   Bean salad* (prepared at home)

Bahamian bananas*

BEAN SALAD:

1 16-ounce can lima beans

1 16-ounce can green beans

1 16-ounce can red kidney
beans

1 16-ounce can yellow wax
beans

1 16-ounce can black-eyed peas

Marinade

Drain and rinse vegetables. Put into bowl. Pour marinade over vegetables. Cover and refrigerate at least 12 hours. Drain and serve.

MARINADE:

½ cup sugar

½ cup wine vinegar

½ cup salad oil

1 teaspoon salt

½ teaspoon dry mustard

½ teaspoon tarragon

Mix all ingredients until well blended.

BAHAMIAN BAKED BANANAS:

6 bananas

3 tablespoons butter

3 tablespoons brown sugar

3 ounces rum

Slice peeled bananas lengthwise and place in pan. Dot with butter. Cover with sugar and rum. Bake at 350 degrees for 20 minutes or until bananas are soft but not mushy. If you do not have an oven, this can be done in a skillet on top the stove.

THIRD DAY:

Breakfast

Juice

Corned beef hash with egg pockets*   Toast and Jelly

Coffee or Milk

Lunch

Canned Sloppy Joes or barbecue on buns

Corn chips   Fruit cocktail

Dinner

Ham

Sweet potatoes and apples*   Asparagus salad

Biscuits*

CORNED BEEF HASH WITH EGG POCKETS:

2 tablespoons butter   Eggs

Canned corned beef hash

Melt butter in a skillet; add hash and cook until hot. Make pockets in the hash, add an unbeaten egg to each pocket, cover, and simmer several minutes until egg is set.

SWEET POTATOES AND APPLES:

Butter   Orange juice (or instant

1 16-ounce can sliced apples   orange-flavored drink)

1 16-ounce can sweet potatoes   Marshmallows

Melt butter in a dutch oven. Add apples. Mash potatoes with orange juice; spread over apples. Top with marshmallows and heat until marshmallows melt.

BISCUITS:

For cooking biscuits without an oven, use biscuit mix and cook in a dutch oven, turning the biscuits so they will brown on both sides.

INDEX

A

Alice Eleanora Nesby's Picante Sauce, 33
Allie's Yacht Club Margaritas, 6
Almond Chicken, 149
Almond Cookies, Chinese, 282
Almonds, Deviled, 63
Ambrosia Mold, Congealed, 98
Ann Lively's Ranchero Sauce, 18
APPETIZERS, 45-64
  Bean Dip, 12
  Ceviche, 75
  Chili con Queso, 10
  Chili Dip, 11
  Curried Crab in Shells, 128
  Gateau Fromage, 117
  Guacamole Salad, 17
  Jackie's Shrimp, 135
  Jalapeño Dip, 10
  Jalapeño Pie, 19
  Nachos, 13
  Picadillo, 11
  Pizza Snacks, 71
  Queso y Carne, 12
  Saucy Meat Balls, 179
  Seafood Mold, 90
  Sea Heiress Oysters, 132
APPLES
  Apple Cobbler, 256
  Apple Pie Superb, 255
  Apple-Vegetable Relish, 229
  Fresh Apple Cake, 264
  Sweet Potatoes and Apples, 298
Apricot Balls, 287
Apricot Drink, Hot, 44
Artichoke Casserole, Crab Meat and, 130
Artichoke Hearts, Crab Meat and, 87
Artichoke Hearts, Tomatoes with, 106
ASPARAGUS
  Asparagus Mold, 107
  Chicken Asparagus Casserole, 156
  Eggs and Asparagus au Gratin, 204
  Ham and Asparagus, 188
  Sweet and Sour Asparagus, 101
Aspic, Avocado, 107
Aspic, Party, 90
AVOCADOS
  Avocado Aspic, 107
  Avocado Salad, 108
  Guacamole Salad, 17
  Hot Avocado Sandwiches, 70
  Hot Sauce for Avocados, 110

B

BACON
  Bacon Dip, 60
  Bacon Green Beans, 210
  Bean-Bacon-Onion Broil, 70
  Broiler Bacon and Tomato
    Sandwiches, 69

Gateau Fromage, 117
Quiche Lorraine, 116
Bahamian Baked Bananas, 297
Baked Beans, Crider's, 204
Baked Carrots, 206
Baked Chicken Breasts, 147
Baked Crab and Shrimp, 50
Baked Crab Dip, 50
Baked Doves, 201
Baked Eggs for Brunch, 115
Baked Fish for Lazy Fishermen, 141
Baked Fish Veracruz, 140
Baked Flounder in Cream Sauce, 143
Baked Ham, 185
Baked Quail, 199
Baked Rice, 121
Baked Summer Squash, 220
Baked Yellow Squash, 220
BANANAS
  Bahamian Baked Bananas, 297
  Banana Bread, 244
  Banana Butterscotch Sticky Buns, 243
  Banana Pie, 254
  Cranberry Banana Bread, 245
Barbecue Sauce, 225
Barbecue Sauce, Bob's, 164
Barbecue Sauce for a Crowd, 224
Barbecued Beef, Smoked, 164
Barbecued Beef Tenderloin, 165
Barbecued Chicken, 148
Barbecued Chicken, Oven, 149
Barbecued Shrimp, Lemony, 133
Barnett's Cheese Spread, 58
Basic Fruit Punch, 42
BEANS — See also GREEN BEANS
  Bean-Bacon-Onion Broil, 70
  Bean Dip, 12
  Bean Salad, 297
  Chili-Bean Casserole, 29
  Crider's Baked Beans, 204
  Frijoles, 32
  Louisiana Red Beans and Rice, 217
  Refritos, 32
  Spicy Bean Soup, 84
  Three Bean Salad, 100
  Winter Salad, 101
BEEF
  Barbecued Beef Tenderloin, 165
  Beef Stew Elaborate, 173
  Beef Stroganoff, 174
  Beef Tips Creole, 174
  Boeuf Bourguignon, 173
  Busy Day Brisket, 166
  Chili Casserole, 29
  Chili-Bean Casserole, 29
  Chili con Carne, 14
  Chili Dip, 11
  Chinese Pot Roast
    Company Style, 168
  Connie's Pot Roast, 167
  Corned Beef Hash with
    Egg Pockets, 298
  Cowboy Stew, 172
  Dried Beef Cornucopias, 59

Dried Beef Log, 59
Easy Stew, 172
Ester's Enchiladas, 26
Family Favorite Meat Loaf, 176
Flautas, 27
Football Feed, 67
French Hamburger Steaks, 177
Green Chili Lasagna, 178
Hamburger-Hominy Pie, 181
Hamburger and Sour Cream
  Casserole, 175
Hash, 175
J. R.'s Special Port Aransas
  Steak, 169
Lucy's Flank Steak, 171
Mamie's Calabaza, 30
Mamie's Tamales, 24
Mary Hutchens' Brisket, 167
Manicotti, 179
Mexican Beef Casserole, 25
Mexican Meat Loaf, 29
Mother's Chili, 15
Oniony Meat Balls, 180
Peggy's Chili, 14
Peggy's Enchiladas, 26
Pepper Steak, 171
Peppered Rib Eye of Beef, 166
Picadillo, 11
Pizza Meat Loaf, 176
Pizzaz Hamburgers, 68
Queso y Carne, 12
Quick Tortilla Stuffer, 27
Roast Brisket, 167
Sailor's Sandwich, 296
Sauerbraten, 169
Saucy Meat Balls, 179
Savory Lasagna, 177
Scrambled Eggs with
  Chipped Beef, 295
Sloppy Joes, 68
Smoked Barbecued Beef, 164
South of the Border Spaghetti, 28
Spanish Pot Roast, 168
Standing Prime Rib, 165
Steak Diane, 170
Steak Kabobs, 170
Steaks Korean, 169
Stuffed Cabbage Leaves, 180
Stuffed Peppers Italiano, 181
Swedish Meat Balls, 47
Tacos, 28
Beef Marinade Sauce, 224
Bell Peppers, Pickled, 229
Berried Quail, 199
Best Stuffed Crabs Ever, 128
Betsy's Shrimp Gumbo with Curry, 77
BEVERAGES, ALCOHOLIC, 37-41
Allie's Yacht Club Margaritas, 6
Border Buttermilk, 6
Coffee Liqueur, 8
Juan's Tequila Sour, 7
Sangria, 7
Sangrita, 7
Tequila Brandy, 8

Tequila Sunrise, 6
BEVERAGES, NON-ALCOHOLIC, 41-44
Bill Shuart's Okra and
  Tomato Dish, 212
Biscuits, Mother's, 242
Bisque, Neely's Oyster, 79
Bisque, Shrimp, 78
Black Bottom Pie, 259
Blender Gazpacho, 83
Blender Hollandaise Sauce, 226
Blender Mayonnaise, 227
Bloody Mary, 39
"Bloody Shame," 40
Blue Cheese Wafers, 62
Blueberry Muffins, 246
Blueberry Sauce, 273
Bob's Barbecue Sauce, 164
Boeuf Bourguignon, 173
Boiled White Icing, 271
Border Buttermilk, 6
Border-Style Eggs, 17
Bourbon Ice Cream, 281
BREADS, QUICK, 240-246
Jalapeño Corn Bread, 34
Josefinas, 34
BREADS, YEAST, 233-239
Bride's Bowl, 41
Bridge Club Dessert, 270
BROCCOLI
  Broccoli and Rice Casserole, 205
  Broccoli Puff, 205
  Gray's Hot Broccoli Dip, 55
  Marinated Broccoli, 102
  Myra's Chicken-Broccoli
    Casserole, 157
  Nana's Spinach and Broccoli
    Casserole, 219
Broiler Bacon and Tomato
  Sandwiches, 69
Brown Sugar Squares, 286
Brownie Mounds, 285
Brownie Pie, 261
Brownies, 286
Brussels Sprouts and Grapes
  Casserole, 206
Brussels Sprouts Cartier, 206
Busy Day Brisket, 166
Butter, Garlic, 229
Buttermilk Candy, Nunna's, 289
Buttermilk Ice Cream, 280
Buttermilk Pancakes, 247
Buttermilk Pecan Pie, 252
Buttermilk Pie, Evelyn's, 251
Butterscotch Brownie Pie, 261
Butterscotch Surprises, 288

C

Cabbage Leaves, Stuffed, 180
Cajeta, 36
Caesar Salad, 99
CAKE FROSTINGS and
  FILLINGS, 271, 272
CAKES, 262-270

Calabaza con Pollo, 23
Cam's Lime-Pine Salad, 96
Candied Orange Cookies, 284
CANDY, 288, 289
  Nogada Amador Ayala, 35
Captain Max Luther's Fish
  Chowder, 74
Caramel Ice Cream, 279
Caramels, Mother's, 289
CARROTS
  Baked Carrots, 206
  Carrot Cake, 264
  Carrot Casserole, 207
  Carrot Relish, 230
  The Kings' Copper Penny
    Carrots, 103
Carolyn Lasater's Mourning
  Doves, 201
Caviar Cheese Ball, Frosted, 48
Celery, Creamed, 207
Celestial Chicken Salad, 92
Cereal, High Protein, 248
Ceviche, 75
Chalupas Compuestas, 13
CHEESE
  Barnett's Cheese Spread, 58
  Blue Cheese Wafers, 62
  Cheese Log, 58
  Cheese Puff Soufflés, 63
  Cheese Snacks, 61
  Cheese Soufflé, 117
  Cheese Straws, 61
  Cheese Toasties, 62
  Chili con Queso, 10
  Cindy Ryder's White Smash, 20
  Cocktail Party Cheese Ball, 57
  Croque Monsieur, 69
  Curry Chutney Cheese Ball, 57
  Ella Lee's Shrimp con Queso, 138
  Fail-Safe Rarebit, 118
  Gateau Fromage, 117
  Green Chili Enchiladas, 20
  Hot Cheese and Crab Dip, 49
  Hot Cheese Squares, 62
  Hot Chutney Cheese Ball, 56
  Jalapeño Dip, 10
  Jalapeño Pie, 19
  Libby's Cheese Casserole, 118
  Nachos, 13
  Olive Cheese Ball, 57
  Olive-Cheese Puffs, 61
  One-Two-Three's, 60
  Pizza Snacks, 71
  Queso y Carne, 12
  Quiche Lorraine, 116
  Toasted Cheese and Egg Cups, 116
  Tomato-Cheese Soufflé, 118
Cheese Cake, 258
Cheese Cake, Lilia's Strawberry, 257
Cherry Cobbler, 256
Cherry Pie, Pineapple-, 260
Chess Pie, Pineapple, 251
CHICKEN
  Almond Chicken, 149

Baked Chicken Breasts, 147
Barbecued Chicken, 148
Calabaza con Pollo, 23
Celestial Chicken Salad, 92
Chicken a la King, 154
Chicken and Dumplings, 151
Chicken and Shrimp Bechamel, 156
Chicken Asparagus Casserole, 156
Chicken Breasts with Wild Rice, 150
Chicken Casserole, 158
Chicken Casserole Mexico, 21
Chicken Crepes, 159
Chicken Curry, 151
Chicken Divan, 157
Chicken Enchiladas, 22
Chicken Mousse, 93
Chicken Parmesan, 147
Chicken Puff, 153
Chicken Rosemary, 146
Chicken Spaghetti, 154
Chicken Tortilla Casserole, 23
Chicken Tetrazzini, 155
Chicketti for 20, 155
Company Chicken Dinner, 158
Creamed Chicken Tacos, 21
Crown Jewel Ham and
  Chicken Molds, 92
Hawaiian Luau Chicken, 150
Hot Chicken Salad, 91
Lib MacMillan's Chicken with
  Salad, 148
Mandarin Orange Chicken, 146
Marca's Enchiladas Suissas, 22
Myra's Chicken-Broccoli
  Casserole, 157
Oven Barbecued Chicken, 149
Rumaki, 47
Seafood Gumbo with Chicken and
  Veal, 78
Sherried Chicken, 147
Southern Fried Chicken, 152
Virginia Conolly's Chicken
  Casserole, 153
Chicken Salad, Celestial, 92
Chicken Salad, Hot, 91
Chicketti for 20, 155
CHILI
  Chili con Carne, 14
  Mother's Chili, 15
  Peggy's Chili, 14
Chili-Bean Casserole, 29
Chili Casserole, 29
Chili con Queso, 10
Chili Dip, 11
Chili Pequin Sauce, 33
Chili Sauce, Northern, 225
Chili Soufflé, 19
Chinese Almond Cookies, 282
Chinese Pot Roast Company Style, 168
Chocolate Cake, Colston, 263
Chocolate Chip Cake, 263
Chocolate Cookies, 281
Chocolate Cup Cakes, 270
Chocolate Dreams, 288

Chocolate Frosting, Great, 271
Chocolate Ice Box Cake, Mother's, 270
Chocolate Pie, Mama's, 253
Chocolate Sauce, 274
Chris' Oyster Loaf, 51
Christmas Cookies, 283
Christmas Fudge Milly, 288
Christmas Party Punch, 43
Christmas Tree Salad, 96
Chutney Cheese Ball, Curry, 57
Chutney Cheese Ball, Hot, 56
Cindy Ryder's White Smash, 20
Citrus Dressing, 109
Clam Sauce for Spaghetti,
  Egan's White, 225
Claudine's Yeast Rolls, 236
Cobbler, Apple, 256
Cobbler, Cherry, 256
Cocktail Party Cheese Ball, 57
Cocktail Water Chestnuts, 56
Coconut Frosting, 272
Coffee Cake, Danish, 244
Coffee Cake, Hungarian, 239
Coffe Cake, Sour Cream, 267
Coffee Can Yeast Bread, 235
Coffee Liqueur, 8
Coffee Punch, 43
Cold Cucumber Soup, 81
Cold Poached Fish, 144
Cole Slaw, 102
Colston Chocolate Cake, 263
Company Chicken Dinner, 158
CONFECTIONS, 287, 288
Confetti Slaw, 103
Congealed Ambrosia Mold, 98
Congealed Cranberry Mold, 97
CONGEALED SALADS — See
  MOLDED SALADS
Congealed Shrimp Salad, 88
Connie's Pot Roast, 167
COOKIES, 281-287
  Pan de Polvo, 35
Coquina Broth, 75
Corinne's Hot Cakes, 247
CORN
  Corn Casserole, 208
  Cream of Corn Soup, 81
  Creamy Corn Scallop, 207
  Hauser Corn, 208
Corn Bread, 240
Corn Bread, Jalapeño, 34
Corn Dodgers, 241
Corn Fritters, 241
Corned Beef Hash with
  Egg Pockets, 298
Cornish Game Hens, Glazed, 162
Cornish Game Hens, Stuffed, 162
Cowboy Stew, 172
CRAB
  Baked Crab and Shrimp, 50
  Baked Crab Dip, 50
  Best Stuffed Crabs Ever, 128
  Crab Burgers, 66
  Crab Casserole, 129

Crab Lorenzo, 127
Crab Louis, 87
Crab New Orleans, 86
Crab Meat and Artichoke
  Casserole, 130
Crab Meat and Artichoke
  Hearts, 87
Crab Meat au Gratin, 126
Crab Meat Dewey, 129
Crab Meat Lonnie, 128
Curried Crab in Shells, 128
Easy Crab Spread, 49
Gray's Crab Dip Provencal, 49
Gulf Coast Poor Boys, 66
Hot Cheese and Crab Dip, 49
Mother's Crab Dish, 127
Seafood Aransas, 139
Shellfish Casserole, 140
Vol au Vent, 126
Cranberry Banana Bread, 245
Cranberry Mold, Congealed, 97
Cranberry Punch, 42
Cream Cheese Frosting, 272
Cream Cheese Jelly Roll, 269
Cream Gravy, 152
Cream of Corn Soup, 81
Cream of Potato Soup, 81
Creamed Celery, 207
Creamed Chicken Tacos, 21
Creamy Corn Scallops, 207
Creme Brulée, 274
Crepes, Chicken, 159
Crider's Baked Beans, 204
Croque Monsieur, 69
Crown Jewel Ham and Chicken
  Molds, 92
Crown Pork Roast, 182
CUCUMBERS
  Cold Cucumber Soup, 81
  Cucumber Mold, 108
  Cucumber Sandwiches, 71
  Gray's Cucumber Dip, 55
  Pineapple-Cucumber Salad, 96
  Shrimp on Cucumber a la
    San Miguel, 54
Cup Cakes, Chocolate, 270
CURRY
  Chicken Curry, 151
  Curried Crab in Shells, 128
  Curried Fruit, 232
  Curried Shrimp, 138
  Curry Chutney Cheese Ball, 57
  Curry Salad Dressing, 110
  Turkey Curry, 161

D

Daiquiri, Frozen, 38
Daiquiri, Vickie's Strawberry, 38
Dana's Dilly Dip, 60
Danish Coffee Cake, 244
Date Bread, 245
Date-Filled Oatmeal Bars, 286
Date Squares, 287

DESSERTS, 274-278 — See also CAKES, COOKIES, CANDIES, DESSERT SAUCES, ICE CREAMS, PIES
Bahamian Baked Bananas, 297
Cajeta, 36
Flan with Caramel Topping, 36
DESSERT SAUCES, 273, 274
Deviled Almonds, 63
Deviled Eggs, 116, 136
Deviled Eggs with Ham, 115
Deviled Oysters, 132
Deviled Shrimp, 53
Dick Picton's Gumbo, 77
Dilly Casserole Bread, 235
Dr Pepper Salad, 97
Doves, Baked, 201
Doves, Carolyn Lasater's Mourning, 201
Dried Beef Cornucopias, 59
Dried Beef Log, 59
Dressing, Turkey and, 160
DRINKS — See BEVERAGES
Duck, Drunken, 202
Duck, Stuffed Wild, 202
Drunken Duck, 202
Dumplings, Chicken and, 151

E

Easy Crab Spread, 49
Easy Creamed Spinach, 218
Easy Elegant Baked Fish, 142
Easy Scallop Casserole, 133
Easy Stew, 172
Egan's White Clam Sauce for Spaghetti, 225
Eggplant, Elegant, 208
Eggplant Extraordinaire, 209
Eggplant, Mama's, 209
EGGS
Baked Eggs for Brunch, 115
Border-Style Eggs, 17
Corned Beef Hash with Egg Pockets, 298
Deviled Eggs, 116, 136
Deviled Eggs with Ham, 115
Eggs and Asparagus au Gratin, 204
Eggs Benedict, 114
Egg Salad Sandwich Filling, 72
Herbed Eggs, 115
Huevos Rancheros, 18
Omelette Basquaise, 114
Scrambled Eggs with Chipped Beef, 295
Shrimp and Egg Casserole, 136
Toasted Cheese and Egg Cups, 116
Elegant Eggplant, 208
Ella Lee's Shrimp con Queso, 138
ENCHILADAS
Chicken Enchiladas, 22
Ester's Enchiladas, 26
Green Chili Enchiladas, 20
Marca's Enchiladas Suissas, 22

Peggy's Enchiladas, 26
Enid's Pressed Veal, 93
Ester's Enchiladas, 26
Evelyn's Buttermilk Pie, 251

F

Fail-Safe Rarebit, 118
Family Favorite Meat Loaf, 176
Fig Cake, 265
FISH
Baked Fish for Lazy Fishermen, 141
Baked Fish Veracruz, 140
Baked Flounder in Cream Sauce, 143
Captain Max Luther's Fish Chowder, 74
Ceviche, 75
Cold Poached Fish, 144
Easy Elegant Baked Fish, 142
Fish au Gratin, 144
King Fish in Creole Sauce, 142
Stuffed Flounder, 141
Succulent Baked Fish, 143
Fish House Punch, 41
Flaky Pie Crust, 251
Flan with Caramel Topping, 36
Flautas, 27
Football Feed, 67
Ford Hook Lima Bean Dish, 211
Frances' Fruit Cake, 268
Frank Sandwich, Tasty, 69
French Hamburger Steaks, 177
French Onion Soup, 84
French 75's, 40
Fresh Apple Cake, 264
Fresh Fruit Ice Cream, 279
Fresh Strawberry Pie, 255
Fresh Vegetable Soup, 80
Fried Quail, 199
Fried Rice, 120
Frijoles, 32
Frog Legs Provencale, 130
Frosted Caviar Cheese Mold, 48
FROSTINGS — See CAKE FROSTINGS
Frozen Daiquiri, 38
Frozen Lemon Dessert, 277
Frozen Mocha Soufflés, 277
Frozen Salad, Individual, 95
Fruit Cake, Frances', 268
Fruit Cake, Uncle John R's Norwegian, 269
Fruit Salad Dressing, 108
FRUIT SALADS
Cam's Lime-Pine Salad, 96
Christmas Tree Salad, 96
Congealed Cranberry Mold, 97
Congealed Ambrosia Mold, 98
Dr Pepper Salad, 97
Fruit Salad, 95
Individual Frozen Salad, 95
Mandarin Orange Salad, 95
Mango Mousse, 99
Midsummer Salad, 94

Pineapple-Cucumber Salad, 96
Twenty-Four-Hour Salad, 94
Wine Salad, 98
Yum Yum Salad, 97
FRUITS
Curried Fruit, 232
Grecian Pears, 278
Hot Fruit Compote, 278
Fudge Milly, Christmas, 288
Fudge Pudding, 275

G

Garlic Butter, 229
Garlic Mayonnaise, 227
Garnelen Bollen, 52
Gateau Fromage, 117
Gazpacho, Blender, 83
Gazpacho, Glorious, 82
Gazpacho, Luella's, 82
Giblet Gravy, 160
Ginger Pickled Shrimp, 53
Gingerbread Muffins, Hattie's
    Refrigerator, 246
Glazed Cornish Game Hens, 162
Glorious Gazpacho, 82
Golden Risotto, 120
Golden Surprise Acorn Squash, 221
Golden Wedding Punch, 42
Gluehwein, 41
Grace's Pickled Vegetables, 231
Graham Cracker Crust, Zwieback or, 250
Grape Juice, Mulled, 44
Grape Sherbet, 281
Grapefruit Jelly, 231
Grapes Casserole, Brussel
    Sprouts and, 206
Grated Potato Casserole, 214
Gravy, Cream, 152
Gravy, Giblet, 160
Gray's Crab Dip Provencal, 49
Gray's Cucumber Dip, 55
Gray's Hot Broccoli Dip, 55
Gray's Pickled Mushrooms, 56
Gray's Salmon Party Mound, 52
Gray's Shrimp Dip, 54
Great Chocolate Frosting, 271
Grecian Pears, 278
GREEN BEANS
    Bacon Green Beans, 210
    Bean Salad, 297
    Green Beans en Casserole, 210
    Sweet and Sour Beans, 210
    Sweet and Sour Salad, 102
    Winter Salad, 101
Green Chili Enchiladas, 20
Green Chili Lasagna, 178
Green Lobster Salad, 88
Green Rice Delight, 119
Green Salad Dressing, 111
GREEN SALADS — See VEGETABLE
    SALADS
Grilled Lobster, 131
Grits Casserole, 122

Guacamole Salad, 17
Guaranty Cake, The, 267
Gulf Coast Casserole, 139
Gulf Coast Poor Boys, 66
GUMBOS
    Betsy's Shrimp Gumbo with
        Curry, 77
    Dick Picton's Gumbo, 77
    Seafood Gumbo with Chicken
        and Veal, 78
    Spicy Seafood Gumbo, 76

H

HAM
    Baked Ham, 185
    Croque Monsieur, 69
    Crown Jewel Ham and Chicken
        Molds, 92
    Ham and Asparagus, 188
    Ham Hash, 186
    Ham Loaf, 186
    Ham Loaf with Sauce, 187
    Jambalaya, 137
    Mushroom and Ham Stuffed
        Tomatoes, 188
    Orse Lee's Coke and Honey
        Ham, 186
    Zesty Ham and Rice Casserole, 189
Hamburger and Sour Cream
    Casserole, 175
Hamburger-Hominy Pie, 181
Hamburger Steaks, French, 177
Hamburger, Pizzaz, 68
Hash, 175
Hash, Ham, 186
Hash with Egg Pockets, Corned
    Beef, 298
Hattie's Refrigerator Gingerbread
    Muffins, 246
Hauser Corn, 208
Hawaiian Luau Chicken, 150
Hearts of Palm Salad, 104
Heavenly Dressing, 111
Herbed Eggs, 115
Herbed Spinach Bake, 219
High Protein Cereal, 248
Holiday Pilaf, 119
Hollandaise Sauce, 127
Hollandaise Sauce, Blender, 226
Hominy Casserole, 211
Hominy Pie, Hamburger-, 181
HORS D'OEUVRES — See
    APPETIZERS
Horseradish Sauce, 226
Hot Apricot Drink, 44
Hot Avocado Sandwiches, 70
Hot Cheese and Crab Dip, 49
Hot Cheese Squares, 62
Hot Chicken Salad, 91
Hot Chutney Cheese Ball, 56
Hot Fruit Compote, 278
Hot Mustard, 227
Hot Potato Salad, 105

Hot Sauce for Avocados, 110
Hot Spiced Percolator Punch, 44
Huevos Rancheros, 18
Hungarian Coffee Cake, 239
Hush Puppies, 240

I

Ice Box Cookies, 285
ICE CREAMS and
  SHERBETS, 279-281
Iced Tomato Soup with Dill, 83
ICINGS — See CAKE FROSTINGS
Individual Frozen Salad, 95
Italian Cream Cake, 262

J

J. R.'s Special Port Aransas Steak, 169
Jack's Sautéed Quail, 201
Jackie's Shrimp, 135
Jalapeño Corn Bread, 34
Jalapeño Dip, 10
Jalapeño Jelly, 33
Jalapeño Pie, 19
Jambalaya, 137
Janet Harte's Whole Wheat Bread, 234
Jelly, Grapefruit, 231
Jelly, Jalapeño, 33
Jelly, Lime, 232
Jelly Roll, Cream Cheese, 269
Joan's Shrimp, 134
Josefinas, 34
Juan's Tequila Sour, 7

K

Kalista's Onion Soufflé, 213
Kay's Calabaza, 31
Kay's Wild Rice Casserole, 121
King Fish in Creole Sauce, 142
Kings' Copper Penny Carrots,
  The, 103
Kolaches, 238

L

LAMB
  Leg of Lamb Supreme, 191
  Leg of Lamb with Plum Sauce, 191
  Marinated Leg of Lamb, 190
  Navarin of Lamb, 192
  Roast Leg of Lamb, 190
Lasagna, Green Chili, 178
Lasagna, Savory, 177
Leg of Lamb Supreme, 191
Leg of Lamb with Plum Sauce, 191
Lemon Delicious, 275
Lemon Dessert, Frozen, 277
Lemon Dessert, Mrs. E's, 276
Lemon Jelly, Miss Alice O'Grady's, 273
Lemon Posset, 276
Lemon Pound Cake, 266
Lemony Barbecued Shrimp, 133
Lettuce and Green Pea Soup, 80
Lib MacMillan's Chicken with
  Salad, 148

Libby's Cheese Casserole, 118
Lilia's Strawberry Cheese Cake, 257
Lima Bean Dish, Ford Hook, 211
Lime Jelly, 232
Lime Punch, 42
LOBSTER
  Green Lobster Salad, 88
  Grilled Lobster, 131
  Shellfish Casserole, 140
Louise's Rum Pie, 259
Louisiana Red Beans and Rice, 217
Luella's Gazpacho, 82
Lucy's Flank Steak, 171

M

Macaroni Salad, Shrimp and, 89
Mama's Chocolate Pie, 253
Mama's Eggplant, 209
Mamie's Calabaza, 30
Mamie's Tamales, 24
Mandarin Orange Chicken, 146
Mandarin Orange Salad, 95
Mango Mousse, 99
Manicotti, 179
Marca's Enchiladas Suissas, 22
Margaret Walsh's Hopping John, 213
Marinade Sauce, Beef, 224
Marinade for Flank Steak, 172
Marinade for Smoked Turkey, 159
Marinated Broccoli, 102
Marinated Leg of Lamb, 190
Marinated Peas, 104
Marty's Pork Roast, 182
Mary Hutchens' Brisket, 167
Mary's Shrimp and Macaroni Salad, 89
Mary's Shrimp Mold, 89
Mayonnaise, Blender, 227
Mayonnaise, Garlic, 227
MEAT — See BACON, BEEF, HAM,
  PORK, SAUSAGE, VEAL, and
  VENISON
Meat Balls, Oniony, 180
Meat Balls, Saucy, 179
Meat Balls, Swedish, 47
Meat Loaf, Family Favorite, 176
Meat Loaf, Mexican, 29
Meat Loaf, Pizza, 176
Mexican Beef Casserole, 25
Mexican Chef Salad, 16
Mexican Meat Loaf, 29
Mexican Pork Chop Supper, 30
Mexican Spiced Pecans, 290
Midsummer Salad, 94
Millionaire Pie, 260
Mincemeat Cheese Pie, 258
Mincemeat for Pie, Pear, 257
Minted Nuts, 290
Miss Alice O'Grady Lemon Jelly, 273
Miss Ella's Pecan Pie, 252
Mixed Vegetable Salad, 101
MOLDED SALADS
  Asparagus Mold, 107
  Avocado Aspic, 107

Avocado Salad, 108
Cam's Lime-Pine Salad, 96
Chicken Mousse, 93
Christmas Tree Salad, 96
Congealed Ambrosia Mold, 98
Congealed Cranberry Mold, 97
Congealed Shrimp Salad, 88
Crown Jewel Ham and Chicken
    Molds, 92
Cucumber Mold, 108
Dr Pepper Salad, 97
Enid's Pressed Veal, 93
Mandarin Orange Salad, 95
Mango Mousse, 99
Mary's Shrimp Mold, 89
Party Aspic, 90
Pimiento-Tuna Molded Salad, 91
Pineapple-Cucumber Salad, 96
Seafood Mold, 90
Spring Salad Soufflé, 106
Wine Salad, 98
Yum Yum Salad, 97
Mother's Biscuits, 242
Mother's Caramels, 289
Mother's Chili, 15
Mother's Chocolate Ice Box Cake, 270
Mother's Crab Dish, 127
Mother's Pumpkin Pie, 253
Mother's Waffles, 248
Mousse, Chicken, 93
Mousse, Mango, 99
Mrs. E's Lemon Dessert, 276
Muffins, Blueberry, 246
Muffins, Hattie's Refrigerator
    Gingerbread, 246
Mulled Grape Juice, 44
Mushroom and Ham Stuffed
    Tomatoes, 188
Mushrooms, Gray's Pickled, 56
Mushrooms, Spinach-Stuffed, 218
Mushrooms, Stuffed, 212
Mustard, Hot, 227
Myra's Chicken Broccoli Casserole, 157

N

Nachos, 13
Nana's Spinach and Broccoli
    Casserole, 219
Navarin of Lamb, 192
Neely's Oyster Bisque, 79
Nogada Amador Ayala, 35
Noodles Antin, 124
Noodles Romanoff, 124
Northern Chili Sauce, 225
Nunna's Buttermilk Candy, 289
Nut Bread, Raisin, 237
Nuts, Minted, 290
Nuts, Sherry's Indian, 64

O

Oatmeal Bars, Date Filled, 286

Oatmeal Cake, 268
Oatmeal Cookies, 283
Off Shore Salad, 296
Oil Pastry, 250
Okra and Tomato Dish,
    Bill Shuart's, 212
Old Fashioned Pound Cake, 267
Olive Broiler Sandwiches, 72
Olive Cheese Ball, 57
Olive-Cheese Puffs, 61
Omelette Basquaise, 114
One, Two, Three, Four Cake, 262
One-Two-Three's, 60
ONIONS
    Bean-Bacon-Onion Broil, 70
    French Onion Soup, 84
    Kalista's Onion Soufflé, 213
    Onion Cake, 236
    Onion-Poppy Seed Dressing, 109
    Oniony Meat Balls, 180
    Rice-Onion Dish, 121
Open-Faced Turkey Sandwich, 70
Orange Cookies, Candied, 284
Orse Lee's Coke and Honey Ham, 186
Oven Barbecued Chicken, 149
OYSTERS
    Chris' Oyster Loaf, 51
    Deviled Oysters, 132
    Gulf Coast Poor Boys, 66
    Neely's Oyster Bisque, 79
    Oysters Box Ranch, 51
    Oyster Tidbits, 50
    Scalloped Oysters, 131
    Sea Heiress Oysters, 132

P

Pan de Polvo, 35
PANCAKES and WAFFLES, 247, 248
Paris Potatoes, 215
Party Aspic, 90
Paté de Fois Gras in Aspic, 48
Patt's Vanilla Ice Cream, 279
Pauline's Venison Stroganoff, 195
Pear Mincemeat for Pie, 257
Pears, Grecian, 278
PEAS
    Margaret Walsh's Hopping John, 213
    Lettuce and Green Pea Soup, 80
    Marinated Peas, 104
    Ranch Style Black-Eyed Peas, 214
    Winter Salad, 101
PECANS
    Buttermilk Pecan Pie, 252
    Mexican Spiced Pecans, 290
    Miss Ella's Pecan Pie, 252
    Pecan Meringue Pie, 261
    Roquefort Pecans, 64
Peggy's Chili, 14
Peggy's Enchiladas, 26
Pepper Steak, 171
Peppered Rib Eye of Beef, 166
Peppermint Ice Cream, 280
Picadillo, 11

Picante Sauce, Alice
  Eleanora Nesby's, 33
Pickled Bell Peppers, 229
Pickled Mushrooms, Gray's, 56
Pickled Shrimp, Ginger, 53
Pickled Vegetables, Grace's, 231
PIES, 251-261
PIE CRUSTS, 250, 251
Pimiento-Tuna Molded Salad, 91
PINEAPPLE
  Cam's Lime-Pine Salad, 96
  Pineapple-Cherry Pie, 260
  Pineapple Chess Pie, 251
  Pineapple-Cucumber Salad, 96
  Pineapple Filling, 272
  Pineapple Refresher, 39
Pizza Meat Loaf, 176
Pizza Snacks, 71
Pizzaz Hamburgers, 68
Plantation Fried Shrimp, 134
Popovers, 243
Poppy Seed Bread, 242
Poppy Seed Dressing with Honey, 109
Poppy Seed Dressing, Onion-, 109
PORK — See also BACON, HAM, and
  SAUSAGE
  Crown Pork Roast, 182
  Mamie's Tamales, 24
  Marty's Pork Roast, 182
  Mexican Pork Chop Supper, 30
  Pork Chop Casserole, 184
  Pork Chops, 183
  Pork Chops a l'Orange, 184
  Pork Chops with Rosemary, 185
  Pork Roast in Mustard, 182
  Sweet and Sour Pork, 183
POTATOES
  Cream of Potato Soup, 81
  Grated Potato Casserole, 214
  Hot Potato Salad, 105
  Paris Potatoes, 215
  Potatoes Deluxe, 216
  Potato Puffs, 214
  Potato Salad, 104
  Sweet Potatoes and Apples, 298
  Sweet Potato Casserole, 216
  Tomato-Scalloped Potatoes, 215
Pot de Créme, 274
POULTRY — See CHICKEN and
  TURKEY
Pound Cake, Lemon, 266
Pound Cake, Old Fashioned, 267
Pound Cake, Sour Cream, 266
Pralines, Quick, 289
Prune Cake, 264
Pumpkin Pie, Mother's, 253
PUNCH — See BEVERAGES
Purée of Vegetable Soup, 79

Q

QUAIL
  Baked Quail, 199

Berried Quail, 199
Fried Quail, 199
Jack's Sautéed Quail, 201
Quail in Wine Sauce, 200
Smothered Quail, 200
Queso y Carne, 12
Quiche Lorraine, 116
Quick Pralines, 289
Quick Tortilla Stuffer, 27

R

Raisin-Nut Bread, 237
Raisin Pie, Sour Cream, 254
Ranch Style Black-Eyed Peas, 214
Ranchero Sauce, 19
Ranchero Sauce, All Lively's, 18
Rarebit, Fail-Safe, 118
Ray's Bread, 243
Red Sauce, 228
Refrigerator Sand Tarts, 285
Refritos, 32
Relish, Apple-Vegetable, 229
Relish, Carrot, 230
Relish, Shawnee, 230
Relish, Stuffed Pepper, 229
Remoulade Sauce, 228
Renee's Salad Dressing, 112
RICE — See also WILD RICE
  Baked Rice, 121
  Fried Rice, 120
  Golden Risotto, 120
  Green Rice Delight, 119
  Holiday Pilaf, 119
  Rice-Onion Dish, 121
  Spanish Rice, 31
Rich Ice Cream, 280
Roast Brisket, 167
Roast Leg of Lamb, 190
Rolled Cookies, 284
Rolls, Claudine's Yeast, 236
Romano-Cheese Salad Dressing, 112
Roquefort Dressing, 111
Roquefort-French Salad Dressing, 112
Roquefort Pecans, 64
Rose's Sour Cream Orange Sauce, 273
Rum Pie, Louise's, 259
Rumaki, 47
Russian Tomato Salad, 105

S

Sailor's Sandwich, 296
SALAD DRESSINGS
  Citrus Dressing, 109
  Curry Salad Dressing, 110
  Fruit Salad Dressing, 108
  Green Salad Dressing, 111
  Heavenly Dressing, 111
  Hot Sauce for Avocados, 110
  Onion-Poppy Seed Dressing, 109
  Poppy Seed Dressing with
    Honey, 109
  Renee's Salad Dressing, 112

Romano Cheese Salad Dressing, 112
Roquefort Dressing, 111
Roquefort-French Salad
  Dressing, 112
Tarragon-Anchovy Dressing, 110
SALADS — See CHICKEN SALADS,
  MOLDED SALADS, FRUIT
  SALADS, SEAFOOD SALADS, and
  VEGETABLE SALADS
Salmon Party Mound, Gray's, 52
Sand Tarts, 282
Sand Tarts, Refrigerator, 285
SANDWICHES
  Bean-Bacon-Onion Broil, 70
  Broiler Bacon and Tomato
    Sandwiches, 69
  Crab Burgers, 66
  Croque Monsieur, 69
  Cucumber Sandwiches, 71
  Egg Salad Sandwich Filling, 72
  Football Feed, 67
  Gulf Coast Poor Boys, 66
  Hot Avocado Sandwiches, 70
  Olive Broiler Sandwich, 72
  Open-Faced Turkey Sandwich, 70
  Pizza Snacks, 71
  Pizzaz Hamburgers, 68
  Sailor's Sandwich, 296
  Sandwich Loaf, 72
  Sloppy Joes, 68
  Tasty Frank Sandwich, 69
  Tuna Fish Spread, 67
Sangria, 7
Sangrita, 7
SAUCES — See also DESSERT
  SAUCES, BARBECUE SAUCES,
  and MARINADES
  Alice Eleanora Nesby's Picante
    Sauce, 33
  Ann Lively's Ranchero Sauce, 18
  Blender Hollandaise Sauce, 226
  Chili Pequin Sauce, 33
  Egan's White Clam Sauce for
    Spaghetti, 225
  Hollandaise Sauce, 127
  Hot Sauce for Avocados, 110
  Horseradish Sauce, 226
  Northern Chili Sauce, 225
  Ranchero Sauce, 19
  Red Sauce, 228
  Remoulade Sauce, 228
  Sauce for Venison, 197
  Tartar Sauce, 228
  Tomato Sauce, 226
Saucy Meat Balls, 179
Sauerbraten, 169
SAUSAGE
  One-Two-Three's, 60
  Sailor's Sandwich, 296
  Sausage and Wild Rice Casserole, 189
  Spicy Sausage Balls, 46
  Venison Sausage and Wild Rice, 198
  Venison Sausage Supper, 198
Savory Lasagna, 177

Scallop Casserole, Easy, 133
Scalloped Oysters, 131
Scrambled Eggs with Chipped Beef, 295
Sea Heiress Oysters, 132
SEAFOOD SALADS
  Congealed Shrimp Salad, 88
  Crab Louis, 87
  Crab New Orleans, 86
  Crab Meat and Artichoke Hearts, 87
  Green Lobster Salad, 88
  Mary's Shrimp and Macaroni
    Salad, 89
  Mary's Shrimp Mold, 89
  Party Aspic, 90
  Pimiento-Tuna Molded Salad, 91
  Seafood Mold, 90
  Shrimp Salad New Orleans, 88
SEAFOOD — See CRAB, FISH,
  LOBSTER, OYSTERS, and SHRIMP
Seafood Aransas, 139
Seafood Gumbo, Spicy, 76
Seafood Gumbo with Chicken and
  Veal, 78
Seafood Mold, 90
Shawnee Relish, 230
Shellfish Casserole, 140
Sherried Chicken, 147
Sherry Flip, 40
Sherry's Indian Nuts, 64
SHRIMP
  Baked Crab and Shrimp, 50
  Betsy's Shrimp Gumbo with
    Curry, 77
  Chicken and Shrimp Bechamel, 156
  Congealed Shrimp Salad, 88
  Curried Shrimp, 138
  Deviled Shrimp, 53
  Ella Lee's Shrimp con Queso, 138
  Garnelen Bollen, 52
  Ginger Pickled Shrimp, 53
  Gray's Shrimp Dip, 54
  Gulf Coast Casserole, 139
  Gulf Coast Poor Boys, 66
  Jackie's Shrimp, 135
  Jambalaya, 137
  Joan's Shrimp, 134
  Lemony Barbecued Shrimp, 133
  Mary's Shrimp and Macaroni
    Salad, 89
  Mary's Shrimp Mold, 89
  Party Aspic, 90
  Plantation Fried Shrimp, 134
  Seafood Aransas, 139
  Shellfish Casserole, 140
  Shrimp and Egg Casserole, 136
  Shrimp Bisque, 78
  Shrimp Canapés, 52
  Shrimp Casserole, 136
  Shrimp Creole, 137
  Shrimp Dip, 54
  Shrimp on Cucumber a la San
    Miguel, 54
  Shrimp Puff, 134
  Shrimp Salad New Orleans, 88

Shrimp Wiggle, 138
Simple Shrimp, 133
Wild Rice and Shrimp Casserole, 135
Simple Shrimp, 133
Slaw, Cole, 102
Slaw, Confetti, 103
Sloppy Joes, 68
Smoked Barbecued Beef, 164
Smothered Quail, 200
Sopa de Fideo, 123
Sopa de Flor de Calabaza, 15
Soufflé, Cheese, 117
Soufflé, Chili, 19
Soufflé, Kalista's Onion, 213
Soufflé, Spring Salad, 106
Soufflé, Tomato-Cheese, 118
Soufflés, Frozen Mocha, 277
Betsy's Shrimp Gumbo with
SOUPS
    Curry, 77
    Blender Gazpacho, 83
    Captain Max Luther's Fish
        Chowder, 74
    Ceviche, 75
    Chili con Carne, 14
    Cold Cucumber Soup, 81
    Coquina Broth, 75
    Cream of Corn Soup, 81
    Cream of Potato Soup, 81
    Dick Picton's Gumbo, 77
    Fresh Vegetable Soup, 80
    French Onion Soup, 84
    Glorious Gazpacho, 82
    Iced Tomato Soup with Dill, 83
    Lettuce and Green Pea Soup, 80
    Luella's Gazpacho, 82
    Mother's Chili, 15
    Neely's Oyster Bisque, 79
    Peggy's Chili, 14
    Purée of Vegetable Soup, 79
    Seafood Gumbo with Chicken
        and Veal, 78
    Shrimp Bisque, 78
    Sopa de Flor de Calabaza, 15
    Spicy Bean Soup, 84
    Spicy Seafood Gumbo, 76
Sour Cream Cake, 265
Sour Cream Coffee Cake, 267
Sour Cream Pound Cake, 266
Sour Cream Orange Sauce, Rose's, 273
Sour Cream Raisin Pie, 254
South of the Border Spaghetti, 28
Southern Fried Chicken, 152
Southern Spoon Bread, 241
Spaghetti Carbonara, 123
Spaghetti, Chicken, 154
Spaghetti, South of the Border, 28
Spanish Pot Roast, 168
Spanish Rice, 31
Spicy Bean Soup, 84
Spicy Sausage Balls, 46
Spicy Seafood Gumbo, 76
SPINACH
    Easy Creamed Spinach, 218

Herbed Spinach Bake, 219
Nana's Spinach and Broccoli
    Casserole, 219
Spinach in Pimiento Cream, 217
Spinach Kitty, 218
Spinach Salad, 105
Spinach-Stuffed Mushrooms, 218
Spoon Bread, Southern, 241
Spring Salad Soufflé, 106
SQUASH
    Baked Summer Squash, 220
    Baked Yellow Squash, 220
    Calabaza con Pollo, 23
    Golden Surprise Acorn Squash, 221
    Kay's Calabaza, 31
    Sopa de Flor de Calabaza, 15
    Mamie's Calabaza, 30
    Squash and Things, 219
    Stir-Fried Vegetables, 222
    Stuffed Acorn Squash, 221
    Zucchini Casserole, 222
Standing Prime Rib, 165
Steak Diane, 170
Steak Kabobs, 170
Steaks Korean, 169
Stew Elaborate, Beef, 173
Stew, Cowboy, 172
Stew, Easy, 172
Stir-Fried Vegetables, 222
Strawberry Cheese Cake, Lilia's, 257
Strawberry Daiquiri, Vickie's, 38
Strawberry Pie, Fresh, 255
Stroganoff, Beef, 174
Stroganoff, Pauline's Venison, 195
Stuffed Acorn Squash, 221
Stuffed Cabbage Leaves, 180
Stuffed Cornish Game Hens, 162
Stuffed Flounder, 141
Stuffed Mushrooms, 212
Stuffed Pepper Relish, 229
Stuffed Peppers Italiano, 181
Stuffed Venison Round Steak, 195
Stuffed Wild Duck, 202
Succulent Baked Fish, 143
Sunday Night Pancakes, 247
Swedish Cookies, 282
Swedish Meat Balls, 47
Sweet and Sour Asparagus, 101
Sweet and Sour Beans, 210
Sweet and Sour Pork, 183
Sweet and Sour Salad, 102
Sweet and Sour Venison, 196
Sweet Potatoes and Apples, 298
Sweet Potato Casserole, 216

T

Taco Salad, 16
Tacos, 28
Tacos, Creamed Chicken, 21
Tamales, Mamie's, 24
Tarragon-Anchovy Dressing, 110
Tartar Sauce, 228
Tasty Frank Sandwich, 69

Tawhiri Buster, 38
Tequila Brandy, 8
Tequila Sunrise, 6
Tetrazzini, Chicken, 155
Three-Bean Salad, 100
Toasted Cheese and Egg Cups, 116
TOMATOES
  Bill Shuart's Okra and Tomato
    Dish, 212
  Blender Gazpacho, 83
  Broiler Bacon and Tomato
    Sandwiches, 69
  Glorious Gazpacho, 82
  Iced Tomato Soup with Dill, 83
  Luella's Gazpacho, 82
  Mushroom and Ham Stuffed
    Tomatoes, 188
  Russian Tomato Salad, 105
  Tomato-Cheese Soufflé, 118
  Tomato Sauce, 226
  Tomato Scalloped Potatoes, 215
  Tomatoes with Artichoke Hearts, 106
Tortillas de Harina #1, 9
Tortillas de Harina #2, 9
Tossed Salad, 100
Tuna Fish Spread, 67
Tuna Molded Salad, Pimiento-, 91
TURKEY
  Open-Faced Turkey Sandwich, 70
  Turketti, 161
  Turkey and Dressing, 160
  Turkey Curry, 161
Turketti, 161
Twenty-Four-Hour Salad, 94

U

Uncle John R's Norwegian
  Fruit Cake, 269

V

Vanilla Ice Cream, Patt's, 279
Vanilla Sticks, 287
Vanilla Wafer Crust, 250
Veal, Enid's Pressed, 93
VEGETABLE SALADS
  Asparagus Mold, 107
  Avocado Aspic, 107
  Avocado Salad, 108
  Bean Salad, 297
  Caesar Salad, 99
  Cole Slaw, 102
  Confetti Slaw, 103
  Cucumber Mold, 108
  Guacamole Salad, 17
  Hearts of Palm Salad, 104
  Hot Potato Salad, 105
  Kings' Copper Penny Carrots,
    The, 103
  Lib MacMillan's Chicken with
    Salad, 148
  Marinated Broccoli, 102

Marinated Peas, 104
Mexican Chef Salad, 16
Mixed Vegetable Salad, 101
Off Shore Salad, 296
Potato Salad, 104
Russian Tomato Salad, 105
Spinach Salad, 105
Spring Salad Soufflé, 106
Sweet and Sour Asparagus, 101
Sweet and Sour Salad, 102
Taco Salad, 16
Tomatoes with Artichoke
  Hearts, 106
Three Bean Salad, 100
Tossed Salad, 100
Winter Salad, 101
VEGETABLES — See individual
  vegetables
Vegetable Soup, Fresh, 80
Vegetable Soup, Purée of, 79
Vegetables, Stir-Fried, 222
VENISON
  Chili con Carne, 14
  Mamie's Tamales, 24
  Pauline's Venison Stroganoff, 195
  Picadillo, 11
  Sauerbraten, 169
  Steak Kabobs, 170
  Stuffed Venison Round Steak, 195
  Sweet and Sour Venison, 196
  Venison Backstrap, 196
  Venison Cutlets Italiano, 197
  Venison Diane, 194
  Venison Ham, 194
  Venison Sausage and Wild Rice, 198
  Venison Sausage Supper, 198
Vickie's Strawberry Daquiri, 38
Virginia Conolly's Chicken
  Casserole, 153
Vol au Vent, 126

W

Waffles, Mother's, 248
Wassail, 43
Water Chestnuts, Cocktail, 56
Wild Rice, 122
Wild Rice and Cheese, 122
Wild Rice Casserole, Kay's, 121
Wild Rice and Shrimp Casserole, 135
Wine Salad, 98
Winter Salad, 101
Whiskey Sour Old South, 39

Y

Yum Yum Salad, 97

Z

Zesty Ham and Rice Casserole, 189
Zucchini Casserole, 222
Zwieback or Graham Cracker
  Crust, 250